Sexualities Research

How is sexuality studied methodologically? How are we innovating, methodologically, in the study of sexuality? What impact, if any, has the increase in mixed methodologies had on the study of sexuality?

Sexualities Research is a collection of original chapters by emerging and world-leading scholars of sexuality. Through this volume the authors seek to address how theoretical and methodological choices enable wider dissemination and social impact of sexualities research. Indeed, covering a diverse range of theoretical perspectives and methodologies to provide important new insights into human sexuality, the chapters cover an array of topics from the experience of researching sexuality, to using theories in new and innovative ways. With an international scope, Sexualities Research also builds on the re-emergence of the European Sociological Association Sexuality Research Network and asks important questions about the study of sexuality in contemporary societies against the background of political upheaval and economic troubles. Certainly, this collection shows the importance and vitality of sociological understandings of human sexuality in the 21st century.

An enlightening volume consisting of a variety of case studies and theoretical research, Sexualities Research will appeal to undergraduate and postgraduate students, as well as postdoctoral researchers who are interested in fields such as Sociology, LGBT/Queer Studies and Gender Studies.

Andrew King is a senior lecturer in Sociology at the University of Surrey, UK

Ana Cristina Santos is a sociologist and senior researcher at the Centre for Social Studies, University of Coimbra, Portugal

Isabel Crowhurst is a lecturer in Sociology and Criminology at the University of Essex, UK

Routledge Advances in Critical Diversities
Series Editors: Yvette Taylor and Sally Hines

www.routledge.com/sociology/series/RACD

Sexualities Research

Critical Interjections, Diverse
Methodologies, and Practical Applications

**Edited by
Andrew King, Ana Cristina Santos and
Isabel Crowhurst**

NEW YORK AND LONDON

First published 2017
by Routledge
711 Third Avenue, New York, NY 10017

and by Routledge
2 Park Square, Milton Park, Abingdon, Oxon OX14 4RN

Routledge is an imprint of the Taylor & Francis Group, an informa business

British Library Cataloguing-in-Publication Data
A catalogue record for this book is available from the British Library

Library of Congress Cataloging-in-Publication Data
A catalog record for this book has been requested

ISBN: 978-1-138-85164-1 (hbk)
ISBN: 978-1-315-72401-0 (ebk)

Typeset in Times New Roman
by Apex CoVantage, LLC

Contents

Tables

Contributors

Pam Alldred is based at Brunel University, London, UK in the Department of Clinical Sciences. Her work is predominantly on gender, sexuality and youth work, informed by post-structuralism, feminist theory and new materialism. Pam is co-editor of the forthcoming Sage Handbook of Youth Work Practice (2017). Alldred and Fox have been working together since 2011 on projects developing new materialist and Deleuzo Guattarian analyses of sexuality, masculinities and social inquiry. Their book *Sociology and the New Materialism* was published by Sage in 2017.

Chiara Bertone is Associate Professor of Sociology of Cultural Processes at the Department of Law and Political, Economic and Social Sciences, University of Eastern Piedmont. She is currently Lead Co-ordinator of the European Sociological Association Sexuality Research Network. She has researched widely in the field of sexualities, including projects on LGBT youth and their families. She is co-editor (with Raffaella Ferroro Camoletto) of Le fragilità del sesso forte. Medicalizzare la maschilità [The weakness of the stronger sex. Medicalizing masculinity]", published by Mimesis in 2016.

Raffaella Ferrero Camoletto is an Assistant Professor based in the Department of Culture, Politics and Society at the University of Torino, Italy. She has undertaken funded research in the area of medicalization of sexuality, especially with Chiara Bertone. Together they are the editors of "Le fragilità del sesso forte. Medicalizzare la maschilità [The weakness of the stronger sex. Medicalizing masculinity]", published by Mimesis in 2016.

Isabel Crowhurst is lecturer in Sociology and Criminology at the University of Essex. Her research is concerned with the shifting and contested knowledge(s) produced around non-normative sexual practices and intimate lives, how these inform and are informed by laws and policies, and how they are negotiated and made sense of in everyday lived experiences. She is the chair of COST Action IS1209 'Comparing European Prostitution Policies: Understanding Scales and Cultures of Governance (ProsPol)', and is currently developing her work on the governance of sex work, and on the complex processes of doing research on these very aspects.

Roma Dey is a trained social worker and sociologist. She has a Master's in Philosophy from the Centre for the Study of Social Systems, School of Social Sciences, Jawaharlal Nehru University, Delhi. Her paper in this volume is from her dissertation Engaging Exclusions: A Socio-Political Study of Body, Sexuality and Selfhood of Dalit Women based on Dalit women's autobiographies. Her PhD on "Interpreting Motherhood: A Study on the Meanings and Practices" is a multimethod study to understand how women make meaning of motherhood through their own experiences and cultural representations in myths, films, policy discourse and political activism of mothers.

Vulca Fidolini has a PhD in Sociology and is Temporary Lecturer at the University of Strasbourg. His main research topics are in youth, masculinities, sexuality, Islam, social norms and modernity/modernities. His last contributions are focused on constructions of masculinity in a migrant milieu and on religious issues linked to sexual behaviour in Islam context. Publications include: "When Religion Reshapes Identities: Young Moroccan Adults, Sexual Behavior and Islamic Modernities" in Taylor Y., Snowdon R., *Queering Religion, Religious Queers* and Fidolini, V (2015) "Self-Construction and multiple-modernities. A sociological approach to the condition of the individual in contemporary Morocco", *Contemporary Social Science*, vol. 10, n° 1, pp. 15–25.

Nick Fox is honorary professor of sociology at the University of Sheffield. Nick has researched and written widely on postmodern and new materialist social theory, with books and many papers focusing upon health and embodiment, and more recently on topics including sexuality, creativity and emotions. A collaboration with Pam Alldred since 2011 around the development of a materialist sociology has been highly productive: their new book *Sociology and the New Materialism* was published by Sage in 2017.

Beatrice Gusmano is a research fellow at the University of Coimbra (Portugal). She is currently employed on "INTIMATE—Citizenship, Care and Choice: The Micropolitics of Intimacy in Southern Europe" (2014–2019), funded by the European Research Council. Within the project, her fieldwork regards LGBTQ ethical non-monogamies, assisted reproduction for lesbian mothers, and living with LGBTQ friends in adult life. Positioning herself as a queerfeminist activist, she has undertaken research regarding the management of non-heterosexual identities at work; LGBT local public policies in Europe and in Italy; work access networks for ex-convicts; bullying and gender education; diversity management.

Brian Heaphy is Professor of Sociology at the University of Manchester, UK. His research and publications have focused on the implications of social change for living with HIV; same sex intimacies; 'given' and chosen' families; ageing sexualities; friendships and other critical associations; theorising personal life; the links between sexualities and class; marriage and formalised partnerships, and qualitative research methods. He has published widely on these topics including: "Same Sex Marriages: New generations, New Relationships" and "Late Modernity and Social Change: Reconstructing Social and Personal Life".

Susann Huschke is a postdoctoral research fellow at the African Centre for Migration and Society (ACMS) and the School of Public Health at the University of the Witwatersrand, Johannesburg. She received her PhD in Social and Cultural Anthropology at Freie Universität Berlin in 2012. Building on a collaborative study on the sex industry in Northern Ireland, Susann's current research focuses on the everyday lives and struggles of sex workers in Soweto, South Africa. As part of the research, Susann facilitated the participatory film and photography project KNOW MY STORY

Stevi Jackson is Professor in the Centre for Women's Studies, University of York, UK and has been involved in the development and teaching of Women's Studies since the early 1970s. She has retained her interest in sexuality throughout her career, but has also worked on broader aspects of feminist theory, on family relationships and on childhood. In recent years she has begun to develop collaborative relationships with Asian scholars and an interest in comparative work on gender, sexuality and social change. She has supervised 30 PhDs to completion, most of which have been concerned with aspects of family, sexual and intimate relationships.

Joanna Jamel is a Senior Lecturer in Criminology and also lectures in Forensic Psychology at Kingston University, UK. A key focus of her previous research was on male rape within different contexts such as evaluating the specialist policing response of Sexual Offences Investigative Technique (SOIT) officers of the Metropolitan Police Service to male victims of rape. Her current research interests include the policing of transphobic hate crime and transgender offenders in prison and is the author of *Transphobic Hate Crime* (Palgrave MacMillan, 2017). She is a member of the Male Sexual Violation Research Networking Group based at Anglia Ruskin University, Cambridge.

Andrew King is a Senior Lecturer and Deputy Head of the Department of Sociology, University of Surrey, UK. He is an internationally recognised scholar of LGBT ageing and has researched and published widely in that field, including a recently published monograph, "Lesbian, Gay and Bisexual Adults: Identities, Intersections and Institutions" (Routledge, 2016). Andrew is the former Chair of the European Sociological Association Sexuality Research Network (2011–2015) and Co-Editor of "Sociology", a leading journal of the British Sociological Association.

Ana Cristina Marques is a sociologist/researcher/teacher who has held posts at Soran University, Arbil Governate, Iraq and University College, London, UK. As a doctoral student, at the University Institute of Lisbon, Portugal, she conducted research exploring young people's understandings of sexuality during their transition to adulthood in Portugal, using qualitative methods.

Elizabeth McDermott is a Senior Lecturer in the Faculty of Health and Medicine, Lancaster University, UK. Her research is concerned with mental health inequality especially in relation to age, sexuality, gender and social class. She has conducted studies investigating suicide, self-harm, emotional distress, wellbeing and happiness and published widely in this area. She has recently completed a Dept of Health funded project, Queer Futures, a national study examining LGBTQ youth, suicide, self-harm and help-seeking (www.queerfutures.co.uk). Her current Wellcome Trust study is focused on the impact of family relationships on LGBTQ youth mental health and wellbeing. She has co-authored a book titled *Queer Youth, Suicide, and Self-harm: Troubled Subjects, Troubling Norms (2016).*

Alžběta Možíšová received a Master's degree in Sociology at Masaryk University in Brno, Czech Republic. Her research interests include representations of gender and sexuality in the media, coming out within family, and domestic violence. Her dissertation project focuses on intimate partner violence in lesbian relationships in the Czech Republic. She lectured on gender, media and sexuality. Since 2007 she has participated in several non-profit projects, advocating for LGBT rights and gender equality.

Paul Ryan is a lecturer in the Department of Sociology at Maynooth University where his research is located within the sociology of intimate life. He is the author of "Asking Angela Macnamara: an intimate history of Irish lives" (Dublin & Portland, Irish Academic Press) and has published on sex work (Gender, Place and Culture, Qualitative Health Research), sexual citizenship and the LGBT movement and qualitative research. Paul is currently a member of the Cost Action—Comparing European Prostitution Policies: Understanding Scales and Cultures of Governance. He can be contacted at paul.ryan@nuim.ie.

Ana Cristina Santos is a Sociologist. She is Senior Researcher at the Centre for Social Studies, University of Coimbra, Portugal. Coordinator of the International PhD Program Human Rights in Contemporary Societies, Cristina is also the PI on the international research project INTIMATE—Citizenship, Care and Choice: The micropolitics of intimacy in Southern Europe, funded by the European Research Council between 2014 and 2019 (www.ces.uc.pt/intimate). Her most recent book is "Social Movements and Sexual Citizenship in Southern Europe" (Palgrave Macmillan).

Sue Scott has researched and published widely in the areas of gender; sexuality, risk; the body and childhood. She is the author (with Stevi Jackson) of "Theorizing Sexuality" (2010). She has held academic posts at a number of UK Universities including Professorships at Stirling and Durham. She was also Executive Dean of Humanities and Social Sciences at Keele University and Pro Vice Chancellor

(Research) at Glasgow Caledonian University. She currently holds an Honorary Professorship at the University of York and is a Visiting Professor at the University of Helsinki and undertakes research consultancy and mentoring. She is a Vice President of the European Sociological Association and a Managing Editor of, the online social science magazine Discover Society discover society.org.

Yvette Taylor is Professor of Education at Strathclyde University. She was previously (2011–2015) Head of the Weeks Centre for Social and Policy Research, London South Bank University and was peer nominated for the THES Outstanding Leadership and Management Team (2013) and as Diversity Role Model (2013). She received the Lillian Robinson Fellowship, Concordia University (2009) and a Fulbright Scholarship, Rutgers University (2010–2011). Yvette has conducted ESRC projects related to sexualities and has four sole-authored books based on her funded research: "Working-class Lesbian Life" (2007); "Lesbian and Gay Parenting" (2009); "Fitting Into Place? Class and Gender Geographies and Temporalities" (2012); and "Making Space for Queer Identifying Religious Youth" (2015).

Jill Wilkens achieved her PhD at London South Bank University in January 2017. Her PhD research explored older lesbian and bisexual women's experience of habitus dislocation and revealed the significance of affinity groups throughout their lives. Jill is currently a teacher-educator at the Northern College in South Yorkshire, UK.

Gerardo Zamora has researched LGBT childlessness in Spain for his doctorate in public health with the Public University of Navarra, Spain. His background is in sociology, health and human rights. He works on health and public health-related programs, guidelines and interventions in intergovernmental organisations.

Acknowledgements

As editors of this collection, we are delighted that it has appeared in the 'Advances in Critical Diversities' series, edited by Yvette Taylor and Sally Hines. We would like to thank them for their advice and support during the initial proposal and editing process and we thank them especially for seeing the potential and originality in showcasing contemporary sexualities research in this way. Additionally, we would also like to thank the editorial team at Routledge, for their support and patience, especially Max Novick, Jennifer Morrow, Emily Briggs and Elena Chiu.

This book would not have been possible without the existence of the European Sociological Association (ESA) Sexuality Research Network and we are very much indebted to the ESA and the Sexuality Research Network membership for supporting the conference on which this collection was initially based. It has been a privilege to watch the ESA Sexuality Research Network develop over the last eight years and to see it provide a forum for such exciting and cutting-edge scholarship.

Finally, we would like to thank our respective families and friends for supporting us, in one way or another, over the course of developing and eventually publishing this book.

Chapter 7 "Making Space at the (Queer) Academic Table?" by Yvette Taylor contains some material previously published in Taylor, Y (2015) *Making Space for Queer-Identifying Religious Youth*. London: Palgrave Macmillan. It is reproduced here with the permission of Palgrave Macmillan.

1 Introduction

*Andrew King, Ana Cristina Santos
and Isabel Crowhurst*

This book introduces readers to a wide and exciting range of sexualities research currently being conducted by scholars who have, in one way or another, engaged with the European Sociological Association Sexuality Research Network in recent years. The principal aim of this chapter is to provide a broad overview of the book, situating it within a number of contexts. We begin with a discussion of the place of sexualities research in current European Sociology, explaining how the book emerged at a particular point in time—one dominated by policies and measures associated with economic austerity and embedded in neo-liberalism—which forms the backdrop to a number of the chapters in the book. The subsequent section provides a sketch of some the key theoretical and methodological trends that have proved highly influential to the development of the sociology of sexualities and which, in different ways, are picked up by the contributors to this the book. Whilst not an exhaustive overview of theories and methodologies that can be applied to sexualities research, those used, discussed and sometimes critiqued in this book do illustrate the diverse ways that sociologists, and those who have influenced them, have attempted to study and make sense of human sexuality. In the final section of this chapter, we provide an overview of the chapters that comprise the book.

Putting 'Sexualities Research' in Context

The chapters in this book were generated through a conference organised by the editors as part of the European Sociological Association Sexualities Research Network (ESARN23). The conference, which took place in London in January 2013 was, in many ways, the culmination of the re-establishment of ESARN23, a process which had commenced in 2008. The conference, in which 50 delegates presented and discussed their work, constituted a turning point for the consolidation of this Research Network within ESA, which has been growing in the past nine years and now gathers members across a broad spectrum of geographical locations. Hence, the book is a celebration of that process and the work that has contributed to the development of European sexualities research in the early 21st century. This process of re-emergence occurred at a time when a crisis in the global financial system appeared to gather pace, especially in European and other

Western countries. Whilst reactions to the crisis have been manifold, one of the key responses has been the inculcation of an era of austerity which has in turn impacted on sexuality studies in different ways.

Firstly, austerity has led to restricted budgets within academia making attendance at events, such as the one which led to this publication, more difficult. This is especially the case for Early Career Researchers and those without direct institutional support. Whilst organisations such as the European Sociological Association might be able to offer limited bursaries and support, ensuring that the next generation of sexualities scholars can fully participate in the discipline is essential. This is of course the case for social (and other) research more generally. However, changes in terms of restricting research grant provision, orienting research to the development of larger grants or those only available to specific 'high priority' topics as a consequence of the need to provide 'value for money' impacts on the ability of researchers to undertake research on the sexual. In effect, austerity has the ability to limit the scope of future research into sexualities and thereby a profound effect on knowledge production. In an era where all research must demonstrate its impact, to what extent will sexualities research in the social sciences be funded? Will governments and academies under financial strain reinforce the stigma of sexuality research as 'dirty work'?

Secondly, there is the now well established link between poverty and sexual exclusion, marginalisation and sexual exploitation, homophobia/biphobia/transphobia and precarious jobs or unemployment (Santana 2002, Takács 2006, Armas 2007, Richardson and Monro 2012). In short, how people's sexualities intersect with the material remains an abiding issue. Research from previous periods of economic recession indicates that in such times sexualised inequalities and how they are addressed, or not, may well be magnified (Richardson and Monro 2012). Such a situation requires a robust scholarly response—to be able to undertake rigorous research to highlight these disparities and inequities and help to shape future policy and practical responses. Yet, as we have already suggested, the academic grounds on which this might be formulated is, at the same time, being slowly divested. Although Foucault (1978 103) was not adopting a materialist view of sexuality when he referred to it as "an especially dense transfer point for relations of power"—it is interesting to note that the current flourishing of European sociological research about sexualities occurs in a climate of redistribution of economic resources, which knits together the material, the discursive and the symbolic, as a number of chapters in this book illustrate.

Indeed, the third reason why sexualities research is intimately infused with the economic and financial climate currently being experienced in Europe relates to how austerity affects populations who are defined and surveyed by their sexual identities. A number of chapters in this book make explicit and implicit reference to this—either because funding cuts have led to the withdrawal or alteration of policies and practices that seek to support sexual minorities, or because such initiatives are viewed as embellishments that cannot be afforded when money is scarce. The politics of knowledge about the sexual is impacted by austerity and the need to 'make every penny count'.

The argument we have made above may seem alarming and in some ways unwarranted and rather pessimistic at the beginning of a book that, in many ways, celebrates the vibrancy and diversity of sexualities research in Europe. But, as editors of this book, we believe that it is important to provide a clarion warning call about the future of sexualities research at such a socio-political juncture. We cannot and do not undertake sexualities research divorced from the wider social, economic and political contexts in which those we research live their lives and in which we, as politically engaged scholars, are also situated. We cannot ignore the wider context and its role in shaping such a central part of sociological research and social life.

We now turn to sketch out some key theoretical and methodological trends that have influenced sexualities research, especially in a European context, but which continue to influence the sociology of sexualities and provide a further context to the chapters that are contained within this book.

Sexualities in Theory and Practice

Over the course of its relatively short life, the sociology of sexualities has drawn on an eclectic theoretical and methodological palette. In this section of the chapter we will focus on those that have, arguably, been the most influential, challenging and productive, certainly over the past 50 years in Europe and elsewhere, and which many of the authors in this book utilise to productive effect. As the social historian Jeffrey Weeks (2010) has said, researching sexualities back in the 1960s was a 'virgin field'. Such a dubious pun, is not, of course, only intended to raise a knowing, ironic smile amongst fellow sociologists, but a statement regarding the lack of sociological interest in the study of sexualities at the time. However, the study of sexuality was not missing. Sexology and psychoanalysis were particularly important, but as Weeks (2010) and others (Jackson and Scott 2011) have acknowledged, these broad perspectives have been largely countered by sociologists, although they have weighed heavily on the sociological imagination. It is therefore expedient to consider this legacy and how sociologists have sought to move beyond it, both in theory and practice.

Early sexologists, including Havelock Ellis and Karl Heinrich Ulrichs, sought to categorise sexuality, but also to frame it in positive, indeed utopian terms. To an extent this continued into the 20th century with Magnus Hirschfield's Scientific Humanitarian Committee (established in 1897), which was dedicated to campaigning for the recognition of sexual minorities and led to the establishment of the Institut für Sexualwissenschaft (Institute for Sex Research) in Berlin in 1919 (until it was forcibly closed and its library burned by the Nazis in 1933). However, at the same time other sexologists, notably Richard von Krafft-Ebing, Iwan Bloch and Otto Weininger, offered theorisations of sexuality more akin to the pathological. In this respect, as Hawkes (1996) has previously noted, the pleasure/danger dichotomy of sexuality was manifested theoretically, as well as in terms of morality and behaviour. But, like others who have followed them, the sexologists believed in a scientific (and to an extent, a social scientific) approach to the study of sexuality.

The sexologists' methods were diverse and often contentious. Detailed case studies, psychological therapies, physical examinations, surveys and statistics were all employed to a greater or lesser extent and certainly this diversity has continued over the course of sexualities research. Krafft-Ebing's *Psychopathia Sexualis* (1894) presented hundreds of case studies to substantiate his theories about human sexuality and its pathologies. Hirschfield's Institute was multidisciplinary, in methods as much as scope. Moreover, in the early to mid-20th century, the methods and theoretical approaches used to instantiate a science of sex and sexuality were enormously influenced by Freud and his followers.

Freud's legacy for the sociology of sexualities has been contentious at best, and potentially divisive, although some recent work that has influenced the sociology of sexualities has drawn on psychoanalytic understandings and concepts (as will be discussed later in relation to psychosocial studies and Queer Theory). Creating and then employing the methods of psychoanalysis, Freud challenged existing understandings of sexuality that had emerged from the sexologists; in particular, the simple distinction between pleasure/perversity, the notion that sexual desires emerge in adulthood and perhaps most crucial from a sociological viewpoint, that repression is central to the emergence of modern societies. As Jackson and Scott (2011) have noted, it was the latter that was taken up and revitalised by the sexual radicals of the post-World War II era, such as Wilhelm Reich as well as Hebert Marcuse, who drew Freud's ideas together with Marx to provide a critique of sexuality under capitalism. Subsequently, Freud's ideas were critiqued from within the psychoanalytic tradition, the most radical being in the work of Jacques Lacan (particularly in *Écrits* [1977]). Lacan adopted a profoundly anti-essentialist and anti-humanist view that later informed theoretical understandings of sexuality, particularly Queer Theory.

One line of critique of Freud's work also emerged in the mid-20th century in the guise of the bookkeepers of sexuality: the work conducted in the US by Alfred Kinsey and his colleagues (Jackson and Scott 2011). Kinsey was critical of psychoanalysis and other sexological research because he felt it lacked scientific rigour. Kinsey and colleagues undertook significant survey research, in terms of both scope and public attention. Certainly, Kinsey's work, with its attendant scaling of sexual behaviour on a spectrum from exclusively heterosexual to exclusively homosexual. Yet while this has provided a quantitative foundation to the study of sexualities and, to an extent, recognised sexual diversity and its social construction, Kinsey never fully accepted what we might term a more sociological approach. Indeed, Kinsey retained an essentialist view of sexuality that latter work within sociology would significantly challenge.

Developing both during and after the Kinsey era, however, another significant vein of critique was feminism. One of the principal criticisms of Freud's work and indeed much early psychoanalysis was that it privileged male sexuality, creating a phallocentric view of female sexuality and reinforcing patriarchy. Feminists such as Kate Millet (1970) and later Elizabeth Wilson (1981) offered compelling critiques of psychoanalytic theory, but as Bristow (2011) notes, although a number of European feminists have critiqued Freud, others (Rose 1983) have reconsidered and utilised his work. In these cases, the methods of psychoanalysis and the reinterpretation of texts are frequently employed—leading to a somewhat symbolic view of sexuality. More recently, psychoanalytic ideas have made a resurgence in sexualities research, in their influence upon Queer Theory. Butler (1990), for instance, utilised, albeit in a critical way, Freudian ideas in *Gender Trouble*; whilst Edelman's (2004) *No Future*, which critiqued the notion of reproductive futurity, drew heavily on psychoanalysis. More recently, the emergent field of psychosocial studies has drawn on psychoanalytic and queer theorisations (Johnson 2015).

Since the 1970s, feminists have radically questioned what once were orthodox views about women's sexuality, and have critically examined the role of patriarchy in creating women's sexual oppression, linking of the personal and the political and the relationship between gender and sexuality. In so doing, feminists have engaged with both the structural dynamics of women's oppression through sexuality and, more recently, its cultural manifestations. A range of feminisms have influenced the development of a sociology of sexualities, including lesbian feminism (Rich 1980), radical feminism (Dworkin 1987, MacKinnon 1987) and other structural approaches (Rubin 1975), as Jackson and Scott (2011) have noted. More recently, intersectionality (Taylor, Hines, and Casey 2010), and transgender studies (Hines 2007, Beemyn et al. 2016), have also made important and significant interjections in debates about gender and sexuality. Additionally, masculinities studies have also contributed to these debates (Anderson 2010, Connell and Messerschmidt 2005, Seidler 2003), seeking to understand the complex dynamics between power, sexuality and gender.

Feminism has also been central to sociological critiques of heterosexuality (Richardson 1996, Jackson 1999). Indeed, it is arguable that there would not be a critique of heterosexuality without feminism and in many ways debates about sexual citizenship, in terms of rights, belonging and whose sexuality counts and whose does not (Richardson and Monro 2012, Weeks 2007) have followed from this. Notions of sexual and intimate citizenship have also been central to debates about sexuality, equality and diversity, the rights of non-heterosexuals and debates about changes in relationships and ideas about family across Europe (Ammaturo 2015, Cappellato and Mangarella 2014, Mepschen, Duyvendak, and Tonkens 2010, Roseneil et al. 2012, 2013, Santos 2012, 2013).

Sexual citizenship has been used widely in sexualities research recently, although it has, to an extent, remained at the level of structure. Yet more micro approaches have also been and indeed continue to be influential, such as symbolic interactionism, especially that associated with the work of Ken Plummer (1975, 1995), Gagnon and Simon (2005) and Jackson and Scott (2011). A similar micro-sociological focus can be viewed in the work of ethnomethodologists and conversation analysts (Brickell 2006, Hicks 2008, King 2016, King and Cronin 2010, Kitzinger 2005). All this research has focused on the quotidian, the ordinary and the mundane; the way that sexualities are experienced in everyday life, whilst, to some extent, retaining links with wider social structures and norms. For some, this micro-level is too limited and neglects the work of someone who has been enormously influential to the theorisation of sexuality for at least thirty years: Michel Foucault.

In a series of books, Foucault (1978, 1985, 1986) argued that sexuality was not a universal, a-historic phenomenon, akin to the surging force of psychoanalytic drives; instead, it was a historically specific, discursive formation that constituted a series of objects and associated subject positions, such as 'the homosexual'. Foucault was particularly critical of Freud, once describing psychoanalysis as "another round of whispering on a bed" (Foucault 1978, 5). In this respect, Foucault brought a much needed socio-historical focus to the sociology of sexuality and reoriented it around questions of power and knowledge. There have been, of course, myriad criticisms of Foucault's work on sexuality (for a good overview see Bristow 2011), but there can be no doubt that his theoretical 'toolbox' has been very significant, as attested to by a number of chapters in this collection. Foucault and indeed psychoanalysis were also influential, albeit in an often critical counter-injunctive way, in the work of Deleuze and Guattarri (Bogue 2008), whose work on assemblages has recently been incorporated into studies of sexuality (Fox and Alldred 2013).

Foucault's methods were primarily concerned with the interpretation of historical texts, drawing out the discourses that constitute sexuality. This discursive focus is also central to Queer Theory, which has shaped sociological understandings of sexuality over the past 20 years, although it was primarily manifested in literature and the humanities, as well as the AIDS activism of the late 1980s and identity politics of the 1990s.

Queer Theory is an extremely diverse body of work, which initially took the construction of the heterosexual/homosexual binary as its object of study (Fuss 1991, Sedgwick 1993), extended understandings of the relationship between gender, sexuality and heterosexuality through performative norms (Butler 1990, 1993, 2004), to a critique of nationalism and the racialising of bodies (Puar 2007), reproduction and futurity (Edelman 2004), as well as continuing to radically question the ontological foundations of gender and sexual difference (Halberstam 2005, 2011, 2013). Queer Theory has also been 'read' alongside phenomenology (Ahmed 2006), critical humanism (Plummer 2011), postcolonial theory (Hawley 2001) and disability studies, particularly Crip Theory (McRuer 2006).

While Queer Theory has a radically deconstructionist orientation, one that has at times been criticised for being overly theoretical, abstract and ignoring materiality (Green 2007), scholars of sexuality have also utilised intersectionality, as both a theoretical perspective and research methodology (Cho, Crenshaw, and McCall 2013, Fotopoulou 2013, Taylor, Hines, and Casey 2010). Originating from the Black Feminist critique of mainstream feminism, of the early 1990s (Crenshaw 1993, Hill-Collins 2000), intersectionality has been used to examine how inequalities associated with sexuality are always constructed in relation to other forms of social division, identity and forms of power and control, such as, but not limited to, race, class, gender, nationality, disability and geopolitical location. And whilst many intersectional studies of sexualities utilise qualitative methods, by no means all do. Indeed, there is a strong quantitative focus to some intersectional sexualities research (Bowleg 2008).

What is clear from this brief sketch is that some theoretical perspectives have been embraced (all those loosely labelled as social constructionist), whilst others have been spurned (all those loosely labelled positivistic). Similarly, methodologically, sexualities scholars have tended to utilise qualitative methods over quantitative. However, such binaries are rarely stable and indeed sexualities researchers have often used more mixed and innovative methods. As the chapters in this collection demonstrate, eclecticism and experimentation are to the fore in contemporary sexualities research and this collection forms part of that conversation.

Overview of the Book

The book is divided into three substantive parts. Part One, 'Critical Intersections', is composed of six chapters that examine the challenges, limitations and opportunities afforded to theorising sexualities. A range of theoretical traditions, perspectives and concepts are used, sometimes as lenses through which to view substantive topics related to sexualities, sometimes more epistemologically to think through how we understand sexualities.

In chapter two, 'Materialism, Micropolitics and the Sexuality-Assemblages of Young Men', Nick J Fox and Pam Alldred adopt a new materialist perspective which shifts the location of sexuality away from bodies and individuals toward the affective flow within assemblages of bodies, things, ideas and social institutions that produce 'sexual' capacities. This is an approach, strongly influenced by the post-structuralist work of Deleuze and Guattari that radically questions how sexuality is conceptualised, which also has implications for doing sexualities research as they show in a case study example of young men's sexualities.

In chapter three, Brian Heaphy turns a theoretical lens on the ordinariness of same-sex sexualities. Heaphy shows how claims to ordinariness underpin contemporary same-sex intimacies and, perhaps more significantly, claims to rights such as civil partnerships and same-sex marriage. Heaphy's central argument is that existing criticisms of the ordinary, from Queer Theorists, amongst others, relies on an overly simplistic and dichotomous view of politics and power with respect to sexuality. Instead, Heaphy suggests that by focussing on the interplay of difference and commonality, embeddedness and agency, and convention and innovation better insights about the flow of power as relates to 'ordinary sexualities' can be achieved.

The subject of chapter four, 'Counting for Equality: Youth, Class and Sexual Citizenship' by Elizabeth McDermott, is how the emerging State 'demography of homosexuality' contributes to circulating neo-liberal homonormative discourses, which, McDermott argues, firmly places the white, middle-class, male, gay, adult on the centre-stage of sexual citizenship and marginalises those who are queerer, female, black, younger and poorer. McDermott's theoretical lens in this chapter is Foucault's ideas about governmentality and she illustrates its usefulness to show that UK Government population surveys represent a new era in sexual knowledge making, one that, she argues privilege certain types of sexual subjectivity and ontologies. This, she contends, has profound consequences for the lived experiences of a range of (other) sexual citizens.

Chapter five, 'The Normative Account: Sexual Experiences and Constructions of Masculinity among Young Moroccan Men in Europe' by Vulca Fidolini shifts attention from questions of epistemology and how knowledge about sexuality is garnered *per se*, towards questions of theorising heterosexual masculinities. Fidolini draws on ethnographic and interview data with young Moroccan men who had come to Europe during adolescence and explores the contestation of hegemonic and normative sexualities. He shows, through detailed readings of interview excerpts, how questions of religiosity, gender and sexuality intersect.

The final chapter in this section is chapter six, 'Practice Theory and Interactionism: An Integrative Approach to the Sociology of Everyday Sexuality? Here Stevi Jackson and Sue Scott seek to overcome problems with interactionist accounts of sexuality by drawing upon practice theory. Specifically, they bring Alan Warde's (Warde 2016) account of practice theory (in relation to eating) into dialogue with Gagnon and Simon's scripting approach, in order to explore the contribution that this theoretical conjunction might make to a sociological understanding of everyday sexual conduct. In so doing, they offer a way of looking at the embodiment of sexuality that differs considerably from the chapter that commenced this section of the book, thereby illustrating the diversity of current theorisations of sexuality.

The second part of the book, 'Critical Methodologies', is composed of five chapters that critically examine the challenges, limitations and opportunities of doing sexualities research. Chapter seven, 'Making Space at the (Queer) Academic Table?' by Yvette Taylor, reflects on the politics, possibilities and problems created by the impact agenda. Taylor draws on two projects; one concerning queer-identified youth and the other LGBT[1] lives in the North-East of England. The chapter offers a nuanced engagement with both the positionalities and power of the research-researcher-researched, and the possibilities of critical academics who seek to think, theorise and understand these, alongside communities.

In chapter eight, 'Challenges in Reflexive Research into Loneliness and Isolation in Older Lesbians' Jill Wilkens reflects on the practice of undertaking qualitative research with a group of women who, amongst other things, included friends. Drawing on a feminist inspired methodology, Wilkens considers the dangers of assuming commonality with participants, the benefits and limitations of 'insider' status and acknowledges the personal cost to the researcher when emotions such as empathy, sadness or guilt are provoked. Wilken's chapter deals sensitively with the issues raised by creating methodologies that attempt to empower in sexualities research, and the balance that is often struck between ethics, reflexivity and practicalities.

A focus on the autobiographical is at the centre of chapter nine, 'Reading Texts and Their Silences: Sexuality and the Autobiographical Method' by Roma Dey. The chapter draws on Western theories of sexuality, principally in the interactionist tradition, and a grounded theory approach to methodology, but applies these to published autobiographies of Dalit women in India. In the chapter, Dey shows how these autobiographies illustrate shifts in Indian society regarding gender and sexualities, but also how forms of oppression and empowerment are enmeshed.

Chapter ten, 'Intimate Partner Violence in Lesbian Relationships: An Interactional-Structural Analysis' by Alžběta Možíšová. The chapter draws on survey and interview data, and Možíšová argues that a purely structural account is not adequate to consider IPV in same-sex relationships because of the different ways that gendered heteronormativity are/not at play. Instead, Možíšová argues for a more grounded, interactional account, which at the same time references wider structures of power.

Finally, in this part of the book is chapter eleven by Ana Cristina Marques, entitled ' "Inside/Out": Researching Young Adults' Sexuality in a(n) (Un)Familiar Space. A Reflexive Approach'. As the title of the chapter indicates, Marques is concerned here with notions of reflexivity and how researchers of sexuality can be positioned as both insiders and outsiders in their research. This is especially so when Marques reflects on her experience of researching younger heterosexual women and LGBT* people in her home town.

Part three of the book, 'Critical Practices', encompasses five chapters, all of which are concerned, one way or another, with how sexualities research is applied in a range of different institutional and national contexts. Chapter twelve, 'Uncomfortable Bargains? Networking Between Local Authorities and LGBT Associations in the Context of Neoliberalism' by Beatrice Gusmano, examines how LGBT issues and national-level politics related to them are translated into local policies. Gusmano considers whether *queerness* can escape the politically tranquillising delivery of a homonormative sexual citizenship. Hence, using the local governance of Turin, Italy, as a case study, the chapter explores the politics of sexual citizenship and draws a number of critical points about the application of contemporary discourses of sexualities.

Sexualities research often references LGBT people without real recourse to considering trans people's lives. In chapter thirteen, Joanna Jamel brings in a much needed focus on trans lives in the context of the criminal justice system and especially the experiences of trans prisoners. Using a range of statistical data from the US, Canada, England and Australia, Jamel's chapter 'Transgender Offenders Within the Prison Estate: A Comparative Analysis of Penal Policy' illustrates how trans prisoners challenge the normative aspects of penal policies based on a socially prescribed gender binary and thus notions of sexual differentiation. A number of practical recommendations, based on research and good practice, are also detailed.

Chapter fourteen, by Paul Ryan and Susann Huschke, also deals with researching sexualities in relation to criminal justice, but takes a more reflective and reflexive overview. The chapter, titled 'Conducting Sex Work Research in a Politically Contentious Climate: Lessons from Ireland', addresses both the personal and professional costs of speaking publically from a position that runs counter to the dominant view about sex work. It deals with how sexualities researchers, including the authors themselves, have navigated relationships with individuals and groups that were often former allies, but now stand in stark opposition to research that advocates a more nuanced 'anti-abolitionist' position concerning sex work. Hence, Ryan and Huschke remind us of the political (and indeed personal) framings of sexualities research and the personal/political costs it can enact.

A focus on expert discourse and its re-framing is central to chapter fifteen, 'Medicalized Virilism Under Scrutiny: Expert Knowledge on Male Sexual Health in Italy' by Raffaella Ferrero Camoletto and Chiara Bertone. In the chapter, they examine how medical experts use discourses concerning age, gender and sexuality to construct male sexuality in certain ways and not others. However, the authors note that there is more ambivalence and negotiation in medical discourse than is often represented. In the chapter they explore these tensions and contradictions.

Finally, chapter sixteen 'Challenging the Use of Heteronormative Categories in Childlessness Studies' by Gerardo Zamora, examines the practicalities of labelling in research. Zamora enters into a sustained critique of the concept of childlessness by way of its largely heteronormative framing. Using interviews with gay men, Zamora argues for a more nuanced and reflective understanding that takes account of LGBTQ lives. The chapter therefore considers the politics of sexualities research and the knowledge that it produces.

Concluding Points

Throughout this book, each of the chapters showcases contemporary sexualities scholarship within sociology, but also draw on other disciplines and theoretical and methodological agendas. In this respect, current research continues the eclecticism established by earlier generations of scholars. Whilst some of the topics may be very specific to contemporary times—issues about same-sex marriage or Viagra, for instance—others continue and extend topics which sociologists of sexuality have been addressing for many years, such as sex work, childlessness and power relations. But in each case, the chapters bring something new and help us to see the continued vitality of a sociology of sexualities in the 21st century. Each chapter demonstrates that the sociology of sexualities, which has always had a strong empirical foundation, as well as a diverse, highly critical and innovative theoretical underpinning, remains important to the wider discipline at this critical juncture.

In this book we hope to provide a space for debates in sexualities research, theoretical, methodological and practical, that readers will find interesting, inspiring and significant for their own work—whether that be as researchers, students, activists, policy-makers or simply interested observers.

Note

1   Different authors use a range of acronyms regarding lesbian, gay, bisexual, transgender (LGBT) and queer (LGTBQ) individuals. This mirrors the diversity both across countries (country-based terminology) but also within LGBTQ politics and research.

References

Ahmed, S. 2006. *Queer Phenomenology: Orientations, Objects, Others.* Durham: Duke University Press.

Ammaturo, F.R. 2015. "The 'Pink Agenda': Questioning and Challenging European Homonationalist Sexual Citizenship." *Sociology* 49 (6): 1151–1166.

Anderson, Eric. 2010. *Inclusive Masculinity: The Changing Nature of Masculinities.* London: Routledge.

Armas, H. 2007. *Whose Sexuality Counts? Poverty, Participation and Sexual Rights.* Brighton: Institute of Development Studies.

Beemyn, G., Rankin, S.R., Park, P., Crawford, L., Keja, V., Chen, J., Beauchamp, T., Burke, N.B., Aizura, A.Z. and M.C. Enriquez. 2016. *Trans Studies: The Challenge to Hetero/ Homo Normativities.* New Brunswick, NJ: Rutgers University Press.

Bogue, R. 2008. *Deleuze and Guattari.* London: Routledge.

Bowleg, L. 2008. "When Black + Lesbian + Woman ≠ Black Lesbian Woman: The Methodological Challenges of Qualitative and Quantitative Intersectionality Research." *Sex Roles* 59 (5): 312–325. doi: 10.1007/s11199–008–9400-z.

Brickell, C. 2006. "The Sociological Construction of Gender and Sexuality." *The Sociological Review* 54 (1): 87–113.

Bristow, J. 2011. *Sexuality.* 2nd ed. London: Routledge.

Butler, J. 1990. *Gender Trouble.* London: Routledge.

Butler, J. 1993. *Bodies That Matter: On the Discursive Limits of Sex.* New York: Routledge.

Butler, J. 2004. *Undoing Gender.* London: Routledge.

Cappellato, V., and T. Mangarella. 2014. "Sexual Citizenship in Private and Public Space: Parents of Gay Men and Lesbians Discuss Their Experiences of Pride Parades." *Journal of GLBT Family Studies* 10 (1–2): 211–230.

Cho, S., Crenshaw, K. and L. McCall. 2013. "Toward a Field of Intersectionality Studies: Theory, Applications, and Praxis." *Signs* 38 (4): 785–810. doi: 10.1086/669608.

Connell, R. and J.W. Messerschmidt. 2005. "Hegemonic Masculinity Rethinking the Concept." *Gender and Society* 19 (6): 829–859.

Crenshaw, K. 1993. "Mapping the Margins: Intersectionality, Identity Politics and Violence Against Women of Color." *Stanford Law Review* 43 (6): 1241–1299.

Dworkin, A. 1987. *Intercourse.* London: Secker and Warburg.

Edelman, L. 2004. *No Future: Queer Theory and the Death Drive.* Durham, NC: Duke University Press.

Fotopoulou, A. 2013. "Intersectionality, Queer Studies and Hybridity: Methodological Frameworks for Social Research." *Journal of International Women's Studies* 13 (2): 19–32.

Foucault, M. 1978. *The Will to Knowledge—The History of Sexuality Vol. 1.* London: Penguin.

Foucault, M. 1985. *The Use of Pleasure: The History of Sexuality Vol. 2.* Translated by R. Hurley. London: Penguin.

Foucault, M. 1986. *The Care of the Self: The History of Sexuality Vol. 3.* Translated by R. Hurley. London: Penguin.

Fox, N.J. and P. Alldred. 2013. "The Sexuality-Assemblage: Desire, Affect, Anti-Humanism." *The Sociological Review* 61 (4): 769–789.

Fuss, D. 1991. "Inside/Out." In *Inside/Out: Lesbian Theories, Gay Theories*, edited by D. Fuss, 1–10. London: Routledge.

Gagnon, J. and W. Simon. 2005. *Sexual Conduct: The Sources of Human Sexuality.* 2nd ed. Piscataway, NJ: Aldine Transaction.

Green, A.I. 2007. "Queer Theory and Sociology: Locating the Subject and the Self in Sexuality Studies." *Sociological Theory* 25 (1): 26–45.

Halberstam, J. 2005. *In a Queer Time and Place: Transgender Bodies, Subcultural Lives.* New York: NYU Press.

Halberstam, J. 2011. *The Queer Art of Failure.* Durham: Duke University Press.

Halberstam, J. 2013. "Queer Betrayals." In *Queer Futures: Reconsidering Ethics, Activism and the Political*, edited by E.H. Yekani, E. Kilian and B. Michaelis, 177–190. Farnham: Ashgate.

Hawkes, G. 1996. *A Sociology of Sex and Sexuality*. Buckingham: Open University Press.

Hawley, J.C. 2001. *Postcolonial, Queer: Theoretical Intersections*. New York: SUNY Press.

Hicks, S. 2008. "Thinking Through Sexuality." *Journal of Social Work* 8 (1): 65–82.

Hill-Collins, P. 2000. *Black Feminist Thought: Knowledge, Consciousness and the Politics of Empowerment*. 2nd ed. New York: Routledge.

Hines, S. 2007. *Transforming Gender: Transgender Practices of Identity, Intimacy and Care*. Bristol: Policy Press.

Jackson, S. 1999. *Heterosexuality in Question*. London: Sage.

Jackson, S. and S. Scott. 2011. *Theorising Sexuality*. Buckingham: Open University Press.

Johnson, K. 2015. *Sexuality: A Psychosocial Manifesto*. London: John Wiley & Sons.

King, A. 2016. "Queer Categories: Queer(y)ing the Identification 'Older Lesbian, Gay and/or Bisexual (LGB) Adults' and Its Implications for Organizational Research, Policy and Practice." *Gender, Work and Organization* 23 (1): 7–18.

King, A. and A. Cronin. 2010. "Queer Methods and Queer Practices: Re-Examining the Identities of Older Lesbian, Gay, Bisexual (OLGB) Adults." In *Queer Methods and Methodologies*, edited by K. Browne and C. Nash, 85–96. Aldershot: Ashgate.

Kitzinger, C. 2005. "Heteronormativity in Action: Reproducing the Heterosexual Nuclear Family in After-Hours Medical Calls." *Social Problems* 52 (4): 477–498.

Krafft-Ebing, R.V. 1894. *Psychopathia Sexualis: With Especial Reference to Antipathetic Sexual Instincts, A Medico-Forensic Study*. London: Rebman.

Lacan, J. 1977. *Écrits: A Selection*. London: Tavistock.

MacKinnon, C.A. 1987. *Feminism Unmodified: Discourses on Life and Law*. Cambridge, MA: Harvard University Press.

McRuer, R. 2006. *Crip Theory: Cultural Signs of Queerness and Disability*. New York: New York University Press.

Mepschen, P., Duyvendak, J.W. and E.H. Tonkens. 2010. "Sexual Politics, Orientalism and Multicultural Citizenship in the Netherlands." *Sociology* 44 (5): 962–979.

Millet, K. 1970. *Sexual Politics*. New York: Doubleday.

Plummer, K. 1975. *Sexual Stigma*. London: Routledge and Kegan Paul.

Plummer, K. 1995. *Telling Sexual Stories*. London: Routledge.

Plummer, K. 2011. "Critical Humanism and Queer Theory: Living With the Tensions." In *The SAGE Handbook of Qualitative Research*, edited by N.K. Denzin and Y.S. Lincoln, 195–207. London: Sage.

Puar, J. 2007. *Terrorist Assemblages: Homonationalism in Queer Times*. Durham, NC: Duke University Press.

Rich, A. 1980. "Compulsory Heterosexuality and Lesbian Existence." *Signs* 5 (4): 631–660.

Richardson, D., ed. 1996. *Theorising Heterosexuality*. Buckingham: Open University Press.

Richardson, D., and S. Monro. 2012. *Sexuality, Equality and Diversity*. Basingstoke: Palgrave Macmillan.

Rose, J. 1983. "Femininity and Its Discontents." *Feminist Review* 14: 5–21.

Roseneil, S., Crowhurst, I., Hellesund, T., Santos, A.C. and M. Stoilova. 2012. "Remaking Intimate Citizenship in Multicultural Europe: Experiences Outside the Conventional Family." In *Remaking Citizenship in Multicultural Europe: Women's Movements, Gender and Diversity*, edited by Beatrice Halsaa, Sasha Roseneil and Sevil Sümer, 41–69. London: Palgrave Macmillan.

Roseneil, S., Crowhurst, I., Hellesund, T., Santos, A.C. and M. Stoilova. 2013. "Changing Landscapes of Heteronormativity: The Regulation and Normalization of Same-Sex

Sexualities in Europe." *Social Politics: International Studies in Gender, State and Society* 20 (2): 165–199.

Rubin, G. 1975. "The Traffic in Women: Notes on the 'Political Economy' of Sex." In *Toward an Anthropology of Women*, edited by R. Reiter, 157–210. New York: Monthly Review Press.

Santana, P. 2002. "Poverty, Social Exclusion and Health in Portugal." *Social Science and Medicine* 55 (1): 33–45.

Santos, A.C. 2012. "The Politics of Sexuality in Portugal: Confronting Tradition, Enacting Change." In *Sexualities: Past Reflections, Future Directions*, edited by Sally Hines and Yvette Taylor, 168–185. London: Palgrave Macmillan.

Santos, A.C. 2013. *Social Movements and Sexual Citizenship in Southern Europe*. Basingstoke: Palgrave Macmillan.

Sedgwick, E.K. 1993. "Epistemology of the Closet." In *The Lesbian and Gay Studies Reader*, edited by H. Abelove, M.A. Barale and D.M. Halperin, 45–61. New York: Routledge.

Seidler, V.J. 2003. *Rediscovering Masculinity: Reason, Language and Sexuality*. London: Routledge.

Takács, J. 2006. *Social Exclusion of Young Lesbian, Gay, Bisexual and Transgender (LGBT) People in Europe*. Belgium: ILGA Europe Brussels.

Taylor, Y., Hines, S. and M.E. Casey, eds. 2010. *Theorizing Intersectionality and Sexuality*. London: Palgrave Macmillan.

Warde, A. 2016. *The Practice of Eating*. Cambridge: Polity Press.

Weeks, J. 2007. *The World We Have Won: The Remaking of Erotic and Intimate Life*. London: Routledge.

Weeks, J. 2010. *Sexuality*. 3rd ed. London: Routledge.

Wilson, E. 1981. "Psychoanalysis: Psychic Law and Order?" *Feminist Review* 8: 63–78.

Part I
Critical Interjections

2 Materialism, Micropolitics and the Sexuality-Assemblages of Young Men

Pam Alldred and Nick J Fox

This chapter explores what is gained (and lost) in a sociology of sexuality that applies a materialist and posthuman perspective. It establishes a Deleuze-inspired language of sexuality using the concepts of 'assemblage', 'affect', 'productive desire' and 'territorialisation'. Sexuality is re-located away from bodies and individuals, on to the affective flow within the sexuality-assemblages of bodies, things, ideas and social institutions that produce sexual capacities in bodies and collectivities. The chapter re-thinks conceptions such as sexual desire, sexual response, sexual preferences, sexual codes of conduct, sexual identity and sexuality itself. The chapter develops and illustrates both this ontology and its translation into a methodology for social inquiry using two disparate datasets to explore the sexuality of young men: a series of interviews with higher education students and two focus groups with white working-class teens.

Introduction

Sexual desire, sexual arousal and sexual pleasure seem so interior to a body, so typically focused 'outwards' on to objects of desire that are not the body itself, that it may seem counter-factual to question sexuality's status as an attribute of an organism. Internalised accounts of sexual desire and sexual identity have strongly influenced lay and social science ontologies of sexuality: within the latter, an individual's sexuality is regarded as revealed, released or repressed by culture (Lambevski 2005; Rasmussen 2012). As Burman (2003), Grosz (1995), and Weeks (1998) pointed out, sexual essentialism has underpinned aspirational and liberationist identity-politics, for instance in struggles for same-sex marriage rights or to counter homophobic bullying (Monk 2011; Rasmussen 2008). And while Foucault's (1981, 1988, 1990) studies have revealed how sexuality, sexual subjectivity and sexual orientation are shaped by socially contingent systems of thought, this does not in itself challenge 'anthropocentric' (Braidotti 2006, 40) conceptions of the human body and human 'individual' as the privileged locus where sexuality happens. Sexual identities and subject-positions are regarded as relatively stable social discourses inscribed on individual bodies (Lambevski 2005).

Doubts over the prioritised status of the body and the human subject in the social sciences, and unease over the nature/culture dualism underpinning much sociology (Barad 1996) have fuelled interest in 'new materialist' approaches that move beyond both agency/structure and animate/inanimate dualisms (Braidotti 2006; Buchanan 1997; Clough 2008; DeLanda 2006, Grosz 1995). This 'turn to matter' has decentred ontological status from a body or conscious subject in favour of 'pre-human or even non-human elements that compose the web of forces, intensities and encounters' (Braidotti 2006: 41); it is these—according to materialist theorists, that produce subjectivities, bodily capacities, and by extension, sexualities. This approach suggests that aspects of existence often considered as properties of an individual body or subject, such as creativity, emotions, development, health and—by extension, sexuality, should be re-conceptualised (Buchanan 1997; Fox 2012; Fox and Alldred 2013).

In this chapter, we wish to explore a sociology of sexuality that takes this ontological step, shifting the location of sexuality away from bodies and individuals toward the affective flow within assemblages of bodies, things, ideas and social institutions that produce 'sexual' capacities. We establish a language and landscape for a materialist 'sexuality-assemblage'; and use this understanding of sexuality to explore some empirical data on the sexuality-assemblages of young men.

New Materialism, Sexuality and the Sexuality-Assemblage

'New' materialism has emerged over the past 20 years as an approach concerned fundamentally with the material workings of power, but focused firmly upon social production rather than social construction (Coole and Frost 2010; Taylor and Ivinson 2013). Unease over the 'textualisation' of bodies in post-structuralism led new materialist scholars including Barad (1996), Braidotti (2006) and Clough (2008) to propose an ontology of subjectivity that asserts a central role for matter (Braidotti 2013). These new materialisms extend materialist analysis beyond traditional concerns with structural and 'macro' level social phenomena (van der Tuin and Dolphijn 2010: 159), addressing issues of how desires, feelings and meanings also contribute to social production (Braidotti 2000; DeLanda 2006).

For Coole and Frost (2010, 29), materiality is plural, open, complex, uneven and contingent; new materialist ontologies "understand materiality in a relational, emergent sense", with a focus that extends from globalisation to issues of identity, and dissolving boundaries between the natural and the cultural, mind and matter (Braidotti 2013). Barad's (1996, 181) 'agential realism' similarly dissolves the distinction between nature and culture, rejecting an opposition found in both realist and idealist ontology when she states that "constructedness does not deny materiality". Matter is not inert, nor simply the background for human activity, but "is conceptualised as agentic" (Taylor and Ivinson 2013, 666), with multiple non-human as well as human sources of agency with capacities to affect.

A number of authors have applied new materialist perspectives to sexuality (Beckman 2011; Braidotti 2006; Fox and Alldred 2013; Holmes et al. 2010; Lambevski 2005; Probyn 1995, Renold and Ringrose 2011; Ringrose 2011), in many cases founded in the philosophy and social critique of Deleuze and Guattari (1984, 1988). Braidotti (2011, 148) has described sexuality as a "complex, multi-layered force that produces encounters, resonances and relations of all sorts", while we theorise sexuality as "an impersonal affective flow within assemblages of bodies, things, ideas and social institutions, which produces sexual (and other) capacities in bodies" (Fox and Alldred 2013, 769), and argue that a 'sexuality-assemblage' (rather than the individual sexual body) should be the focus of study. Sexuality-assemblages bridge 'micro' and 'macro', private and public, intimacy and polity, and establish the capacities of individual bodies to do, feel and desire. They shape the eroticism, sexual codes, customs and conduct of a society's members, as well as the categories of sexuality such as 'hetero', 'homo' and so forth (Linstead and Pullen 2006). In short, it is a sexuality-assemblage that is productive of all phenomena associated with the physical and social manifestations of sex and sexuality. We will now swiftly develop our understanding of the sexuality-assemblage, and the DeleuzoGuattarian concepts underpinning it.

First, conceptualising a sexuality-assemblage emphasises the fundamental *relationality* of all matter: bodies, things and social formations gain their apparent 'is-ness' only when in relation. Rather than taking the body or thing or the social organisation as a pre-existing unit of analysis, we should attend to the fluctuating assemblages that produce both events and the apparent stability of the relations that they comprise. For example, a sexuality-assemblage accrues around an event such as an erotic kiss, which comprises not just two pairs of lips but also physiological processes, personal and cultural contexts, aspects of the setting, memories and experiences, sexual codes and norms of conduct, and potentially many other relations particular to that event.

Second, a sexuality-assemblage is analysed not in terms of human or other agency, but by looking at its 'affective economy' (Clough 2004). We use the term 'affect' simply to indicate an ability to affect or be affected; an assemblage's affect economy can be understood as shifting bodies and other assembled relations "from one mode to another, in terms of attention, arousal, interest, receptivity, stimulation, attentiveness, action, reaction, and inaction" (Clough 2004, 15). Within a sexuality-assemblage, human and non-human relations affect (and are affected by) each other to produce material effects, including sexual capacities and desires, sexual identities and the many 'discourses' on sexualities.

Third, and importantly for the study of sexuality, desire is understood as part of the affective flow in the sexuality-assemblage (Deleuze and Guattari 1988), to the extent that desire produces specific capacities to act or feel in a body or bodies, be it arousal, attraction, sexual activity, rejection or whatever. Productive desire is the creative capacity (Jordan 1995, 127) of a body to act, feel or otherwise engage with other bodies and the physical and social world; the conditions of possibility for "what a body can do". Put another way, desire is nothing more nor less than the capacity of a body to affect or be affected.

Finally, an emphasis on affect economies and the changes they produce in relations and assemblages provides a dynamic focus for the empirical study of sexuality and sexuality assemblages. Studying a body's, a thing's or a social formation's capacities (and the limits and the possibilities for such capacities and capabilities) supplies a means to explore affect economies empirically. We may ask what a body can do within a relational sexuality-assemblage, what it cannot do and what it can become. This opens to scrutiny both the affect economy within a sexuality-assemblage, and its internal micropolitics, which produces sexual desires, sexual responses, codes of sexual conduct, sexual identities and so forth.

The Micropolitics of Sexuality-Assemblages

We turn now to the application of this materialist ontology of sexuality-assemblages to sociological purposes. In an approach that focuses on how bodies affect and are affected, rather than what they are, analytical attention must address the "relations between bodies, their configurations within specific assemblages and the dynamic of the interrelations of their intensive capacities" (Gatens 1996, 170). As noted earlier, assemblages connect multitudinous relations from physical, biological, cultural and abstract realms, while the flows of affect between and among these relations produce bodily desires and capacities. These capacities are products of flows of affect within assemblages, creating the conditions of possibility for sexual desire, sexual responses, codes of sexual conduct, sexual identities and so forth, and hence a *micropolitics* of sexuality: of how bodies, things, social institutions and abstract concepts interact and of the power relations within assemblages.

The micropolitics of sexuality-assemblage is key to a materialist analysis of sexuality, and we will attend briefly to two DeleuzoGuattarian conceptions of how assemblage micropolitics work: 'territorialisation' and 'aggregation', which we will apply when we turn to analysis of empirical data on sexuality-assemblages later.

Territorialisation (Deleuze and Guattari 1988) describes the relational and affective contextualisation of a body or other element in an assemblage. One or more affects can territorialise a body, establishing it within a specific context and thereby defining context-specific capacities. Other affects may subsequently 'de-territorialise' or 're-territorialise' it, re-shaping the possibilities and limits of what a body can do, continuously and unendingly. Sexual arousal, attraction, preferences and conduct (variously understood as the interaction of biology, psychology and culture in anthropocentric sciences and social sciences) can be seen as territorialisations produced by affects and desires in a sexuality-assemblage. So for instance, a kiss may territorialise a body into sexual arousal, while marketing aimed at children may territorialise ('sexualise') their bodies into adult sexual identities and choices (Bale 2011). Other affects may de-stabilise or de-territorialise. For example, that same kiss, if delivered by a new lover, might open up a radically de-territorialising "line of flight" (Deleuze and Guattari 1988, 277) that propels a body into possibilities, such as polyamory, or a new life begun elsewhere.

We replace Deleuze and Guattari's (1984) obscure (physical chemical) terminology of 'molar' and 'molecular' affects as, respectively, 'aggregative' and 'singular' (Fox and Alldred 2015). Aggregating affects act similarly on multiple bodies, organising or categorising them to create converging identities or capacities. In the field of sexuality, ideas and concepts such as love, monogamy, chastity or sexual liberation, prejudices and biases, conceptual categories such as 'women', 'heterosexual' or 'perverted', along with the discourses on human sexuality documented by Foucault (1981) all aggregate bodies, producing (among other outputs) the pervasive social relations between bodies that sociology has summarised as 'patriarchy', 'heteronormativity' and the familialisation of sexuality and reproduction (Deleuze and Guattari 1984). By contrast, other affects (for instance, a gift, smile or a caress from a lover) produce a singular effect or capacity in just one body, with no significance beyond itself, and without aggregating consequences. Singular affects may be particularly significant as micropolitical drivers of de-territorialisation, enabling bodies to resist aggregating or constraining forces, and opening up new capacities to act, feel or desire.

These two micropolitical processes provide a means to explore why sexuality manifests as it does in different social and cultural settings. Flows of affect in sexuality-assemblages (including sexual desires) connect bodies to other relations, and territorialise body capacities, producing the sexual body and all its anatomical, physiological, emotional and cognitive capacities. This sexual body is not pre-existing, but entirely produced (territorialised) out of materials in a sexuality-assemblage. Territorialisations produce body capacities including comportments, identities and subjectivities that establish 'masculinity' and 'femininity'. Sexual attraction, sexual preferences and proclivities are similarly territorialisations toward particular objects of desire, consequent upon the particular mix of relations and affects deriving from physical and social contexts, experience and culture. Sexual codes are culture-specific aggregating affects that establish the limits of what individual bodies can do, feel and desire in specific sociocultural settings, and shape the eroticism, sexual codes, customs and conduct of a society's members, as well as the categories of sexual identity such as 'hetero', 'homo', polyamorous, queer and so forth (Barker 2005; Linstead and Pullen 2006). Singular affects produce unique affects within the sexuality-assemblage that may de-territorialise and dis-aggregate these formations, to produce novel and even resistant expressions of sexuality.

Sexuality itself, often almost synonymous in anthropocentric sociology with sexual identity, we radically re-conceptualise, following Deleuze and Guattari (1984) as *the flow of affect in the sexuality-assemblage surrounding a body*. It has two manifestations. On one hand, it is a de-territorialising, nomadic and 'rhizomic' (meaning multiplying, non-linear) affective flow between and around bodies and other relations that has the potential to produce any and all capacities in bodies, different sexual desires, attractions and identities, and those not normally considered sexual at all: nomadic sexuality has nothing to do with reproduction or even genitality (Bogue 2011; Deleuze and Guattari 1984), and consequently may produce "subversive and unforeseeable expressions of sexuality" (Beckman 2011, 11).

On the other hand, this rhizomic flow of affect is continuously subject to restrictions and blockages (Deleuze and Guattari 1984), often produced by aggregating relations that codify, categorise and organise, channelling desire into a relatively narrow range of sexual capacities. Whereas anthropocentric approaches evoke liberal-humanist notions of an 'authentic' sexuality lost or distanced by social and cultural forces (Kitzinger 1987), in this posthumanist perspective, the production of an individual 'sexy' body is always an active territorialisation of this non-human and impersonal, rhizomic sexuality. Despite this territorialisation, new affects still have the capacity to de-territorialise, re-establishing the rhizomic flow and creating possibilities for a sexual line of flight.

The Sexuality-Assemblages of Young Men

We will now apply this ontology of sexuality-assemblages, and analyse empirical data concerning young men's sexuality according to the precepts of new materialism (Fox and Alldred 2015). The data we present here is drawn from two studies, the first an ethnography of sex and relationship education (SRE) teaching in UK secondary schools conducted by the first author (Alldred and David 2007), which included interviews and observations of teenage boys in school or in alternative educational settings; the other a secondary analysis of 32 interviews with male students, employed and unemployed young men undertaken as part of a study of masculinity.[1]

We begin our analysis by exploring similarities and disparities in the range of relations in young men's sexuality-assemblages. However, our main focus is upon the micropolitical movements of territorialisation, de-territorialisation, aggregation and dis-aggregation. We use the data sources to seek out flux and fluidity within the sexuality-assemblage, to disclose the affects and desires that produce young men's sexualities (Ringrose 2011), and crucially, the limits to these capacities.

Relations and Affects

Studies of childhood and development suggest that biology, parents and family, friendships, schooling, early experiences and bodily maturation are all components of a young man's sexuality-assemblage (Bancroft 2003), while sociological studies also point to the contribution of culture and the media (Bale 2011; Frosh et al. 2002). The ethnography of teen boys' SRE classes supplies a snapshot of young male sexuality, revealing the importance of peers, siblings, teachers and the school environment (both in terms of the formal curriculum and the informal interactions in and out of class) for the teen sexuality-assemblage, while disclosing something of the affect economy that links these relations. School nurses were preferred over teachers as sources of sexual health information, while teens resisted values and relationship discussions which they felt were none of the school's business. Boys were also reluctant to discuss emotional issues with teachers, preferring 'mates' or family members such as an older brother. Among a group of teen boys excluded from school, the SRE curriculum had little impact. For this school-excluded group, the embodied pleasures of sexuality were the dominant element in the mix, and a means to resist the tedium of the classroom, and moreover the values that produced them as academic failures, as outcasts from school, and unsuccessful in building their CVs (Alldred and David 2007). Interviews with this all-male group (conducted by a female researcher) were treated as further opportunities for sexual banter and horseplay to subvert an adult agenda.

The second dataset offers a second cross-section of relations, when young men were at university, at work or unemployed. These 32 young men were generally sexually active, ranging from occasional sexual encounters, reports of frequent casual relationships with partners met in social venues, through to steady relationships, and for one respondent, marriage. Dredging these data revealed a broad range of material (animate and inanimate; physical, psychological, social and abstract) relations in young men's sexuality-assemblages: significant others (mates, girlfriends, parents, teachers); the physical spaces where they interact and socialise, the alcohol and drugs they consume; sport and fitness activities and the ideas surrounding them; sexual partners; cultures and backgrounds. Also in the mix were abstract concepts such as monogamy, love, sexual fidelity and honesty, all of which have the capacity to affect bodies.

While these disparate data sources suggest the idiosyncratic, unstable and fluctuating composition of sexuality-assemblages, it also identifies relations and affects that occur more generally. From the teenage boys in the school dataset— who focused primarily upon the embodied pleasures that sexual arousal could provide, to the university students for whom alcohol, clubs and pubs, and abstract ideas of love and fidelity often appeared in the affect economy, there were recurrent threads that cut across individual sexuality-assemblages. To explore this further, we now consider the micropolitics of these sexuality-assemblages.

The Micropolitics of Young Men's Sexuality

The fluxes, stabilities and instabilities produced in sexuality-assemblages as the affect economies within them shift and re-configure, disperse or re-form can be further analysed in terms of *territorialisations* that specify relatively stable capacities in young men, *de-territorialisations* that undermine these and establish different sexual or other capabilities, *aggregations* that group or unify aspects of young men's sexualities, and the *singular* affects that occasionally offer new capacities and possibilities for sexuality or subjectivity.

Both datasets provided evidence of the ways in which boys' and young men's bodies and sexual subjectivities were territorialised and aggregated. For the boys, this was the product of a competitive and hierarchical affect economy between peers that ranked their own bodies, cars and girlfriends, and was sometimes bolstered by the exercise of physical or social displays of machismo or intimidation. Bodily maturation, height, voices that had 'broken' and facial hair were relations that mediated claims by boys to heterosexual prowess, as did competitive homophobic posturing and (hetero)sexualised banter (for example, one boy's suggested improvement to his school's SRE classes: 'I reckon we should have a fit bird come in and then talk about all the male [body] parts').

In the older group, competition for what one young man called 'the best girl', or the acquisition of a steady girlfriend reflected relational micropolitics that territorialised young men's bodies into a heterosexual and heteronormative assemblage. Scott described his efforts to be 'the person who's had a lot of sexual partners. . . who attracts the best looking girl in the bar'. Andrew entertained his 'mates' with details of his sex life, while Najib's sexual encounters were part of an assemblage with his male friends:

> They were all on my case, all of them, like 'Come on. We want to see you in action', and I was like 'No, no. I'm all right', you know. And they were all calling me chicken. And I thought 'Oh no, here we go again'. You know, the ego thing, I was listening to part of them: 'Pick the best girl in the club, and I'm going to get with her'. So he [a mate] picks out the—I mean this woman was amazing. You know, she was gorgeous. And all night I'm trying to pull this girl. . . you know, and I finally do.

This competitiveness contributed to the production of a sexual subjectivity: for Lester, heterosexual encounters defined his capacities as a man.

> I suppose it is quite an important marker your first girlfriend, or your first pull, or the first time you get laid. I suppose it is quite important as, like, a yeah 'Now I am. . . more than I was yesterday', just because of that. It's kind of a rite of passage, maybe.

Both datasets thus illustrate a similar, strongly aggregative, territorialisation that drew teen boys and young men into an assemblage that framed their masculinity and (hetero)sexuality within what some scholars have described as 'compulsory heterosexuality' and 'hegemonic masculinity' (Holland et al. 1998; Mac an Ghaill 1994). In part these aggregations derived from the physical and social materialities of clubs, pubs and alcohol that provided a backcloth for the students' sex lives. Other aggregative territorialisations of sexuality derived from religious, moral or cultural relations. Stephen, a devout Christian, described sex before marriage as 'real rubbish', while Najib's sexuality was territorialised by notions of physical and moral hygiene that prescribed with whom he had sex. However, some territorialisations were non-aggregative or singular, inasmuch as they produced unique capacities in particular bodies. Sonny reflected on the unpredictable effects of sexual encounters:

> When I crave sex, when I'm single I crave, like, sort of, hot passionate sex with someone I love. So when I have that it's very important. It's like. . . it's like drip-feeding you or something, it's just like pure, you know, it's just great. . . . . That's what I crave all the time, and if I've not got that then I can get disenchanted.

Sexual relationships felt double-edged for some of these young men. Tim described the territorialisation associated with a steady girlfriend, and joked that relationships were very bad for his social life. However, Paul considered that the territorialisation of his sexuality into a steady relationship was an acceptable trade-off to meet physical and emotional needs.

> I think having a girlfriend outweighs, um, not having a girlfriend. You know, my mates are always desperate for it, and not getting any, and . . . and aside from the physical needs, I find that there, there's the emotional needs as well. And I, I think I'd be quite lonely if I . . . You know, I've come to spend, like, any night I'm not busy I'm with my girlfriend. So I'm never on my own. Whereas if all of a sudden I was on my own I think I would get lonely, because I don't really like my own company that much.

Set against these multiple territorialising and aggregating movements in the sexuality-assemblage, the data also revealed de-territorialising flows of affect that produced new capacities and opened up possibilities for action and interaction. While Paechter (2006) noted that school is typically a space where children's bodies are sidelined or even erased as part of the disciplinary regime, in the SRE classes we describe here, rather than erasing them, bodies in the abstract became the focus of attention. Sexual desire and arousal were both the topic of the class and the potential means whereby educational agendas could be substituted by displays of pubescent male sexuality, banter, sexist and homophobic jokes (Alldred and David 2007). While this behaviour indeed may be part of territorialisation into a narrow 'hegemonic' masculinity, the physiology of male sexual desire and heterosexual experience or prowess offered a line of flight for the boys excluded from school, away from their unsuccessful educational identities into alternative 'adult' sexual identities:

Interviewer: Would you rather do sex education with the girls or [just with] the boys?
Boy 2: The girls
Interviewer: Is that just so you can flirt with them?
Boy 2: No, not really, [*laughing*] you just sit next to them until you can get a stiff on!

The data from the older respondents also suggested how affective flows could produce de-territorialisations. Some were quite minimal and negative: Ghalib sought out female company (though he said he found it constraining and unnatural), in an effort to avoid being overly territorialised and aggregated by male companionship, which he feared might lead "to becoming gay or something". Marco (like some other students in the sample) resisted territorialisation into a steady heterosexual relationship, which he worried might constrain his future development. By contrast, some students described singular affects associated with a steady relationship that had de-territorialising consequences. For instance, Neil hesitantly revealed how his relationship had produced capacities to mitigate debilitating threats and risks in his daily life:

> You can talk to your girlfriend unlike the way you can talk to pretty much any other person. Like, there's just . . . there's a bond that forms . . . like you can literally just say what's, whatever is on your mind. And, ah. . . and just, I don't know, that feeling of trust as well, that someone actually is thinking about you all the time. . . and you're thinking about them. . . It's like, it's like a, it's like a kind of bubble amongst the ah. . . I don't know, because the world's pretty. . . I don't want to say dark, because that's a bit unfair. But it's not. . . it's kind of like. . . scary sometimes. Like when you, when you think about how much shit is going on on the earth, and how many wars and all that. And I think loving. . . one other person is a, it's a good way of just, kind of, finding a meaning. You know, it feels like it's not all for nothing, and that there is a point.

Together, these data suggest the movements of territorialisation and de-territorialisation, aggregation and dis-aggregation in the sexuality-assemblage of boys and young men, reflecting continual shifts in the micropolitical flows of power and resistance between and within bodies, and the instability of young men's sexualities. Territorialisations and aggregation that reproduce 'hegemonic masculinity' are countered by flows that fracture these dominant forms, and open up new possibilities: we consider the significance of this for understanding young men's sexuality in the following discussion.

Discussion

Our analysis is distinctive in its focus upon a sexuality-assemblage surrounding the bodies of young men that is neither unitary nor stable. Rather, this assemblage is constantly in flux, awash with flows of affect that aggregate and dis-aggregate relations, and that territorialise bodies into conventional desires or identities, but may then loose these bodies on a sexual line of flight. Data from two disparate sources suggests that young men's bodies and sexualities are territorialised by myriad affects deriving variously from physiology, from social interactions with peers or sexual partners, with institutions such as schools or clubs, and by things such as condoms and alcohol. However, what is a territorialisation from one perspective can also be de-territorialising when viewed from a different angle, and we have seen how the territorialising and aggregating heteronormative banter and disruption of SRE classes is also a means by which some boys used their usually 'silenced' sexual bodies to de-territorialise themselves from being failed subjects educationally. Similarly the territorialisation of a 'steady' sexual relationship can be a de-territorialisation from the rituals of 'the pull'.

While territorialisation and de-territorialisation are an inevitable feature of social life, the distinction between aggregating and singular affects is of more significance for our understanding of sexuality. A body's sexuality may be highly aggregated: by psychological, social and cultural inscription into a hetero or homo-sexual orientation; into a structured manifestation, such as monogamy, celibacy or promiscuity; by cultural codes surrounding sexual conduct (Foucault 1981); or by scientific knowledge. On the other hand, expressions of a body's sexuality can harness powerful singular affects deriving from physical or emotional inti-macy, or from embodied and psychological pleasures, that may stand not only in place of aggregation but even disrupt an aggregated affect economy, radically de-territorialising a body into a sexual line of flight (cf. Renold and Ringrose 2008).

Such analysis offers a more optimistic perspective on how sexuality has been considered in terms of power and resistance than in either Foucault's work (which sees sexual pleasure as progressively encircled by a *scientia sexualis*), or in per-spectives that emphasise hegemonic forms of masculinity characterised by homo-phobia, misogyny and compulsory heterosexuality (Frosh et al. 2002; Mac an Ghaill 1994). In our new materialist analysis, 'hegemonic masculinity' is not to be treated as the explanation of young men's heterosexual identities, but a consistent and frequent emergent affectivity, explained at the level of actions, interactions and events. It is a social form reproduced by a complex mix of affects deriving from biology and culture, including the affects in the school environment, the cultures of laddism, popular and online media (Bale 2011) and in stereotyped pat-terning of sexual encounters. But these affect economies and micropolitics also contain within them singular affects which have the capacity to break bodies and subjectivities free from aggregations. Though sexuality is typically highly con-strained, there is always the possibility for it to become other.

Our findings reveal young men's sexuality-assemblages whose micropolitics are highly conventional and narrowly defined. These assemblages produce an impoverished sexuality that is aggregated and territorialised by cultural norms of sexual behaviour imbued with patriarchal and heteronormative biases; by daily interactions with boys and girls, men and women (be this a misogynistic teen peer group or a ritualised dating game fuelled by alcohol and male bravado); by the genitalisation of sexuality; and by broader social and economic processes. But beneath this depleted sexuality always lurks the possibility for new desires, pleasures and capacities, ruptures and resistances. The value of this materialist approach rests in revealing the sexuality-assemblage not as an attribute of an individual body or human subject, but as a micropolitical, material field within which young male bodies and subjectivities are assembled, from which norma-tive forms of masculinity and sexuality are produced and reproduced, but within which resistance and becoming-other are always possible.

Conclusion

Our intention in this chapter has been to develop and illustrate the framework for a new materialist sociology of sexuality that focuses on relations, assemblages and flows of affect and desire, rather than upon human bodies, subjectivities and social interactions and practices. The notable features of this approach are: that sexual-ity is not a characteristic of a body or an individual, but a flow of affect that links human and non-human; while sexuality is potentially unbounded and rhizomic, in practice it is highly territorialised into a limited repertoire of practices, identities and registers; resistance may be theorised without recourse to essentialism or individual agency; sexuality links the public and the private, macro and micro; and, that the approach invites methodological pluralism to explore, document and analyse sexuality assemblages. Together, these features supply the sociology of sexuality with the capacity to generate novel insights that are limited neither by a focus upon the experiential or the social structural. We have also shown how this translates into a methodology for exploring sexuality-assemblages that generates insights into how sexualities emerge and mutate, and an understanding of young male sexuality that is more complex and labile than has sometimes been suggested.

Note

1 Data gathered by Roger deVisser and Jonathon Smith as part of the ESRC-funded Young Men, Masculinities and Health study (2003–2004); UK Data Archive, University of Essex (UKDA 5371). Pseudonyms were applied by the original researchers.

References

Alldred, P. and M. David. 2007. *Get Real About Sex*. Maidenhead: Open University Press.
Bale, C. 2011. "Raunch or Romance? Framing and Interpreting the Relationship Between Sexualized Culture and Young People's Sexual Health." *Sex Education* 11 (3): 303–313.
Bancroft, J. 2003. "Introduction." In *Sexual Development in Childhood*, edited by J. Bancroft, xi–xiv. Bloomington: Indiana University Press.
Barad, K. 1996. "Meeting the Universe Halfway: Realism and Social Constructivism Without Contradiction." In *Feminism, Science and the Philosophy of Science*, edited by L.H. Nelson and J. Nelson, 161–194. Dordrecht: Kluwer.
Barker, M. 2005. " 'This is my partner, and this is my partner's partner': Constructing a Polyamorous Identity in a Monogamous World." *Journal of Constructivist Psychology* 18 (1): 75–88.
Beckman, F. 2011. "Introduction: What Is Sex? An Introduction to the Sexual Philosophy of Gilles Deleuze." In *Deleuze and Sex*, edited by F. Beckman, 1–29. Edinburgh: Edinburgh University Press.
Bogue, R. 2011. "Alien Sex: Octavia Butler and Deleuze and Guattari's Polysexuality." In *Deleuze and Sex*, edited by F. Beckman, 30–49. Edinburgh: Edinburgh University Press.
Braidotti, R. 2000. "Teratologies." In *Deleuze and Feminist Theory*, edited by I. Buchanan and C. Colebrook, 156–172. Edinburgh: Edinburgh University Press.
Braidotti, R. 2006. *Transpositions*. Cambridge: Polity.
Braidotti, R. 2011. *Nomadic Theory*. New York: Columbia University Press.
Braidotti, R. 2013. *The Posthuman*. Cambridge: Polity.
Buchanan, I. 1997. "The Problem of the Body in Deleuze and Guattari, or, What Can a Body Do?" *Body and Society* 3: 73–91.
Burman, E. 2003. "From Difference to Intersectionality." *European Journal of Psychotherapy, Counselling and Health* 6 (3): 293–308.
Clough, P.T. 2004. "Future Matters: Technoscience, Global Politics, and Cultural Criticism." *Social Text* 22 (3): 1–23.

Clough, P.T. 2008. "The Affective Turn: Political Economy, Biomedia and Bodies." *Theory, Culture and Society* 25: 1–22.

Coole, D.H. and S. Frost. 2010. "Introducing the New Materialisms." In *New Materialisms: Ontology, Agency, and Politics*, edited by D.H. Coole and S. Frost, 1–43. Durham, NC: Duke University Press.

DeLanda, M. 2006. *A New Philosophy of Society*. London: Continuum.

Deleuze, G. and F. Guattari. 1984. *Anti-Oedipus: Capitalism and Schizophrenia*. London: Athlone.

Deleuze, G. and F. Guattari. 1988. *A Thousand Plateaus*. London: Athlone.

Foucault, M. 1981. *The History of Sexuality Vol.1: The Will to Knowledge*. Harmondsworth: Penguin.

Foucault, M. 1988. *The Use of Pleasure (Vol. 2 of the History of Sexuality)*. Harmondsworth: Penguin

Foucault, M. 1990. *The Care of the Self (Vol. 3 of the History of Sexuality)*. Harmondsworth: Penguin.

Fox, N.J. 2012. *The Body*. Cambridge: Polity.

Fox, N.J. and P. Alldred. 2013. "The Sexuality-Assemblage: Desire, Affect, Anti-Humanism." *Sociological Review* 61: 769–789.

Fox, N.J. and P. Alldred. 2015. "New Materialist Social Inquiry: Designs, Methods and the Research-Assemblage." *International Journal of Social Research Methodology* 18 (4): 399–414.

Frosh, S., Phoenix, A. and R. Pattman. 2002. *Young Masculinities*. Basingstoke: Palgrave Macmillan.

Gatens, M. 1996. "Through a Spinozist Lens: Ethology, Difference, Power." In *Deleuze: A Critical Reader*, edited by P. Patton, 162–187. Oxford: Blackwell.

Grosz, E. 1995. *Space, Time and Perversion*. London: Routledge.

Holland, J., Ramazanoglu, C., Sharpe, S. and R. Thompson. 1998. *The Male in the Head*. London: Tuffnell Press.

Holmes, D., O'Byrne, P. and S.J. Murray. 2010. "Faceless Sex: Glory Holes and Sexual Assemblages." *Nursing Philosophy: An International Journal for Healthcare Professionals* 11 (4): 250–259.

Jordan, T. 1995. "Collective Bodies: Raving and the Politics of Gilles Deleuze and Felix Guattari." *Body and Society* 1 (1): 125–144.

Kitzinger, C. 1987. *The Social Construction of Lesbianism*. London: Sage.

Lambevski, S.A. 2005. "Bodies, Schizo Vibes and Hallucinatory Desires—Sexualities in Movement." *Sexualities* 8 (5): 570–586.

Linstead, S. and A. Pullen. 2006. "Gender as Multiplicity: Desire, Displacement, Difference and Dispersion." *Human Relations* 59 (9): 1287–1310.

Mac an Ghaill, M. 1994. *The Making of Men*. Buckingham: Open University Press.

Monk, D. 2011. "Challenging Homophobic Bullying in Schools: The Politics of Progress." *International Journal of Law in Context* 7 (2): 181–207.

Paechter, C. 2006. "Reconceptualizing the Gendered Body: Learning and Constructing Masculinities and Femininities in School." *Gender and Education* 18 (2): 121–135.

Probyn, E. 1995. "Queer Belongings: The Politics of Departure." In *Sexy Bodies*, edited by E. Grosz and E. Probyn, 1–18. London: Routledge.

Rasmussen, M.L. 2008. *Becoming Subjects: Sexualities and Secondary Schooling*. London: Routledge.

Rasmussen, M.L. 2012. "Pleasure/Desire, Sexularism and Sexuality Education." *Sex Education* 12 (4): 469–481.

Renold, E. and J. Ringrose. 2008. "Regulation and Rupture: Mapping Tween and Teenage Girls' Resistance to the Heterosexual Matrix." *Feminist Theory* 9 (3): 313–338.

Renold, E. and J. Ringrose. 2011. "Schizoid Subjectivities? Re-Theorizing Teen Girls' Sexual Cultures in an Era of 'sexualization'." *Journal of Sociology* 47 (4): 389–409.

Ringrose, J. 2011. "Beyond Discourse? Using Deleuze and Guattari's Schizoanalysis to Explore Affective Assemblages, Heterosexually Striated Space, and Lines of Flight Online and at School." *Educational Philosophy and Theory* 43 (6): 598–618.

Taylor, C.A. and G. Ivinson. 2013. "Material Feminisms: New Directions for Education." *Gender and Education* 25 (6): 665–670.

van der Tuin, I. and R. Dolphijn. 2010. "The Transversality of New Materialism." *Women: A Cultural Review* 21 (2): 153–171.

Weeks, J. 1998. "The Sexual Citizen." *Theory Culture and Society* 15 (3): 35–52.

3   Ordinary Sexuality

Brian Heaphy

What does it mean to say that queer sexualities are becoming ordinary? How are theoretical and personal accounts of 'ordinary' lesbian, gay and bisexual lives linked to power? In what way do claims about 'queer ordinariness' reinforce or trouble gendered and sexual conventions? Drawing on a UK study, this chapter considers the ways in which younger civil partners emphasised their ordinariness in their accounts of their gender, sexual and relational identities and practices. It might be tempting to view such accounts as providing evidence for how queer lives are becoming more conventional or, alternatively, for the ways in which heterosexual lives are being reflexively transformed. The chapter, however, suggests something else: that personal accounts of ordinariness provide insights into how gendered and sexual lives are being reformed through 'reflexive convention'.

Introduction

The terminology of 'ordinariness' is entering the lexicon of academic and political discussions of sexual minority lives. However, it is often used in inconsistent and contradictory ways to support or critique developments in lesbian and gay lives and same-sex relationships, especially same-sex marriage. Through an analysis of younger civil partners' relational biographies, this chapter explores younger lesbians and gay men's narratives of their everyday lives, as well as their aspirations and claims to ordinariness. In doing so, it seeks to illuminate the historical and generational dynamics underpinning new claims to lesbian and gay ordinariness, as well as the need for more situated analyses of how these claims emerge from both embedded *and* vital experience.

The chapter begins by briefly highlighting some of the ways in which 'ordinariness' has been a feature of recent discussions of lesbian and gay lives and relationships, how it is theoretically and politically framed, and how it is linked to historical-generational developments. Following a brief discussion of the study that generated the relational biographies that are the focus of the chapter, I consider younger same-sex partners' accounts of their everyday lives, and their more or less successful claims to sexual and intimate citizenship on the basis of their ordinariness. In so doing, I consider the diverse ways in which partners articulated the significance of their sexualities to their everyday lives, and in particular their family, friendship and formalised couple relationships.

The majority of partners' narratives suggest that interlinked developments in the increasing cultural visibility, social acceptance and legal recognition of sexual minorities have opened up new possibilities for successful claims to citizenship on the basis of lesbian and gay ordinariness. However, a notable minority of partners' narratives suggest that the recognition of their ordinariness could be limited by socio-cultural positioning as it was linked to factors such as race and ethnicity, disability, religion, class and economic resources, geographical location and so on. On the basis of this I argue against the idea that lesbian and gay men's accounts of their ordinary lives, or their aspirations to be recognised as ordinary, can be viewed as evidence for either side of debates about whether 'more ordinary' lesbian and gay lives are indicative of a new homonormativity or of radical political gains. Instead, I argue for a more vital conception of the ordinary that takes into account the multifarious and seemingly contradictory workings of power to comprehend the situated possibilities that are available for contemporary lesbian and gay lives.

The New Ordinary

'Ordinariness' is emerging as a significant concept in discussions of lesbian and gay lives, and especially same-sex marriage. In the political sphere, for example, lesbian and gay claims to 'rights' on the basis of their ordinariness have been powerful ones. This is evident from the ways in which individuals and groups have campaigned for and supported same-sex marriage. As the then-Governor of Massachusetts, Deval Patrick, wrote in 2013: "Gays and lesbians [. . .] want nothing more than to be ordinary' and 'When [what] people seek is to be ordinary, government ought to step back and let them be" (*The Washington Post*, May 16th, 2013). In the British media as well, same-sex marriage has been associated with 'more ordinary' lesbian and gay lives, as the headline of an article in *The Independent* newspaper implies: "A life more ordinary: Two gay couples reflect on their first two married months" (Quine, 2014). Elsewhere, Rauch (2004, 8) has also argued that "homosexuals are increasingly [. . .] ordinary", and as we shall see later on in this chapter, in a UK study that I undertook with colleagues many younger civil partners believed that, together with changing social attitudes, legislative developments from the mid-2000s onwards allowed them to live more ordinary lives.

Despite this, the tendency in queer theory is to equate 'the ordinary' with homonormativity. Warner (2000,113) for example, has suggested that same-sex marriage risks constructing 'good' and 'bad' gays, where the former do "not insist on living differently from ordinary folk". In a similar vein, in discussing civil partnership ceremonies, Peel and Harding (2004, 45) have equated the desire "to be ordinary" with the desire to "be heterosexual". Also discussing same-sex marriage, Lenon (2011) argues that the pursuit of the ordinary fits well notions of citizenship that hold whiteness as an aspirational ideal. In this respect, lesbian and gay aspirations to ordinariness are understood as part of the development of the 'new homonormativity' (Duggan 2002), a concept that is used denote how the focus on consumption and couple and family rights as the route to sexual equality promotes the integration of heterosexual norms into 'homosexual' lives. Duggan (2002, 179) discusses the politics of homonormativity as one:

> that does not contest dominant heteronormative assumptions and institutions but upholds and sustains them by promising the possibility of a demobilized gay constituency and a privatized, depoliticized gay culture anchored in domesticity and consumption.

Amongst theorists of homonormativity, the creation of new social hierarchies is a key concern. Generally, the concern is with the basis on which certain sub-groups of lesbians and gay are afforded 'rights' at the expense of gender, sexual or racialised 'others'. Inevitably, the focus is usually on how privileged and elite lesbians and gay men conform to and incorporate heteronormative standards to construct a 'new' regulatory homonormative order.

In contrast to theorists of homonormativity, Weeks (2008) has been critical of queer theoretical arguments that suggest recent legislative developments such as civil partnership and same-sex marriage work in favour of a new hierarchy amongst sexual minorities, and serve the interests of a privileged elite. Weeks (2008, 792) argues that we should never underestimate "the importance of being ordinary", suggesting that grassroots claims to ordinariness have been at the heart of queer gains in politics and in everyday life. Brown (2012, 1065) has also argued against homonormativity as a concept, because of the way it denigrates "ordinary lesbian and gay lives". Viewed in this way, homonormativity is a concept derived from the relatively extraordinary experiences of elite cosmopolitan queers, and that ignores the social, economic, cultural and spatial constraints that shape 'ordinary' non-cosmopolitan lives. In addition to this, homonormativity, derived as it is from the master concept heteronormativity, is a concept that cannot fully rid itself of an attachment to an oppressive and omnipotent concept of institutional power, and thus cannot adequately account for the flow of power in the situated contexts in which diverse lesbian and gay lives are lived. For example, from a privileged urban and cosmopolitan queer position civil partnership and same-sex marriage may well be seen as the capitulation to oppressive power, but from less privileged socio-cultural locations it can also be seen as a radical engagement with resistive, transgressive and productive operations of power.

Recognising the *flow* of power also involves recognising that the oppressive, productive and enabling aspects of power interact with each other in vital and unpredictable ways. Thus, arguments about civil partnership and same-sex marriage that posit them as evidence for either oppressive homonormativity *or* radically critical developments are unconvincing to the extent that they are embedded in simple and dichotomous analyses of politics and power as they concern sexuality.

Perhaps one of the major drawbacks of analyses of the homonormative nature of lesbian and gay claims to ordinariness is the failure to satisfactorily address new commonalities in 'homosexual' and 'heterosexual' experience, and to fully grapple with the historical dynamics underpinning these and their generational implications. In terms of the commonalities, Bech's (1997) analysis of the conditions that have made same-sex marriage possible highlights that it is mistaken to argue that homosexual forms of existence have become more like heterosexual ones. Rather, he argues, heterosexual forms of existence have become more like modern homosexual ones. Thus, it is the *changing* nature of heterosexuality that needs to be placed at the heart of analyses of the new commonalities between homosexual and heterosexuals and of developments such as same-sex marriage:

> 'The heterosexuals' [. . .] know that the family is not an eternal institution into which they have entered once and for all; they may divorce, establish another family, live outside the family, use the world of strangers as a resource, a place where one can go and find other people to build up new kinds of relationships. They, too, experience promiscuity, broken relationships and serial monogamy, and they have established networks of friends other than relatives.
> (Bech 1997, 195–6)

Bech argues against the idea that same-sex marriage should be seen as 'normalisation', 'bourgeosification' or 'straightification'. On the contrary, same-sex marriage is indicative of the ways in which there is a "basic *homo*-genisation of ways of life" (Bech 1997, 203), where experiences that were once distinctive to homosexuals are now ordinary ones for both homosexuals and heterosexuals. This raises the historical and generational dynamics of 'new' lesbian and gay claims to ordinariness. Theoretically at least, claims to be ordinary are not necessarily about following heterosexual *or* new homosexual norms and conventions. Rather, they could also be interpreted as an implicit recognition that the economic, social and cultural conditions that shape late modern experience have led to radical de-institutionalisation of distinct heterosexual and homosexual ways of living. From this perspective, claims about the possibilities that exist for more ordinary lesbian and gay lives reflect a historical shift in the life conditions of lesbians and gay men, where the homogenisation of previously distinctive heterosexual and non-heterosexual ways of living is a new reality for some generational sub-sectors, especially younger ones.

However, the homogeneity of heterosexual and homosexual experience is only part of the story. At the same time there are differences that cut across heterosexual and homosexual experience that also need to be taken into account, such as those linked to class and economic resources, race and ethnicity, religion, geographical location and so on. Research-wise, Brown (2012, 1069) argues "there is a need to research and theorize ordinary homosexualities as they are lived and understood in ordinary [. . .] locations". He further suggests that "by studying the specific relations that produce ordinary homosexualities [. . .] sexualities research might move beyond the exceptional and contribute to a new sexual politics rooted in the heterogeneity of everyday social relations" (Brown 2012, 1071). With respect to same-sex marriage, Harding (2006, 512) also suggests the need to investigate the attitudes and perceptions of 'ordinary' lesbians and gay men, as does Hull (2006, 1) who argues that the that "voices of ordinary same-sex couples" can be difficult to hear, suggesting that despite the widespread media coverage "we know very little about what marriage means to ordinary gays and lesbians" (ibid.). However, if lesbian and gay meanings of marriage are unclear, so are lesbian and gay meanings of the ordinary. So far, the ways in which the notion of the ordinary is deployed in theoretical, political and research accounts of lesbian and gay experience has done little to clarify the diverse ways in which ordinariness is given meaning on the ground.

In light of this lack of clarity, I suggest that lesbian and gay ordinariness can be fruitfully explored in three different but overlapping ways. First, by distinguishing and considering the links between the *ordinary (or everyday) lives* of lesbians and gay men and *claims to citizenship on the basis of ordinariness*. Second, by exploring the possibilities and obstacles encountered by specific sub-generations of lesbians and gay men in making successful claims to citizenship on the basis of *their* ordinariness. Third, in contrast to current debates about the implications of lesbian and gay ordinariness that rely on an overly simplistic and dichotomous view of politics and power with respect to sexuality, I suggest that by focussing on the *interplay* of difference *and* commonality, embeddedness *and* agency, and convention *and* innovation we can begin to generate better insights into the flow of power as relates to 'ordinary sexualities'.

The Study

The reminder of this chapter draws on personal narratives of relating that were generated through joint and individual interviews with 50 couples, where partners were aged up to 35 when they entered civil partnership. The study that generated the interviews was funded by the Economic and Social Research Council (ESRC reference: RES-062–23–1308) and was undertaken with Carol Smart and Anna Einarsdottir (see Heaphy et al. 2013). The study was carried out between 2009–11, before the UK government's plan to introduce same-sex marriage was announced. Equal numbers of male and female civil partners were recruited with the help of registrar offices in urban and rural settings in England and Wales, and through the General Registrar Office of Scotland. Fifty partners were aged between 25 and 30 when they entered into civil partnership, 43 partners were aged between 30 and 35, and the remaining number were aged under 25. Ages at the time of interview ranged from the early 20s to the late 30s. The sample was mainly white (91 participants), but was mixed in terms of the indicators of social class, rural/urban location and religion. Eight female couples had children in their care, but none of the men did. Relationship length ranged from less than six months to over ten years, and civil partnership length from one month to five years. Couples were first interviewed together and then separately. Joint interviews were focused on the 'couple story' of the relationship, and individual interviews were focused on personal relational histories and socio-biographically shaped orientations to relating.

The cohorts included in the study are those that were born between the mid-1970s and the late-1990s. They had entered into their teens between the mid- to late-1980s and the early-2000s, and entered into their 20s between the mid-1990s and the late-2000s. If one of the defining experiences of earlier cohorts was that of a more or less absolute heterosexual landscape (where the public visibility of homosexuality was highly policed and enforced), one of the differentiating aspects of younger cohorts' experience is the increasing visibility of sexual minorities. By the mid-1980s homosexuality had entered the public consciousness through AIDS, but also through battles against negative representations of lesbian and gay relationships. By the late 1980s, public debates about lesbian and gay families were in full swing and Denmark had legalised same-sex unions. By the mid-1990s (when the oldest of the younger cohorts were aged in their mid-20s and the youngest were still young children) same-sex relationships were being represented in the media and television programmes like *Friends, Ellen, Brookside, Queer as Folk* and the like. By the mid-2000s civil partnership was culturally constructed as akin to marriage in the UK. Thus, these cohorts have to a greater or lesser degree grown up with the cultural visibility of lesbian and gay identities and same-sex relationships, and will have legal recognition for their identities and relationships (in variety of ways) for most of their adult lives.

Ordinary Lives and Claims to Ordinariness

There is little doubt that the possibilities for constructing openly lesbian or gay lives have altered radically in many Western societies in recent decades. For much of the latter part of the 20th century, personal, academic, critical community and political narratives emphasised how lesbian and gay lives and same-sex relationships were defined by family hostility and social and legal marginalisation, as well as by resistance, creativity and experimentation. Because they lacked personal, social and institutional supports and cultural guidelines for their identities and relationships, lesbians and gay men's everyday lives were framed by the experience of ontological disruption, social relocation and everyday experimentation. Put another way, in the face of personal, socio-cultural and legal hostility, lesbians and gay men had little choice but to engage in a process of self-reinvention involving a shift away from the heterosexual relational contexts in which they had grown up and the creation of new ways of living. Because of this, lesbian and gay claims to citizenship on the basis of their ordinary lives implied that notions of what constituted both 'citizenship' and 'ordinary lives' needed to be expanded: the former to include the sexual and the intimate, and the latter to include the diversity of practices associated with non-heterosexual relationships such emotional and sexual non-monogamy, families of choice, elective communities and so on.

In contrast, a striking feature of the relational narratives of younger civil partners was the comfort the majority displayed with respect to more narrowly defined conceptions of sexual and intimate citizenship and the ordinary. In discussing the significance of their families in their everyday life, for example, most partners referred to their 'given' families of origin, their partners and their children where they existed. Hanna (aged 26) and Tammy (aged 29) described how their relationship was embedded in everyday practices linked to mutual family commitments and care, which included providing emotional, material and financial support to their parents, siblings and other kin. Theirs was also a story of receiving support for their relationship from their families of origin, which included living with one partner's parents as they could not afford their own home, and receiving financial and material support so that they could afford to get 'married' and have a small wedding.

Hanna and Tammy's relationship story, like those told by many other civil partners, is a relatively unexceptional—if not wholly conventional—one of the dynamic life-contexts in which couple and family commitments are formed, develop and are lived. It is partly a romantic story—of a chance meeting with the right partner, falling in love, moving in together and making a formal commitment. It is also a story of financial constraints that limit how ordinary lives can be lived, of everyday achievements and challenges, as well as major crises linked to one partner's illness and the death of a sibling. Their narrative is indicative of the ways in which biologically and/or legally 'given' kin can nowadays be accepting of sexual difference, of how families or origin remain significant for many younger lesbians and gay men, and of the possibilities that now exist for lesbian and gay identities and relationships to be *embedded in*, as opposed to being the cut free from, the heterosexual contexts in which lesbians and gay men grew up.

Like many other younger partners, Hanna and Tammy's narrative suggests that heterosexual and homosexual difference is not the primary organising frame as it was in previous generations' accounts of lesbian and gay experience. This was also evident where partners commonly referred to the similarities between their friends' and their own lives. While previous generations of lesbians and gay men tended to emphasise the difference between their lives and heterosexual ones, younger partners tended to emphasise the similarities. Eric (aged 36) for example, noted that "all our other friends are just normal heterosexuals couples", while Kathryn (aged 37) recounted that "the majority of our friends are married and heterosexual and we just [don't see any difference]" and Mark (aged 25) commented that "you would never know that we were any different to the straight friends that we've got".

Young partners rarely suggested that there were any very significant differences between their everyday lives, and those of their heterosexual peers. This was underscored by the common belief that lesbians and gay men had been granted 'equal rights' through the host of legislative developments that had taken place in the mid-2000s (see Heaphy et al. 2013 for details) and especially the introduction of civil partnerships. It was unsurprising therefore that partners and their families and friends tended to view civil partnerships as a form of marriage and as a relatively ordinary way to acknowledge the primacy of the couple relationship in partners' lives. Partners commonly and explicitly used the language of 'marriage' to refer to their civil partnerships, and recounted that their families and friends also did so. In line with this, civil partnership ceremonies and celebrations were commonly described as weddings and were often highly conventional. As OJ (aged 27) recounted:

> I wanted it, the ceremony, to sort of represent [. . .] becoming a family [. . .] it was a serious event and I think both of us were very keen that the way the event was organised would show that.

Unlike previous generations of same-sex partners, younger partners like OJ displayed very limited engagement with—or paid limited heed to—arguments against same-sex marriage or critical cultural accounts of the links between marriage, family and inequality. Nevertheless, as conventional as he wanted his and his partner's wedding to be, OJ's narrative also implied a commitment to asserting a political claim: that it is possible for two adult men to be 'a family', and that they should be recognised as ordinary citizens on that basis.

The discussion so far raises three points about younger lesbian and gay men's everyday lives and their claims to ordinariness. First, the historical and socio-cultural conditions in which many contemporary younger lesbians and gay men form their identities and relationships are in many ways significantly different to those that shaped previous generations' experiences. Many lesbians and gay men nowadays, like Hanna and Tammy, construct their ordinary lives in more open, accepting and supportive personal, socio-cultural and legal contexts than those that shaped the ordinary lives of generations of lesbians and gay men. Because of this, there is less of a need to create 'alternative' ways of living, and to distinguish between lesbian and gay and heterosexual forms of existence. Second, while the personal-political gains of this include the diminished sense of marginalisation from given kin, heterosexual friendship networks and the mainstream culture, as well as the availability of legal protections, from the perspective of the politics of previous generations of lesbians and gay men there are also personal-political losses in terms of the relatively narrow and mainstream ways in which younger same-sex partners conceive 'the ordinary' and 'citizenship' (see Weeks et al. 2001).

This raises the third point: despite the historical, socio-cultural and legal developments that have changed the contexts in which many lesbians and gay men construct their everyday lives, and the ways in which the everyday lives of heterosexuals cannot simply be reduced to 'the conventional', there are also historical continuities in mainstream conceptions of the ordinary. This was especially evident in the ways in which younger same-sex partners, who believed they were now 'full' citizens on the basis of their 'marriages', deployed monogamy as a key indicator of an ordinary marriage commitment. As Annabel (aged 29) put it "I wouldn't have it any other way. I just don't think, especially in a marriage. I don't think there's any other way for it. There's no room for anybody else". While previous generational sub-sectors of lesbians and gay men claimed sexual and intimate citizenship on the basis of their everyday experiments in relating, including non-monogamy, polyamory, families of choice, elective communities and so on, the generational sub-sector represented by the majority of partners in our study asserted their citizenship on the basis of narrowly-defined and often 'conventional' conceptions of the ordinary.

Lives Less Ordinary

Despite the fact that lesbian and gay identities and same-sex relationships are increasingly becoming a more visible and accepted aspect of the contemporary relational landscape our interviews attest to the fact that same-sex couples and partners could still experience instances of invalidation. While parents, families and personal communities mostly validated our young partners' identities, relationships and formalised partnerships, this was not always the case. For example, a small minority of families were hostile about their relative's non-heterosexuality and while partners mostly emphasised their acceptance over their marginalisation, some did recount instances of symbolic violence, where their identities and relationships were explicitly deemed unworthy of recognition and respect.

This raises the issue of differences *within* younger civil partners' experience, how these were linked to the situated personal circumstances that shape lesbian and gay everyday lives, and how less recognised claims to ordinariness were linked to socio-cultural positioning. Here I discuss these in terms race and ethnicity, class and economic resources, disability, and religion (for a detailed discussion of gender see Heaphy et al. 2013). My concern here is with the ways in which socio-cultural positioning could feature as a critical interpretive frame for understanding 'personal' possibilities with respect to everyday life.

Few partners explicitly linked the constraints or challenges they encountered in being openly lesbian or gay or in a same-sex relationship to institutionalised prejudice. Of those who did, Maria (aged 33) told a story of the intense stresses that living a non-heterosexual life as a black co-parent with a white partner could entail. For Maria, being black and in a same-sex 'bi-racial' parenting relationship promoted a sense of distance from what she termed 'traditional black families', 'traditional gay couples' and 'traditional straight relationships'. Her and her family's distinctive position minimised the supports that were available for the relationship and led to a strong sense of marginalisation. She recounted how her family was often viewed as strange by her and her partner's own families of origin, other black families, and by straight and gay couples. As well as the institutionalised prejudice Maria and her partner encountered as a bi-racial couple, the fact that they were same-sex parents meant that 'the system' wasn't set up to deal with them and that they were marked as 'different' by other (heterosexual and white same-sex) parents. For Maria, black families, straight relationships and lesbian and gay communities had distinctive values, norms and practices that were at odds with hers. Discussing lesbian and gay relationships, she recounted: "In the gay community, if a relationship doesn't work then you just leave and that's that and it's not that simple, we don't have enough money for starters to just leave".

While Maria emphasised the limited supports for her ordinary life as a mother in bi-racial same-sex relationship, in the above quotation she also refers to financial resources required to live in accordance with cultural ideals. In this respect

she highlights how economic resources represent a limit to equality and satisfaction in relationships as they constrain the power of partners to leave it. The
constraints that limited financial resources place on shaping ordinary lesbian and
gay lives also featured highly in other partners' stories, most notably those who
were from the most disadvantaged class backgrounds. Economic constraints and
struggles featured highly in Callum's (aged 21) and Mark's (aged 25) and Hanna's
(aged 26) and Tammy's (aged 29) accounts of their ordinary lives, relationships
and their strong connections to their families of origin. Both couple's recounted
how the very possibilities of living independently and later on living as married
couples were constrained by financial resources. Money worries were a shadow
against which both couples narrated their ordinary lives and relationships. As
indicated earlier on in this paper, for Hanna and Tammy, dealing with money
worries was part of a wider family project, where economic constraints implied
a strong sense of mutual responsibility for family care. Economic constraints are
not only linked to class, but also to other factors like disability and illness. In this
respect, access to citizenship in the form of same-sex marriage could exacerbate
these constraints, and recognition as an ordinary couple could come at cost. As
Kurt (aged 34), a disabled man, recounts:

> It sounds terrible [. . .] but [. . .] if they didn't have [. . .] equality for [. . .]
> gay couple[s] then Henry and I would be [. . .] a lot better off than we are
> [. . .] because we'd be classed as two single men [for benefits] and we'd have
> everything [. . .] the fact is that because we have equal rights, and I agree with
> having equal rights [. . .] means that we are incredibly near the breadline and
> struggling incredibly.

Others partners pointed to how their religious family and cultural backgrounds,
Christian and Muslim, continued to enforce gendered and heterosexual meanings
of ordinariness. In one exceptional case a partner discussed how because of familial and cultural expectations it was impossible to be open about her non-heterosexual identity and 'marriage' to family members and community associates, and
how this would inevitably shape her life:

> My parents will expect me to marry [a man]. At some point I will get married.
> And that will be my life [. . .] If things were different, if my parents knew of
> this relationship and were accepting of it, then this would be my proper life.
> But because that's not the situation [. . .] later I'm probably going to get mar-
> ried again [to a man].
>
> (Josha, aged 22)

Josha's narrative emphasised the difficulties of being open about her sexuality and
relationship in the context of her Muslim family and community background. The
stigma and shame this would imply was not simply hers, but also her broader family. Intensely religious backgrounds were mostly associated with the intense regulation of sexuality. Those who were most likely to struggle to view their sexualities

and same-sex desires as ordinary, and were inclined to experience coming out as personally and relationally problematic were from these backgrounds. Nevertheless, despite residual guilt and shame, most partners claimed to have more or less overcome the obstacles that religion placed in being open about their same-sex relationships, and to have achieved a degree of parental and familial tolerance—even if this did not extend to their acceptance as ordinary.

In summary, where partners alluded to the *impossibilities* of living 'fully' ordinary lives as lesbians and gay men, this was commonly linked to their multiple positioning in terms of sexuality combined with race and ethnicity, class and economic resources, religion, disability and/or other axes of difference. In other words, it seemed that a sense of being ordinary in a way that afforded recognition as legitimate sexual and intimate citizens seemed more achievable for same-sex couples on the basis of being white, able-bodied and from religiously liberal or secular backgrounds. Economic resources could also facilitate a fuller sense of ordinariness. This was evident where depleted resources constrained the possibilities of achieving the ideals of a mature and financially self-sufficient 'married' couple. Given that some couples were better placed than others to achieve a full sense of their ordinariness, this could be seen as a privilege that is *not* simply or automatically given by virtue of the legal recognition of minority sexual identities and relationships. The situated circumstances in which partners live their everyday lives clearly influences the extent to which they can achieve the kind of ordinariness required for a sense of 'full' citizenship. Consequently, this raises the links between everyday lives, ordinariness and the flow of power with respect to sexuality.

Ordinariness and Situated Everyday Lives

Given the wealth of insights that sexualities theory and research has generated into complex and multifarious workings of power, it is rather odd that current arguments about lesbian and gay ordinariness tend to be structured in terms of a dichotomy between homonormativity and radical political change. On the one hand, critical theoretical discussions of the new possibilities that appear to have opened up for lesbians and gay men tend to focus on the murky workings of constraining power behind the scenes. On the other hand, more celebratory analyses of these new possibilities tend to focus on the liberating power of developments on the ground. However, new possibilities co-exist and interact with new and established constraints and the working of power with respect to these requires what Butler (2002) terms 'double thinking' or, more accurately, multiple thinking.

Amongst our young same-sex couples, ordinariness was a claim about difference *and* commonality. Ordinariness was valued by those who believed they have been afforded its privileges *and* by those who believed they had not. Ordinariness is not only the ideal of the privileged; it is *also* the ideal of the marginalised although they may be less well positioned to fully achieve it. Thus claims about the possibilities and impossibilities of living ordinary lives and relationships are political claims: about the (in)validation of lives and relationships as they are lived in diverse contexts in line with socio-cultural positioning. Claims about ordinariness are not neutral ones, as Savage and his colleagues (2000) have illuminated with respect to class identities (see also Heaphy 2011). They can be political in that they deny social differences, inequalities and hierarchies, but they are also political in claiming citizenship on the basis of a refusal of social distinctions between the mainstream and the marginal. Viewed in this way, the ideals of ordinariness as they concern lesbian and gay sexualities cannot simply be equated with either 'homonormativity' or 'radical political gains'. Rather the power of the ideals of ordinariness are linked to the ways they further fragment and divide the politics of sexuality by setting up a false dichotomy between the radical and the conservative. In truth, if we accept the proposition that queer theoretical analyses of homonormativity and ordinariness represent elite cosmopolitan experiences and interests, then they are no more or less radical than those deemed to be homonormative elites who support the politics of ordinariness: both are engaged in the construction of new hierarchies (one with elite queer 'cosmopolitans' at the top, the other with the elite 'ordinary' at the top).

Meanwhile, the power dynamics that inform continuing and reconfiguring (in) equalities as they emerge in situated ways in everyday life are ignored—such as those linked to the interactions between non-heterosexuality, class and economic resources, race and ethnicity, disability, religion, gender and geographical location. In this respect, a convincing analysis of lesbian and gay ordinariness needs to be set within research on the situated ways in which lesbian and gay lives are changing over time and across generations. This is necessary so as to develop a *vital* conception of the ordinary that is linked to a vital sense of power that is perhaps more suitable for comprehending new, generationally situated possibilities for lesbian and gay lives. The analysis of lesbian and gay ordinariness can only be a very partial analysis if it does not take sexuality as it interacts with other axes of difference into account. For my own part, I have found a focus on relational biographies a fruitful way to explore the situated ways in which younger same-sex partners' conceptions of—and aspirations to—ordinariness are personally, economically and socio-culturally embedded, and the ways in which constraining *and* enabling power works in situated ways.

References

Bech, H. 1997. *When Men Meet: Homosexuality and Modernity*. Cambridge: Polity.

Brown, G. 2012. "Homonormativity: A Metropolitan Concept That Denigrates 'Ordinary' Gay Lives." *Journal of Homosexuality* 59 (7): 1065–72.

Butler, J. 2002. "Is Kinship Always Already Heterosexual?" *Differences: A Journal of Feminist Cultural Studies* 13 (1): 14–44.

Duggan, L. 2002. "The New Homonormativity: The Sexual Politics of Neoliberalism." In *Materializing Democracy: Toward a Revitalized Cultural Politics*, edited by R. Castronovo and D.D. Nelson, 175–194. Durham and London: Duke University Press.

Harding, R. 2006. " 'Dogs Are "Registered", People Shouldn't Be': Legal Consciousness and Lesbian and Gay Rights." *Social and Legal Studies* 15 (4): 511–33.

Heaphy, B. 2011. "Gay Identities and the Culture of Class." *Sexualities* 14 (1): 42–62.

Heaphy, B., Smart, C. and A. Einarsdottir. 2013. *Same-Sex Marriages: New Generations, New Experiences*. Basingstoke: Palgrave Macmillan.

Hull, K.E. 2006, *Same-Sex Marriage: The Cultural Politics of Love and Law*. Cambridge: Cambridge University Press.

Lenon, S. 2011. " 'Why is Our Love an Issue?': Same-Sex Marriage and the Racial Politics of the Ordinary." *Social Identities* 17 (3): 351–372.

Patrick, D. 2013. "Gay Marriage and the Right to Be Ordinary." *The Washington Post*, 16th May.

Peel, E. and R. Harding. 2004. "Civil Partnerships: A New Couple's Conversation." *Feminism and Psychology* 14 (1): 41–46.

Quine, O. 2014. "A Life More Ordinary: Two Gay Couples Reflect on Their First Two Married Months." *The Independent*. 6th June.

Rauch, J. 2004. *Gay Marriage: Why It Is Good for Gays, Good for Straights, and Good for America*. New York: Times Books.

Savage, M., G. Bagnall and B. Longhurst. 2000. "Individualization and Cultural Distinction." In *Class Analysis and Social Transformation*, edited by M. Savage, 101–120. Buckingham: Open University Press.

Warner, M. 2000.*The Trouble With Normal: Sex, Politics, and the Ethics of Queer Life*. Cambridge, MA: Harvard University Press.

Weeks, J. 2008 "Regulation, Resistance, Recognition." *Sexualities* 11 (1–2): 27–33.

Weeks, J., Heaphy, B. and C. Donovan. 2001. *Same Sex Intimacies: Families of Choice and Other Life Experiments*. London: Routledge.

4 'Counting' for Equality
Youth, Class and Sexual Citizenship

Elizabeth McDermott

This chapter critically discusses, through the frame of Foucault's (1991) governmentality, the political, epistemological and ontological questions which arise from the production of national data on sexually diverse population groups and the implications this has for the sexual citizens we make possible. Drawing on a review of evidence on measuring young people's sexuality for research and monitoring conducted by the author for the UK Equality and Human Rights Commission, the chapter discusses the dilemmas of creating national statistics on sexuality, which we understand as not reflecting a social reality, but being part of constructing that reality. The chapter considers how sexual identity statistics become state instruments for the control of populations by making them understandable and governable. It examines how they become ways we can know ourselves, that is, state knowledge's work through 'biopower' coercing us to conform to particular ways of being.

Introduction

In this chapter I raise questions about who is made intelligible through the generation of national statistics on sexual diversity. I suggest that the emerging state 'demography of homosexuality' contributes to circulating neo-liberal homonormative discourses which firmly places the white, middle-class, male, gay, adult on the centre-stage of sexual citizenship and marginalises those who are queerer, female, black, younger and poorer. There has been a significant widening acceptance and incorporation of sexual diversity within many countries that has produced via legislation, policy, practice, research and public discourses, a nascent form of sexual citizenship. A major way in which sexual citizenship and equality claims have advanced is through the state, and those working to improve equality, arguing that sexuality needs to be measured, counted and 'known'. The quest for numbers and statistics, it is claimed, is in order that we can generate 'knowledge' about lesbian, gay and bisexual (LGB) people's needs and ways they may be discriminated against or disadvantaged. For example, the UK Equality & Human Rights Commission (EHRC 2012, 628) report 'How Fair is Britain?' stated, "The introduction of a sexual identity question onto the Integrated Household Survey and surveys in Scotland and Wales will create a step-change in our understanding of the issues facing lesbians, gay men and bisexual (LGB) people".

The demand for national statistics on the LGB[1] population was manifest in the debates about whether a sexual identity question should be included in the 2011 UK census (it was not included) (ONS 2006). The argument from those wishing to progress equality was that if we are, indeed, equal citizens then LGB people need to be 'counted' as such so (Mitchell et al. 2009). As a political strategy, equal rights claims to citizenship have been regarded by some as a limited way of improving LGB people's lives. Critics are cautious of the universalising tendencies of sexual citizenship conceptualisations because the demand for equality is founded on 'sameness', rather than 'equality of difference'(Richardson 2005). In other words, citizenship and equality are claimed on the basis that LGB people are 'normal' and want the same rights and responsibilities as heterosexuals (Richardson 2005; Seidman 2002).

In this chapter I critically discuss, through the frame of Foucault's (1991) governmentality, the political, epistemological and ontological questions which arise from the production of national data on sexually diverse population groups, and the implications this has for the sexual citizens we make possible. Drawing from a review of evidence on measuring young people's sexuality for research and monitoring conducted by the author for the Equality and Human Rights Commission, the aim is to discuss the dilemmas of creating national statistics on sexuality which we understand as not reflecting a social reality, but being part of constructing that reality. Sexual identity statistics become state instruments for the control of populations, by making them understandable and governable (Brown and Knopp 2006; Browne 2010) they act as a form of governmentality (Foucault 1991). They also become ways we can know ourselves, that is, state knowledges work, as Foucault (1976) suggests, through 'biopower' coercing us to conform to particular ways of being.

In the next section, I discuss the politics of producing knowledge on sexualities suggesting that large-scale national data collection represents a new era in sexual knowledge making. I concentrate on the UK development of including a sexual identity question on some representative government surveys. I suggest that the use of fixed sexual categories to quantify sexual diversity may only be a 'valid measure' for more privileged LGB people. The subsequent section discusses the specific problems of researching and measuring young people's[2] sexuality. Evidence is presented that indicates that young people use a profusion of sexuality labels (e.g. queer, questioning, pansexual) in addition to heterosexual, lesbian, gay or bisexual; and they may be resistant to, and uncertain or undecided about, sexual categorization. My critique focuses on the fixed nature of the sexual identity categories used for UK surveying and their exclusionary basis in terms of queerer subjectivities, class, youth and race. The penultimate section draws out the ontological implications of this new era of knowledge production for young people's sexual citizenship. I consider the sexual citizens that are made intelligible through population surveys, arguing that there may be a tendency to legitimate LGB citizens as white, gay, male and middle class. In conclusion, I argue that the emergence of a 'homosexual demography' which may marginalise age, race, class, gender and queer contributes to the continuing dominance of neo-liberal sexual politics which favours the privileged.

Sexualities, Knowledges, Politics

It is beyond the scope of this chapter to provide an overview of the different ways that knowledge of sexuality has been created apart from to assert that in the West, 'the homosexual' as a specific type of person did not appear until early 18th century (Foucault 1976). From this point, 'experts' engaged in producing knowledge on the sexually 'perverse', particularly in science, medicine and psychiatry, and exerted the power and authority to define homosexuality as pathological (Seidman 1997). The rise of the LGB movement in the 1970s contested understandings of homosexuality as abnormal and claimed same-sex sexuality as a positive, life-enhancing identity (Weeks 2007). Richardson (2005, 529) argues that this represented a shift in the politics of knowledge production where lesbians and gay men gained the 'authority' to speak from a same-sex sexual identity position. This has led over the last few decades to the generation of a wide range of knowledge on sexuality from both within and outside the academy (Weeks 2007).

I would argue that we are now witnessing a significant shift in the politics of knowledge production as across the West, countries are increasingly producing population statistics on sexual-diverse groups via various government surveys and research tools. In the US, Canada, Australia and the UK national large-scale representative surveys regularly (although not consistently) include a measure of sexual orientation (Byles et al. 2013; Chae et al. 2010; Ridolfo, Miller and Maitland 2012; Saewyc et al. 2004). These surveys are inevitably focused on the population concerns of government—employment, crime, health and education. Other nations, such as Norway and New Zealand, have investigated whether to include sexual identity questions in census and national data collection (Taylor 2008). In the UK, the Office for National Statistics (ONS) has included a sexual identity question on, for example, the British Crime Survey and the Integrated Household Survey (both have nationally representative samples) since 2009, but the question is not included on the UK census (Joloza, Evans and O'Brien 2010).

This developing state production of knowledge on sexually diverse groups is a result of demands for LGB equality, major legislative transformations, seismic changes in attitudes towards homosexuality and new discourses of acceptance and tolerance (Brown 2006). The emergence of a state-sponsored 'homosexual demography' raises serious questions about LGB groups becoming a population as datum i.e. a field of government intervention. For example, including a sexual identity question on a national census has wide implications in terms of citizenship (who belongs) and political economy (how they belong). The desire to be 'known' by the state will bring with it, possibly, a new set of institutions, procedures, analyses, policies and guidelines creating a specific form of power that has as its target the LGB population. It is for this reason that we must critically engage with the new surveying of sexual subjects, keeping at the forefront of our analyses the potential power of state knowledge.

The discussion here is framed by Foucault's notion of governmentality (1991) which refers to the ways that the power of the state regulates populations through numerous governmental 'apparatuses' e.g. age of consent laws, and through the

subjugation of bodies where the individual disciplines the self via these state discourses. Foucault (1976) argues that the regulation of population groups (biopolitics) is done largely through the organisation of power through bodies (biopower)
and the constitution of norms, rather than power solely emanating directly from
the state through laws etc. Foucault (1991) identifies the emergence of demography as a key technique of power to governing. His historical analysis highlights
the process by which government, population and political economy emerge interlinked: the population as an objective of governmental techniques, and political
economy as the "science of intervention" (Foucault 1991, 102). The development
of demography provides '*savoirs*' (i.e. knowledges) of the state which are used
as a tactic of government. It is through the notion of biopower that we comprehend how government statistics or the science of the state can become 'truths',
which provide a powerful compunction for us to become: we discipline ourselves
through these knowledges and truths; they govern us.

Critical geographers have shown with regard to sexuality and population data
in the US (Brown and Knopp 2006) and the UK (Browne 2008, 2010) that how
sexuality is measured and counted in national surveys is a question of politics
and governmentality. As a consequence of governments' requirement for national
data on sexually diverse groups, the state needs to, methodologically, find ways
of counting, defining and categorising sexuality (Browne 2010). Epstein (2003)
suggests that 'counting' becomes pre-occupied with the operationalisation of categories, partly because governments have far less experience of engaging with
sexuality. Measuring sexuality inevitably involves qualitative decisions about
what is counted and how, and Browne (2010) contends that this is a political act
which can create and legitimise particular groups of people. She states:

> The move to establish a sexuality question undeniably (re)constitutes lesbi-
> ans, gay men and bisexuals as citizens in ways that enable particular forms of
> governmental surveillance, as well as invisibilising and excluding and rend-
> ing some subjects and subject positions unintelligible.
>
> (Browne 2010, 246)

In other words, how we 'count' has ontological repercussions for who is made
visible and the norms of sexual citizenship which circulate in wider society. For
example, the UK Office for National Statistics (ONS) standard question on sexual
identity (see table 4.1 below) that has been developed to ask people over 16 years
of age, for interviewer delivered national surveys (face-to-face or by telephone),
illustrates the ways that categories of measurement can exclude certain groups.

The ONS sexual identity question has only four possible question response
options—'Heterosexual/straight', 'Lesbian or gay', 'Bisexual' and 'Other'. His-
torians and sociologists have long recognised that the names given to same-sex
behaviour, desire and identities changes over time and across cultures (Weeks
1991). I would argue that the reliance on such limited discrete sexual identity
categories has a propensity to present sexual identities as stable categories with
fixed meanings. It assumes that LGB people and populations are homogenous

Table 4.1 ONS Standard Sexual Identity Question (based on Haseldon and Joloza 2009)

Which of the following options best describes how you think of yourself?

1. Heterosexual or Straight,
2. Gay or Lesbian,
3. Bisexual,
4. Other

and 'the homosexual' can be known through a unitary sexual self. In Browne's (2008, 2010) insightful analysis of the development of the ONS sexual identity question, she argues that there is a 'disruptive potential' of 'lesbian, gay, bisexual and heterosexual' categories in government social research surveys which can keep in play both deconstructionist and sexual identity politics. My problem with this argument is that it focuses exclusively on the disruption of heteronormativity and ignores the ways LGB people are positioned via other power dynamics of age, class, race and gender. Browne's argument does not consider that there may be unequal gains from a possible disruption of heteronormativity. We need to be far more critical of the sexual identity categories being used to produce under-standings of the LGB population by taking seriously the intersectional nature of sexuality which makes some LGB people more equal than others (Purdam et al. 2008). In the next section I consider the implications of asking young people to categorise their sexuality using fixed sexual identity categories. I ask the question who is *not* being counted? Or in the words of population scientists who is missing or misclassified?

Measuring Young People's Sexuality

The use of discrete sexual identity categories for national data collection has seri-ous ramifications for young people. These categories presume both a fixed unitary sexual self and that individuals identify with *any* label in terms of their sexual attraction, desire, behaviour, etc. A US study that aimed to test sexual orientation survey questions found that a direct sexual identity question was criticised by young people because they were unhappy with the implied 'fixed' identity. Below, a 15-year-old young bisexual woman states that sexual identity questions are:

> forcing you to put yourself into a category. When dealing with adolescents, a lot of people don't know. . . it makes you say what you definitely are, almost like you know.
>
> (Austin et al. 2006, 59)

International evidence shows that there is a great deal of variation in the pro-cesses by which young people develop a sexual sense of self (Clarke et al. 2010). Young people's sexuality is not easily represented in standardised models, and goes beyond simple binaries of gay/straight. There is a diversity of sexual identity labels, and a fluidity in the ways with which young people may ascribe to different categories, behaviours and attractions (Clarke et al. 2010; Diamond 2003; McDermott and Roen 2012). Survey research consistently indicates that there is a discordance between young people's reported attractions, behaviours and sexual identification as heterosexual, lesbian, gay or bisexual. In other words, if young people report same-sex activity they do not automatically identify as LGB and may still identify as heterosexual. For example, Russell and Consolacion's (2003) US study analysed data from the National Longitudinal Study of Adolescent Health, a random, representative sample of 5,872 students (average age 16.5 years old). This survey did not have a question on sexual identity or orientation but an item on romantic attraction. It asked: 'Have you ever had a romantic attraction to a female?' and 'Have you ever had a romantic attraction to a male'? The analyses showed there was considerable overlap between young people's stated romantic attractions and relationships. The 'heterosexual' girls and boys reported that they were in mainly heterosexual relationships, but there was also a small proportion who reported that they were having a same-sex relationship. Similarly, those in the 'sexual minority' girls and boys categories reported both same-sex and heterosexual relationships. In fact, 'heterosexual' girls reported higher numbers of same-sex relationships than those in the 'sexual-minority' girl category. As this suggests, there seems to be some fluidity across the dimensions of young people's sexuality and no automatic relationship between attractions, behaviours, identities and relationships. Survey research clearly shows that fewer young people self-report sexual identity than are willing to report same-sex attractions and behaviour (Remafedi et al. 1998; Savin-Williams 2001; SMART 2009).

In addition, evidence signals three contemporary trends about young people and the ways they are willing to define their sexuality. Firstly, research points to a proliferation of sexuality labels in addition to the conventional categories heterosexual, lesbian, gay and bisexual. UK research found labels such as, Questioning, Queer, Pansexual, Genderqueer, Transboy, Asexual, Panromantic (McDermott and Roen 2012; McDermott, Roen, and Piela 2013). Similarly, in the US (Russell, Clarke, and Clary 2009), young people used a wide range of labels such as Boidyke, Queerboi, Polygendered, Trisexual, Omnisexual, Bi-dyke, Multi-sexual. Secondly, categories such as 'genderqueer' and 'boidyke' blur the boundaries of sexuality and gender and show, perhaps, an unwillingness to use conventional 'adult' labels. Thirdly, research indicates that many young people reject or resist the idea of giving their love, desire, attraction (or lack of it) a name (McDermott 2011, 2010; McDermott and Roen 2012; Yon-Leau and Muñoz-Laboy 2010).

These studies underline the continuing relevance of conventional sexual identity categories of straight, lesbian, gay and bisexual to young people but there is also a newer sexual (and gender) literacy about categories. Some young people may be uncertain about their sexuality, they may be unwilling to assign themselves to a sexual category, or the categories themselves may be inappropriate. The UK's ONS Sexual Identity Project found when they sought young LGB people's views on the validity of the sexual identity question that they suggested other categories should be included such as "unsure", "questioning", "confused", "experimental" and "queer" (Betts 2009, 36) (see also Austin et al. 2006). As British psychologists Clarke et al. (2010, 152) assert, "sexuality and gender identity is often a poor criterion for researching the experiences of, and issues affecting the lives and development of, young people with same-sex attractions."

Furthermore, research on young people's sexuality suggests that gender, race and class are significant to the ways in which same-sex attractions are experienced and reported in surveys. Australian (Dempsey, Hillier, and Harrison 2001) and US (Diamond 2000) research suggests young women display greater fluidity between sexual feelings, behaviours and identities. In young men there is more congruence between gender a-typicality, same-sex attractions and behaviours. This means in surveys, young men are more likely to describe themselves as 100% homosexual compared to young females (Maguen et al. 2002). US research consistently shows that young people from Hispanic, Black and Asian backgrounds tend to report similar levels of same-sexual attractions and behaviours as their white counterparts, but lower than expected levels identify with the categories lesbian, gay or bisexual. The interpretation of these results is that Anglo-Western sexual identity categories LG and B are culturally specific (Dube, Savin-Williams, and Diamond 2001; Rosario, Schrimshaw, and Hunter 2004; Yon-Leau and Muñoz-Laboy 2010).

Social class is rarely reported as a variable for analysis in same-sex youth research. However, there is evidence of social class mediating the reporting of same-sex desire in one large-scale survey. Remafedi et al's (1998) analysis of the US Minnesota Adolescent Health Survey found reporting of homosexual attractions rose with socioeconomic status (measured by parental income and employment) (see table 4.2 below). In the sample of 34,706 young people, 6.8% of young people from the wealthiest ('very high') backgrounds reported homosexual attractions compared to 2.3% of young people from 'very low' income backgrounds. In addition, there is an incremental increase in the proportion of young people reporting homosexual attractions by parental income, i.e. the less your parents earn, the less likely a young person is to report homosexual attractions. This is similar to the ONS Integrated Household Survey (2009) findings reporting that those (aged 16 and over) who categorised themselves as lesbian and gay were more likely to be middle class (degree educated and professionally employed) (Joloza et al. 2010).

The consensus of opinion from US survey research guidance is that multiple measures of sexuality need to be employed in research if samples are to include racially diverse and working-class people. This is because measures of sexual identity that are limited to categories HLGB are not always meaningful to these groups (Chae et al. 2010; Ridolfo, Miller, and Maitland 2012). Where possible all three dimensions of sexual orientation should be assessed (behaviour, attraction, identity) and where space is limited on questionnaires, then a single question on sexual attraction may be the most appropriate measure of sexuality, especially for young people (see Austin et al. 2006; Saewyc et al. 2004; SMART 2009). It is critical to recognise that young people's sexuality is constituted through other categories of inequality such as class, ethnicity and gender and the measures we use

Table 4.2 Proportion of Students Reporting Homosexual Attractions by Socioeconomic
         Status

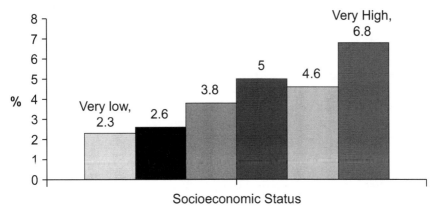

Source: US Minnesota Adolescent Health Survey (Remafedi et al. 1998) (graph author's own)

in national data collection must be attuned to these differences. Decisions about
how we count make huge differences in both knowledge produced and its potential uses. If we fail to understand this, the knowledge we create will tend toward
white, middle-class accounts of young people's sexuality and this has implications for the sexual citizens we make intelligible.

Governing Young Queer Citizens?

> The soul of the young citizen has become the object of government through
> expertise. (Rose 1999, 131)

The move to quantify LGB population groups through national statistics can be
viewed as challenging the heteronormativity of the state by making visible sexually diverse groups. However, in the previous two sections, I have highlighted
epistemological concerns about the narrow categories of HLGB used in sexual
identity questions which have a tendency to capture adult, white, middle-class,
gay men but are less appropriate for queerer subjectivities/identities, youth, working class people, women and the racially 'othered'. In this last section I want
to consider the ontological question of who is being made intelligible and who
is being governed through this newly emerging state-sponsored 'homosexual
demography'? Foucault (1991) contends that the link between state knowledge
and power works to establish the limits within which we view the social and ourselves. Following this, Butler (2004, 58) argues that 'truth' or 'reality' in the form
of scientific statistics, for example, is 'one way power dissimulates as ontology'.
The point here is to think about not only the epistemological basis of LGB population statistics but ask what do they *do*?

Arguably, these knowledges may work to exclude, make unintelligible and govern along predictable and established lines of power and inequality. In some ways this should not surprise us. Political identity claims such as the demand for a sexual identity question on the UK census, have their roots in neo-liberal discourses of rights and assimilation, the basic politics of bourgeois individualism (Brown 1995). This 'sexual politics of neoliberalism' (Duggan 2002) is a market-driven, neo-liberal version of sexual citizenship that aims for equal entitlement of resources (welfare), recognition (civil rights) and consumption (economics) (Duggan 2002; Richardson 2005). These demands require that class, age, gender and race are marginalised or obscured because sexual citizenship is instituted though mainstream norms of social acceptance, legal protection and material comfort (Brown 2001). As Seidman (2002, 133) contends "the normal gay is expected to be gender conventional, link sex to love and a marriage-like-relationship, defend family values, personify economic individualism, and display national pride".

State-sponsored knowledge on the LGB population are state instruments for the control of population by making them understandable and governable, they act as a form of governmentality. These statistics are presented as scientific 'objective facts' that provide the 'truth' about the LGB population and can be used to inform law, policy, guidelines and interventions of the state. They also become ways we can know ourselves, that is, state knowledges work through 'biopower'. The mechanisms by which the state regulates subjects is not through 'an omnipotent and omniscient central state' but by combining the desires of "political, scientific, philanthropic and professional authorities" with the "aspirations of individuals, with the selves each of us want to be" (Rose 1999, 217) i.e. we govern ourselves. The formation of subjects who take responsibility for themselves and their actions is central to state control and there is a heterogeneous assemblage of technologies that provides the means to govern individual subjectivity. LGB population statistics provide the means to govern both through state intervention and by contributing to neo-liberal sexual citizenship discourses that establish the parameters in which sexually diverse people come to understand and regulate themselves.

How might these new LGB population 'truths' impact on the way in which young sexually diverse people come to know and understand themselves? Young people's sexuality is a site of intense regulation, speculation and contention precisely because it is central to citizenship, civil order and the process of governance (Waites 2005; Lesko 2001). Lesko (2001) argues that in order to develop into 'proper' future well-socialized, productive and responsible adult citizens, young people must rationally govern themselves through the 'right' sexual and gender identities; they must become the "heteronormative good future citizen" (Robinson 2012, 257). Therefore, a young person who desires the same (or any, or neither) sex must, as Butler states (2004), negotiate a nexus of norms which ignore, marginalise or confer recognition. Thus norms of recognition function to "produce and deproduce the notion of the human" (p. 32). Butler's form of intelligibility allows us to think about the difficulty of *being* young, working class, black and queer within a neo-liberal version of sexual citizenship which is homo-normative. This homo-normativity may generate social and psychological difficulties for those who do not fit within the white, gay, male and middle-class normative boundaries. I would argue this is a form of homo-normative governance, the regulation of the young and queer to fit within 'acceptable' and civilised categories of homosexuality, which do little to threaten or upset the contemporary social order.

Historically, the generation of classifications of social class and the production of sexuality, age, gender and race have been closely entangled, and durable over time (Lesko 2001; Skeggs 2004). Foucault (1976, 123) clearly argues that the production of sexuality was a class project: "the primary concern was not repression of the sex of the classes to be exploited, but rather the biology, vigor, longevity, progeniture, and descent for the classes that 'ruled'". The production of sexuality from Foucault's perspective was a 'self-affirmation' of the ruling class rather than the 'enslavement' of those below. Skeggs (2004) argues that the production of sexuality and gender as classed and raced categories continues today. My argument is that state population data on LGB people demonstrate the continuing interrelationship between categorisations of sexuality and social class, age, race and gender, where it is those who are most dominant who have the power to authenticate their sexuality. The claim for sexual identity recognition through national statistics may be viewed as the self-affirmation of lesbians, bisexuals and gay men in the most advantaged positions.

Conclusion

> All this garrulous attention which has us in a stew over sexuality, is it not motivated by one basic concern: to ensure population, to reproduce labor capacity, to perpetuate the form of social relations. In short, to constitute a sexuality that is economically useful and politically conservative?
>
> (Foucault 1976, 36)

This chapter is concerned with the ways that new state-sponsored LGB population data may be contributing to constructions of neo-liberal sexual citizenship which is both, as Foucault states above, economically useful and politically conservative. I have argued that using fixed sexual identity categories of HLGB inevitably make some sexualities intelligible and excludes others. The risk is that we institute through quantification, homo-normative categories which only render visible white, middle-class, lesbian, gay and bisexual young citizens. We must take seriously the multiplicity of experience of young LGB people and ensure we use a framework to 'count' sexuality that does not exclude queer sexualities, young people and working-class and black people, amongst others. As Skeggs (2004, 60) states, racism and class inequality "not only remain intact, but are also reproduced through lack of attention".

The purpose of this chapter has been to pay critical attention to the potential power of the state to regulate sexually diverse populations through these emergent knowledges. In terms of biopolitics, LGB population statistics become part of government 'apparatuses'. By making known an 'economically useful' and 'politically conservative' sexual citizen (economic self-sufficient, monogamous, married and nationalistic), they govern and regulate who is accepted and understood as a sexual citizen. They allow for the assimilation of those subjects who disrupt the status quo least, and marginalise those who are more problematic to the economic individualism of neo-liberal sexual citizenship. These new knowledges also potentially operate through biopower. At the centre of claims for recognition are efforts to reassure the state that LGB people are capable of self-governance, they can be rationale and respectable sexual citizens (Richardson 2005). Self-governance is key to the norm of the sexual citizen, the LGB subject through marriage, family and economic self-sufficiency demonstrates the ability to self-govern as a bourgeois individual—an implicitly middle-class assimilation. In a sense, the assimilation of LGB people through rights-claims and sexual citizenship is part of the broader social processes by which class and racial inequalities are occluded and re-constituted.

For queer youth, negotiating the borders between childhood and adulthood, the imagined future as an adult is being shaped by circulating norms of neo-liberal sexual citizenship—monogamy, marriage, family and economic self-sufficiency. This disguises the varying social, economic, cultural and symbolic inequalities which impact on young queer lives. It is crucial that as we work towards improving equality and make demands for sexuality to be 'counted' that we are aware of how systems of knowledge enable some people to be known. The forms of knowledge that are made available to us offer the potential for knowing our sexual selves and others. The sedimentation and ossification of certain categories of sexual identity (Skeggs 2004) or as Wendy Brown (2006) terms the ontologisation of political identity categories, narrows our ways of knowing, and contributes to the exclusionary nature of the concept of sexual citizenship, which is in danger of establishing the deserving gay as white, male and middle class and the undeserving queer as black, female, young and working class.

Notes

1 Terminology for sexuality is notoriously contested, for the purposes of this chapter LGB will used to indicate sexual-diversity and queer to indicate a political and theoretical position.
2 Young people are a contested age group. For this chapter I refer to those aged between 16 and 25 years old as this age group corresponds to definitions used in UK policy and practice.

References

Austin, B., Conron, K., Patel, A. and N. Freedner. 2006. "Making Sense of Sexual Orientation Measures: Findings From a Cognitive Processing Study With Adolescents on Health Survey Questions." *Journal of LGBT Health Research* 3 (1): 55–65.
Betts, P. 2009. *ONS Developing Survey Questions on Sexual Identity: Cognitive/In-Depth Interviews*. London: Office for National Statistics.
Brown, M. and L. Knopp. 2006. "Places or Polygons? Governmentality, Scale, and the Census in the Gay and Lesbian Atlas." *Population, Space and Place* 12 (4): 223–242.

Brown, W. 1995. *States of Injury: Power and Freedom in Late Modernity*. Princeton, NJ: Princeton University Press.

Brown, W. 2001. *Politics Out of History*. Princeton, NJ: Princeton University Press.

Brown, W. 2006. *Regulating Aversion: Tolerance in the Age of Identity and Empire*. Oxford: Princeton University Press.

Browne, K. 2008. "Selling My Queer Soul or Queerying Quantitative Research?" *Sociological Research Online* 13 (1).

Browne, K. 2010. "Queer Quantification or Queerying Quantification: Creating Lesbian, Gay, Bisexual or Heterosexual Citizens Through Governmental Social Research." In *Queer Methods and Methodologies: Intersecting Queer Theories and Social Science Research*, edited by K. Browne and C.J. Nash, 231–249. Farnham: Ashgate.

Butler, J. 2004. *Undoing Gender*. London: Routledge.

Byles, J., Forder, P., Grulich, A. and G. Prestage. 2013. ""It's okay to ask." Inclusion of Sexual Orientation Questions Is Feasible in Population Health Surveys." *Australian and New Zealand Journal of Public Health* 37 (4): 390–391.

Chae, D., Krieger, N., Bennett, G., Lindsey, J., Stoddard, A. and E. Barbeau. 2010. "Implications of Discrimination Based on Sexuality, Gender, and Race/Ethnicity for Psychological Distress Among Working-Class Sexual Minorities: The United for Health Study, 2003–2004." *Work and Health* 40 (4): 589–608.

Clarke, V., Ellis, S., Peel, E. and D. Riggs. 2010. *Lesbian, Gay, Bisexual, Trans and Queer Psychology*. Cambridge: Cambridge University Press.

Dempsey, D., Hillier, L. and L. Harrison. 2001. "Gendered (s)explorations Among Same-Sex Attracted Young People in Australia." *Journal of Adolescence* 24 (1): 67–81.

Diamond, L. 2000. "Sexual Identity, Attractions and Behaviour Among Young Sexual-Minority Women Over a 2-Year Period." *Developmental Psychology* 36 (2): 241–250.

Diamond, L. 2003. "New Paradigms for Research on Heterosexual and Sexual-Minority Development." *Journal of Clinical Child and Adolescent Psychology* 32 (4): 490–498.

Dube, E., Savin-Williams, R. and L.M. Diamond. 2001. "Intimacy Development, Gender and Ethnicity Among Sexual-Minority Youths." In *Lesbian, Gay and Bisexual Identities and Youth*, edited by A. D'Augelli and C. Patterson, 129–152. Oxford: Oxford University Press.

Duggan, L. 2002. "The New Homonormativity: The Sexual Politics of Neoliberalism." In *Materializing Democracy*, edited by R. Castronovo and D. Nelson, 175–194. Durham NC: Duke University Press.

EHRC. 2012. *Triennial Review 2010: How Fair Is Britain?* Manchester: Equality and Human Rights Commission.

Epstein, S. 2003. "Sexualizing Governance and Medicalizing Identities: The Emergence of 'State-Centered' LGBT Health Politics in the United States." *Sexualities* 6 (2): 131–171.

Foucault, M. 1976. *The Will to Knowledge: The History of Sexuality: 1*. London: Penguin Books.

Foucault, M. 1991. "Governmentality." In *The Foucault Effect: Studies in Governmentality*, edited by G. Burchell, C. Gordon and P. Miller, 87–104. Hemel Hampstead: Harvester Wheatsheaf.

Haseldon, L. and T. Joloza. 2009. *Measuring Sexual Identity: A Guide for Researchers*. London: Office for National Statistics.

Joloza, T., Evans, J. and R. O'Brien. 2010. *Measuring Sexual Identity: An Evaluation Report*. London: Office for National Statistics.

Lesko, N. 2001. *Act Your Age! A Cultural Construction of Adolescence*. New York: Routledge Falmer.

Maguen, S., Bakeman, F. and L. Armistead. 2002. "Developmental Milestones and Disclosure of Sexual Orientation Among Gay, Lesbian, and Bisexual Youths." *Journal of Applied Developmental Psychology* 23 (2): 219–33.

McDermott, E. 2011. "Multiplex Methodologies: Researching Young People's Well-Being at the Intersection of Class, Sexuality, Gender and Age." In *Theorizing Intersectionality and Sexuality*, edited by Y. Taylor, S. Hines and M. Casey, 235–254. Hampshire: Palgrave Macmillan.

McDermott, E. 2010. *Researching and Monitoring Young People's Sexual Orientation: Asking the Right Questions at the Right Time.* Manchester: Equality and Human Rights Commission.

McDermott, E. and K. Roen. 2012. "Youth on the 'virtual' Edge: Researching Marginalized Sexualities and Genders Online." *Qualitative Health Research* 22 (4): 560–570.

McDermott, E., Roen, K. and A. Piela. 2013. "Hard-to-Reach Youth Online: Methodological Advances in Self-Harm Research." *Sexuality Research and Social Policy* 10: 125–134.

Mitchell, M., Howarth, C., Kotecha, M. and C. Creegan. 2009. *Sexual Orientation Research Review 2008.* London: NatCen.

ONS. 2006. *The 2011 Census: Assessment of Initial User Requirements on Content for England and Wales-Sexual Orientation.* London: Office for National Statistics.

Purdam, K., Wilson, A., Afkhami, R and W. Olsen. 2008. "Surveying sexual orientation: Asking difficult questions and providing useful answers,." *Culture, Health and Sexuality* 10 (2): 127–141.

Remafedi, G., French, S., Story, M., Resnick, M.D. and R. Blum. 1998. "The Relationship Between Suicide Risk and Sexual Orientation: Results of a Population-Based Study." *American Journal of Public Health* 88 (1): 57–60.

Richardson, D. 2005. "Desiring Sameness? The Rise of a Neoliberal Politics of Normalisation." *Antipode* 37 (3): 515–535.

Ridolfo, H., Miller, K. and A. Maitland. 2012. "Measuring Sexual Identity Using Survey Questionnaires: How Valid Are Our Measures?" *Sexuality Research and Social Policy* 9 (2): 113–124.

Robinson, K. 2012. "'Difficult citizenship': The Precarious Relationships Between Childhood, Sexuality and Access to Knowledge." *Sexualities* 15 (3–4): 257–276.

Rosario, M., Schrimshaw, E. and J. Hunter. 2004. "Ethnic/Racial Differences in the Coming-Out Process of Lesbian, Gay and Bisexual Youths: A Comparison of Sexual Identity Over Time." *Cultural Diversity and Ethnic Minority Psychology* 10 (3): 215–228.

Rose, N. 1999. *Governing the Soul: The Shaping of the Private Self.* 2nd ed. London: Free Association Books.

Russell, S., Clarke, T. and J. Clary. 2009. "Are Teens 'Post-Gay'? Contemporary Adolescents' Sexual Identity Labels." *Journal of Youth and Adolescence* 38 (7): 884–890.

Russell, S. and T. Consolacion. 2003. "Adolescent Romance and Emotional Health in the United States: Beyond Binaries." *Journal of Clinical Child and Adolescent Psychology* 2003 (4): 499–508.

Saewyc, E., Bauer, G., Skay, C., Bearinger, L., Resnick, M., Reis, E. and A. Murphy. 2004. "Measuring Sexual Orientation in Adolescent Health Surveys: Evaluation of Eight School-Based Surveys." *Journal of Adolescent Health* 35 (4): 345.e1–15.

Savin-Williams, R. 2001. "Suicide Attempts Among Sexual-Minority Youths: Population and Measurement Issues." *Journal of Consulting and Clinical Psychology* 69 (6): 983–991.

Seidman, S. 1997. *Difference Troubles: Queering Social Theory and Sexual Politics*. Cambridge: Cambridge University Press.

Seidman, S. 2002. *Beyond the Closet: The Transformation of Gay and Lesbian Life*. London: Routledge.

Skeggs, B. 2004. *Class, Self, Culture*. London: Routledge.

SMART. 2009. *Best Practice for Asking Questions about Sexual Orientation on Surveys*. SMART Sexual Minority Assessment Research team. Los Angeles: The Williams Institute, University of California.

Taylor, T. 2008. *Review of International Organisations' Experiences of Administering Questions on Sexual Identity/Orientation*. London: Office for National Statistics.

Waites, M. 2005. *The Age of Consent: Young People, Sexuality and Citizenship*. Hampshire: Palgrave Macmillan.

Weeks, J. 1991, *Against Nature: Essays on History, Sexuality and Identity*. London: Rivers Oram Press.

Weeks, J. 2007. *The World We Have Won*. London: Routledge.

Yon-Leau, C., and M. Muñoz-Laboy. 2010. "'I Don't Like to Say That I'm Anything': Sexuality Politics and Cultural Critique Among Sexual-Minority Latino Youth." *Sexuality Research and Social Policy* 7 (2): 105–117.

5 The Normative Account

Sexual Experiences and Constructions of Masculinity Among Young Moroccan Men in Europe

Vulca Fidolini

This chapter draws on detailed ethnographic observations and interviews with 68 young Morrocan men who live in France and Italy as migrants, and who are Muslim. It shows that it is a plural context in which they renegotiate their identities, producing an account of their sexual experiences which is often oriented by a 'normative veil'. The chapter argues how this 'normative veil' is becoming more and more a sociological tool in itself, able to offer a solution to interpret sexual conduct, gender construction, as well as young adult condition in modern context. The chapter describes a social scientific path towards the constitution of a reliable sociological instrument to study sexual behaviour and its representations within a specific cultural perspective.

Introduction

Sexuality does not just entail acts, but it is also how people interpret, define and tell sexual experiences within different social scenarios (Gagnon 2004). Consequently, telling sexual stories can also become a narrative context to stage (*mettre-en-scène*) cultural belongings and rhetorical images of one's own culture, to reinforce shared feelings, or perhaps, even, to satisfy the researcher's expectations.

This chapter is based on some of the results that emerged from ethnographic research conducted over three years (2011–2014), in France (Alsace) and Italy (Tuscany). Using in-depth interviews, the study explored the sexual behaviours and constructions of masculinity of a group of 68 young Moroccan Muslim men (aged 20–30 years old), who had come to Europe during their adolescence (when they were aged between 13–19 years old). The decision to work with these young Muslim men was aimed at understanding how they conceived their sexuality during their transition to adulthood, especially in analyzing their premarital life, during which Islam bans any kind of sexual relationship (Bouhdiba 1974).[1] In most cases, the young men interviewed were university students, originally from Moroccan urban centres. In this chapter, I will be using the results of this research to analyze the impact of normativity in the interviewees' sexual accounts. More specifically, in exploring the interviewees' accounts during my research I asked myself the following questions: around which social norms does the sexual account of the interviewee get built? How can norms contribute to shaping one's sexual account? How do normative stories become an instrument to analyze hegemonic representations of sexuality and gender identifications?

In the first section of the chapter, the main problems that emerged in my field-work are introduced and the question of the normative account is outlined. The second section of the chapter then introduces a young interviewee, Bader, whose case is analyzed in detail in order to show, empirically, the impact of the norma-tive account on his sexual experiences and his construction of masculinity. In particular, I will use the case of Bader to show and define the implications that normativity can have on reporting sexual experiences in the context of a research interview, especially when dealing with the influence of heteromasculinity's hegemonic models on sexual accounts (Anderson and McCormack 2014).

In the final section, I argue that normative sexual accounts are not necessar-ily an obstacle to data collection, but can also be interpreted as a form of rich data for the investigation of sexual representations, making normativity itself the primary lens of a sociological analysis. Hence, I will interpret this normativity as a 'synchronic warehouse' (Appadurai 1996) composed of different personal and collective belongings—this allows the study of sexual representations and behaviors, as a field where these young men renegotiate their own culture, their religion, their socialization paths, peer dynamics and family relationships, in new social scenarios abroad.

Are They Telling Me What I Would Like to be Told?

Studying the dynamics of masculinity construction and how they relate to sexual experiences during the transition to adulthood, requires the continuous presence of the researcher in the field in order to establish trust with the research partici-pants. My purpose was not to define the hallmarks of a presumed unique Moroc-can, Arabic or Mediterranean masculinity—as a long tradition of anthropological studies has tried to classify it, often falling into the trap of culturalism and essen-tialism (Davis 1977; Peristiany 1965; Pitt-Rivers 1977). On the contrary, mascu-linity construction was, to me, a further point of observation regarding the sexual conduct of these young men, and especially of their relation to hegemonic models of masculinity (Connell 2005; Connell and Messerschmidt 2005). I wanted to observe masculinity as a process and as a reflexive dynamic of self-construction, dealing with social tensions, which cross the sexual biographies of these young Moroccan men. I did not want to find and define *a* model of masculinity, but rather focus attention on the dialectics that build dominant models of masculinity among these young men, by investigating their condition as migrants, their socialization paths, their peer dynamics and their family relationships. What kinds of mascu-linities did they recognize as 'suitable models of masculinity'? How did they per-form these models? These were some of the questions that I asked in my research.

The start of this exploration was characterized by a first phase entirely dedi-cated to the establishment of friendly relationships with these young men. I did not want to be seen and perceived exclusively as a student in search of infor-mation for his fieldwork, but also as a friend to whom their beliefs, their inner convictions, their personal experiences could be revealed. My initial aim was to look into the sexual experiences of young men who were in a mixed heterosexual couple (more specifically, young Moroccan migrant men in a relationship with a non-Muslim and non-Arabic woman) and not yet married. However, during the early phases of my fieldwork, I realized that narrowing the study to an already preconfigured sample would not allow me to consider a wide range of experiences in my interviewees' lives. Therefore, I also decided to draw attention to other 'categories' of young Moroccan men, including those who were single, those who had not yet had sexual intercourse, those who had an Arabic or a Muslim female partner, those who were married and lived with their spouse, and those who lived apart together with wives based in Morocco. Focusing on the transition to adulthood, my aim was to analyze the hegemonic impact of heteronormative models of sexuality and masculinity on these men's lives.

By using semi-structured interviews, I did not try to rebuild interviewees' entire biographies, but concentrated instead on their sexual experiences, in order to understand the ways in which sexuality could be a tool of identity construction in different socialization scenarios: taking into account their family education in Morocco, their later experiences abroad, their interactions with peers between Morocco and Europe, and their relationships with partners.

At the end of the first phase of interviews (overall more than 20, conducted in Italy and France between the end of 2011 and the first months of 2012), I had also collected several stories through ethnographic observation. I had observed a group of young people both in Italy and in France, sharing with them different everyday life experiences: hanging out with friends, family dinners, holidays in Morocco, meetings with their parents and relatives, wives and girlfriends, friends and acquaintances.

Mostly what surprised me was the ease with which I succeeded in posing questions to the interviewees about their sexual experiences, and their willingness to tell me their stories without embarrassment. It was their openness with me about their private experiences that made me question my methodological approach. I noticed that they tended to emphasise their belonging to a Muslim culture to explain and justify their sexual conduct, even if when they did not seem to abide by the Muslim precepts they evoked. For example, they underlined the importance of Islamic premarital sexual interdicts, whilst engaging in sexual acts despite being unmarried. The questions I asked myself, as a result, were: are they staging their Muslim identity? Do the continuous references to family education and Islamic precepts represent a real scenario of their identity construction, or are these normative representations mobilized only to gratify the researcher's expectations? Does my perceived identity as a young, assumed heterosexual, Mediterranean man[2] contribute to enhancing some aspects of my Moroccan peers' (hetero)sexual accounts? For example, are they underlining stereotyped features of a hegemonic Mediterranean masculinity (La Cecla 2010; Mitchell 1998; Ouzgane 2006; Piña-Cabral 1989)? Why were they always referring to such heteronormatively scripted accounts?

Indeed, two years into my ethnography, none of my interviewees had based their sexual accounts other than on a rather 'standard' heteronormative script;

they even claimed that they did not know young homosexual fellow country-men. A few examples of such normative narratives revolve around the virginity of European women, which was not considered the same as that of Arabic or Muslim women. Similarly, 'deflowering' a Muslim girl implied in their accounts that these young men were assuming a particular responsibility, which would not be comparable at all to the significance of the same act with a non-Muslim Italian or French girl.

> We shouldn't have sex before the marriage. Our Islam says that. What's more, if I do it and I take the virginity of a woman who is Moroccan like me, this would be even worse. It's about cultural matters, you know? [. . .] It's not only because of the girl as such, there's something more. There's a family behind her, who would be involved. I mean, it might happen to my family too, you have to remind yourself that parents are involved and there could not be something sadder for them than to realize their daughter has been mocked. Heaven, for us Muslims, is beneath the feet of women, honor and family values are founded on her figure. If you take advantage of a woman it's like you poke fun at her whole family, not only at her. It's like you make fun of God himself, and if you are a true Muslim like me, you can't do it. I bear the name and the image of my family, my parents made huge efforts for me, I cannot betray their name, our family, our religion, make them ridiculous by fucking virgins wherever I go, you understand? Thus if I want to start something with a woman, I always ask in advance if she's virgin and above all if she's Muslim.
>
> (Yassine, 22 years old, France. Author translation)

Having sex with a 'Muslim girl' was often considered a first step towards more extended marital responsibilities, where the man must play the role of the husband, able to respect his wife and take care of his family according to a patriarchal model of masculinity. In other cases, a clear distinction between the figure of the wife and that of the sexual partner appeared. While the former must not be the object of 'vulgar' sexuality (e.g. anal and oral sex, regardless of the religion of the sexual partner), the latter is a lover with whom it is not necessary to follow restrictive sexual rules, and with whom it is allowed to go 'further, without harming the honorability of the girl' (Khaled, 25 years old, Italy).

The following account of a young Moroccan man, Mohamed, explains what patterns this distinction between wife and sexual partner could entail, always structured around a normative account. At the time of the interview, Mohamed had been sharing the house with his Italian girlfriend for a couple of years. Because of their cohabitation, Mohamed conferred on her the role of wife, despite the fact they were not yet married:

> [. . .] having sex with your wife is *halal*, normal, legal, according to Islam, you know? With regard to my girlfriend, for instance, I don't force her to lie on all fours, I don't tell her 'come on, do this, do that, lick me here, suck it,

take it to me'. She is your wife! You must respect her. In other cases, if I'm
with a woman just for the pleasure of having fun with her, I mean, you know
what I mean!? you know how it is like for a young man! [laughing]. I did
shit in the past with other girls. This is not good for a Muslim. Nevertheless,
since I don't look for the same thing when I want to enjoy myself with other
girls, I don't feel I have to observe rules like with my wife. It's not my right
to make such things happen with my wife. I'm Muslim and I respect this duty,
because my religion says wife must be always respected.

(Mohamed, 27 years old, Italy. Author translation)

Even when concerned with justifying the completely opposite behavior, namely
sexual abstinence, the accounts of these young men seem to be veiled by a sense
of normativity. Some of them admit to preferring to 'turn to God and look at Him'
instead of 'staring at girls who pass by in front of you' (Mustapha, 22 years old,
Italy), while others (like Jalal, 24 years old, France) affirmed 'going out, hearing Koran's readings in earphones of iPod in order not to commit 'the sin of the
glance, since just looking or thinking about sex are sins themselves too'. Still
others declared to being no longer willing to engage sexually with girls, because
of the possible scornful look of other Muslims: according to them, this would
entail the damaging of their image of young Moroccan Muslims, abroad, in front
of other fellow countrymen (Salah, 27 years old, France). The introduction of
Bader's case, in next section of the chapter, will offer a more comprehensive
example of this normativity, showing its impact in supporting model of hegemonic heteromasculinity.

Self-Construction Through Norms: Heteromasculinity,
Muslim Identity and Rhetorical Strategies

Bader is a young university student. At the time of the interview Bader was
20 years old and he had arrived in France, at the age of 18, after gaining a high
school diploma in Morocco. I met him in October 2011 in one of the French university residences where I conducting my ethnography. I had spoken to him about
my project during the first phase of my research, at the end of 2011, but I decided
to conduct a recorded interview with him a year later, after collecting information
about the lifestyle of the young men living in that particular university residence
in the course of a long period of ethnographic observations.

During our recorded interview the mood was relaxed. I was no longer a mere
researcher for him, but thanks to my constant presence at the university residence
I had become a friend. Bader knew the purpose of my study and consented to
answer my questions. From the outset of our conversation he revealed to me that
he had never had sexual or intimate relationships with women, either in Morocco
or France. In asserting this, he referred clearly to his position as an observant
Muslim. In particular, when telling me about his first few months living in France,
he remembered that his experience abroad had helped him reinforce his credo

and contributed to strengthening his conviction about Islam as 'the right path to follow':

> When I arrived here I can tell it's been like a shock for me, I mean, in Morocco I was not used to seeing so many things like here in France. Even if I used to live in Casablanca, I spent a life very close to my parents. . . . I never went out alone and if it happened they went along with me. We are a quite well-off family, I attended private schools and also my friends were, so to say, 'selected'. [. . .] [Here, instead] I've seen boys and girls that are always drunk at parties, people who throw up on board of tram on their way home at night, people who smoke. Islam fosters personal hygiene, respect and purity of your body. It's especially here [in Europe] where I've started to comprehend what my religion actually teaches.
>
> (Bader, 20 years old, France. Author translation)

Regarding sexuality, Bader's ideas were likewise definitive and firm:

> I'm talking about smoking and alcohol. Yet I could say the same for sex as well. Having sex without being seriously committed to someone and out of the marriage is not beneficial to the body. Such an attitude is for Islam a grave sin. [. . .] I try keeping myself out of these bad habits, because I know I can lose the purity of my body only because of a moment of weakness.

Struck by Bader's strong and heartfelt account, I tried to understand his experiences and choices in relation to intimacy and sex more fully. His approach to these aspects was even more surprising to me because he was talking about a crucial period of his life, rich with new experiences and new acquaintances, in another country, far away from his parents and his regulated life in Morocco:

> Listen, I repeat to you exactly what friends of mine often tell me. They ask me if I don't fancy having girl by my side. They say my lack of desire is purely due to the fact I've never tried it before. They think this represents a problem for me. Since I've never tried it, it's obvious I cannot understand what's been talked about. But, on the contrary, this is a matter of responsibility. When we leave our circle of friends and relatives and spend time also with non-Muslim guys like it is for me now, it's only up to you if you want to respect what you've been taught, what your culture embraces [. . .]. [With girls] I say everything clearly from the beginning. So that I avoid girls letting their imagination run free, because I know they can come up with this kind of ideas. I kindly tell her from the beginning I don't want to hurt her. I say I'm Muslim and for me remaining virgin until the marriage is a value, therefore I don't have sex with anyone. Often it ends up badly, in the sense that girls can be of course disappointed, but I personally have friends who didn't behave like me and afterwards were engulfed with regrets. [. . .] Culpability

can kill you, if you know you have committed such a sin [. . .]. Religion in act permits me to avoid all of this diseases, to compromise the purity of my body, lose my virginity. . . everything, everything.

Bader's account does not only refer to his determination to be compliant with Muslim precepts and to respect his virginity[3], it also extends to matters of gender relations: in particular, the construction of his masculinity vis-a-vis the image of 'the woman to marry'. It is at this point that the reference to Islam becomes the prevalent in a larger 'warehouse of belongings', such as family background and educational paths which defined his primary socialization in Morocco. Even without his parents intruding in his independence, Bader talked about the necessity for an individual to respect the 'honor' and 'reputation' of one's family, especially regarding choosing the person who is destined to become one's wife. On this point, Bader emphasized the importance of his parents' opinion on the ideal woman to marry, because she will be the custodian of her husband's masculinity and his family's reputation:

BADER: your parents' opinion is so significant that you ask them to find a wife for you. You don't ask them to find 'a beautiful girl', you ask them to find a 'serious woman', a Muslim woman. It is inevitable and I'll do the same as well.

INTERVIEWER: So, the choice is not up to you?

BADER: Oh no, no, absolutely not! [. . .] It's not important if she is wealthy or poor. She won't only be your wife, she'll be the mother of your sons, she ensures the continuity of your family. In case you find someone who only wants to have fun with you, the game is over. Of course they let you choose, they suggest many women. Then it's impossible that I'll bump into someone who is my opposite. Basically it is a person who is coherent with Muslim ethics who is sought, in other words a good girl.

Aside from the image of the female marriage role—reproducing women's subordinated role in the patriarchal system (Delphy 1998; Mathieu 1973)—what is of interest for my discussion here is the attention paid by this young man to his desire to respect his parents' wishes, and to be compliant with his 'Muslim ethic'. It is exactly through this dialogue with his parent's wishes and his Muslim identity that the (hetero)normative account becomes a synchronic warehouse of his socialization scenarios. The following section of the interview illustrates exactly how his 'past' is fundamental to the reproduction of a hegemonic heteronormative masculinity through which Bader stages his 'sexual role' (Connell 2000). Here Bader spontaneously decides to talk to me about the experience of a homosexual friend of his:

BADER: Among my friends there is one who is homosexual who confessed me: 'At a certain point I'll tell my mum I wish I could get married', but this would be only an excuse not to have troubles and not to tell everybody I'm gay'. In Morocco judgments against gays are fierce; homosexuality is a shame, it's like you're ill, you become the waste of the society because it's said you're against Allah's word. Then you're practically forced to submit yourself to the dominant culture and can be no longer yourself [. . .].

INTERVIEWER: When you say you're going to ask your parents to choose a wife for you, don't you think it's a freedom restriction for you too, and you are no longer yourself?

BADER: I'll have to choose my woman among women, whereas he'll be forced to choose any woman, while he actually longs for a man. I feel pity for him, do you understand? He's not free to do what he wants and this makes me sad.

Whilst it is possible that Bader has used someone else's experience as a rhetorical strategy to talk indirectly about himself and unveil his identity to me, what deserves particular attention in this passage is the use he makes of this episode and heteronormative frame to display his ideal of masculinity, adapting his expression of masculinity to a hegemonic model, which mainly depends on the judgement of the others (Flood 2008).

Bader builds up his masculine identity on the basis of a binary gender representation where social roles are sexually defined and heterosexually oriented (Butler 1990; Rubin 1975). However, in Bader's case, it is not so much his sexual conduct that enables him to express his hegemonic model of (hetero)masculinity, reassuring himself about his sexual orientation—indeed, as he explicitly states at the beginning of his interview that he has never had sexual intercourse. On the contrary, the confirmation of his hegemonic ideal of (hetero)masculinity is based on his identification of a binary and complementary representation of gender relations, where femininity is the opposite pole which allows a man to identify his sexual role and his position in the sex/gender system (Rubin 1975). This model of hegemonic heteromasculinity is specifically validated by the plan of a future marriage through which his role as a man will be demonstrated. In this view, his construction of masculinity is based on the observation of the heterosexual marital union, allowing Bader to justify his sexual orientation, by referring to the model of hegemonic heterosexuality (Hamel 2002; Mitchell 2002), which is shared and expected by his parents.

The social, heterosexual, injunction, conveyed as a standard rule and supported by Islamic precepts, becomes, therefore, a tool to exhibit his masculinity and to manage others' expectations of his biography through the reproduction of a heteronormative account. The possible homosexual 'drift' is then represented as a deviant behaviour, which will have to bend itself anyway to the hegemonic power of a heterosexual model of masculinity: exactly as it happened to the alleged friend to whom Bader makes reference in his interview.

Losing Knots of Normativeness. Interpretations of the Normative Account

The accounts I collected could be analyzed in two different ways. On the one hand, I could consider these as reproductions of a patriarchal discourse. This would correspond to a way of telling sexual biographies and masculinity construction led by the interviewee's intention to reproduce particular Islamic norms and heteronormative gender relation patterns in order to satisfy the expectations of external 'others'. For example, the will to offer an image of 'the good Muslim' specifically to fulfil the expectations of the interviewer. In this sense, the individual seems to disappear in a tangle of encroaching normativity of both monolithic religious and gendered models.

On the other hand, all the collected accounts could be interpreted as a permanent field of individualization strategies (Bozon 2004), where sexual representations and practices are continually negotiated by these young men depending on their personal sexual needs, their religious belonging, their pragmatic aims related to their transition to adulthood in premarital relationships (Fidolini 2014). In this way, the different behaviors that Yassine, Mohamed and Mustapha claimed to have regarding the kind of sexual partner they engaged with, could be seen as a manifestation of a personal bricolage through which they reworked their sense of belonging, especially their Muslim socialization depending on the circumstances and their desires. Here, the individual is at the core of a repossession process, whereby social dependencies and belongings are negotiated according to contingent needs.

According to the first perspective, I initially recognized an artificial construction of their accounts with the purpose of keeping me at a distance from the 'reality' of their experiences and conceptions of sexuality through the adoption of a normative argument, compliant with my own expectations as researcher. The 'religious issue' and the reference to Islamic precepts functioned both as rhetorical tool, for the interviewees, to tell me about themselves, and as an enlightening interpretative key, for me, to analyze their 'sexuality discourse' (Foucault 1979). Later on, I thought that these young men had 'found out' my interest in the role played by their socialization in their country of origin. Maybe, I thought, I had exposed my expectations too overtly, always asking about cultural renegotiation between Morocco and their experiences in Europe, and especially focusing on the role of religion in their lives. As a result, I later thought, their accounts were structured so because they were trying to reproduce *ad hoc* my own expectations, and that I was perceived like an external, alien observer from whom they would have to maintain a distance to protect their most intimate thoughts.

As a result, I saw the second interpretative perspective—where young men negotiate their social and religious belongings as a supposedly reflexive individual strategy the most important aspect of my research. Being persuaded that every single young man could think so painstakingly about his Muslim identity, and the ways in which it could match his own sexual biography, supported this interpretative option.

Therefore, I considered every account from these two opposite perspectives: on the one hand as a rhetorical practice, artificially built in order to indulge the researcher and, on the other hand, as an individual reflexive process. However, this double view soon become a double bind.

Rather than trying endlessly to unravel the knot of this double bind, I decided to make it the first analytical element and the first outcome of my research project. Through a reinterpretation of the normative elements emerging from the collected accounts, I tried to approach them historically and synchronically. The choice of a historical-biographic and a contemporary-synchronic approach is informed by Appadurai's work on the 'synchronic warehouse' (Appadurai 1996): namely the set of cultural scenarios, knowledge and belongings which constitute a 'kind of temporal central casting', to which resource — by the individual—'can be taken as appropriate depending on the movie to be made, the scene to be enacted', the role to be played in a particular interaction framework (Appadurai 1996, 30).

As a result, I shifted my attention to the relationships these young men develop with their scenarios of social, cultural, religious, familiar belongings, in order to comprehend how they make use of these relationships to structure their sexual account. From this perspective, the religious references to Islamic ethics are not exclusively a matter of religion, they also imply familiar education, parents' control on life perspectives, dialectics of 'reflexivity of the self' (Giddens 1991), evolution of personality throughout their transition to adulthood and, last but not least, continuous revision of emotional experiences repertoires (Bozon 2004). Similarly, references to parents' will is not exclusively a matter of family education, but it also involves religion, peers dynamics, homosocial relationships, cultural belongings and images of the self that have to be conveyed also to the researcher.

The 'synchronic warehouse' is never considered as a whole by these young men: it is never a container from which the individual can only take or refuse to take in a dichotomous way. It is instead in the very plurality of opportunities—which can be taken or not—where the cornerstone of the analysis can be developed. Thus, the normative account can turn out to be a tool used to construct sexual biographies and representations of masculinity. As Allen (2005, 53) argues, not telling 'the truth' in describing sexual life does not necessarily represent an obstacle to good data collection for researcher, because a sexual account reveals an individual's hegemonic representations about (his/her) sexuality. Similarly, it is not only by having sex, but also by talking about sex that the social meanings of masculinity are built, gender configurations are reproduced and social and cultural identities are reaffirmed.

In this sense, the question of the presumed truthfulness of the collected accounts seems to decline in importance. The 'synchronic warehouse', on which the normative account is built, is a landmark for these young men. It is a major instrument for the individual construction of the young interviewees and the starting point for data analysis (Fidolini 2015). Regardless of a willful *mise-en-scène* or a truthful account about one's sexuality, or again a simple strategy to justify sexual conduct and representations in front of social, cultural, religious norms, the 'synchronic warehouse' is always present and provides a set of references to negotiate one's role in society. Thus, it is not surprising that the Islamic prohibition of premarital sexuality does not prevent these young men from having sex (by transgressing their own Muslim references). On the contrary, the critical period of transition to adulthood assumes the form of a free zone, where sexuality is tested by affirming that the mistake of premarital sexual intercourse represents just an intermediate phase towards the legitimate sexual practice in the *halal* (licite) marriage (Bouhdiba 1974).

The reference to their Islamic ethics, through which the normativity of the accounts of these young men is built, is not a monotonous and rigid background, but is an opened-up horizon to draw boundaries and ways for a reflexive exercise of the self, which results in being inseparable from everyone's socialization. Not only do the young interviewees play a fundamental role in the reproduction of these normative references, but they also make of these an organizational framework for their behaviors and an interpretative instrument for others' attitudes. It is here where the social and private profile of the young adult takes shape, becoming the object of a personal project of future stability, constructed, once again, on the dominant representation of a 'marital man' forged with reference to the normative model of a patriarchal masculinity.

Notes

1 The research focuses on Moroccan men who define themselves as 'Muslims', despite the fact that not all of them are strictly observant nor 'good Muslims' (as they themselves said in the interviews).
2 I am an Italian man, in my late 20s.
3 Among 68 interviewees, only five of them declared being still virgin.

References

Allen, L. 2005. "Managing Masculinity: Young Men's Identity Work in Focus Groups" *Qualitative Research*, 5 (1): 35–57.
Anderson, E. and McCormack, M. 2014. "Cuddling and Spooning: Heteromasculinity and Homosocial Tactility Among Student-Athletes." *Men and Masculinities*, OnlineFirst, published online 12 March 2014: 1–17.
Appadurai, A. 1996. *Modernity at Large: Cultural Dimensions of Globalization*. Minneapolis: University of Minnesota Press.
Bouhdiba, A. 1974. *Sexuality in Islam*. London: Routledge.
Bozon, M. 2004. "La nouvelle normativité des conduites sexuelles ou la difficulté de mettre en cohérence les expériences intimes." In *Normes et conduites sexuelles. Approches sociologiques et ouvertures pluridisciplinaires*, edited by J. Marquet, 15–33. Louvain-la-Neuve: Academia Bruylant.
Butler, J. 1990. *Gender Trouble: Feminism and the Subversion of Identity*. New York and London: Routledge.
Connell, R. 2000. *The Men and the Boys*. Cambridge: Polity Press.
Connell, R. 2005. *Masculinities*. Cambridge: Polity Press.

Connell, R. and J.W. Messerschmidt. 2005. "Hegemonic Masculinity: Rethinking the Concept." *Gender and Society* 19 (6): 829–859.

Davis, J. 1977. *People of the Mediterranean: An Essay on Comparative Anthropology.* London: Routledge & Kegan Paul.

Delphy, C. 1998. *L'ennemi principal, tome 1, Économie politique du patriarcat.* Paris: Syllepse.

Fidolini, V. 2014. "When Religion Reshapes Identities. Young Moroccan Adults, Sexual Behaviour and Islamic Modernities." In *Queering Religion, Religious Queers*, edited by Y. Taylor and R. Snowdon, 178–193. New York and London: Routledge.

Fidolini, V. 2015. "Idéaux de masculinité et sexualité interdite: Expériences sexuelles au moment de la transition vers l'âge adulte." *Agora—Débats/Jeunesses* 69 (1): 23–35.

Flood, M. 2008. "Men, Sex, and Homosociality: How Bonds Between Men Shape Their Sexual Relations With Women." *Men and Masculinities* 10 (3): 339–359.

Foucault, M. 1979. *The History of Sexuality Volume 1: An Introduction.* London: Allen Lane.

Gagnon, J. 2004. *An Interpretation of Desire: Essays in the Study of sexuality.* Chicago and London: The University of Chicago Press.

Giddens, A. 1991. *Modernity and Self-Identity: Self and Society in the Late Modern Age.* Oxford: Polity Press.

Hamel, C. 2002. "En milieu maghrébin, une question d'honneur." In *Dissemblances: jeux et enjeux du genre*, edited by R-M. Lagrave, A. Gestin, E. Lepinard and G. Pruvost, 37–50. Paris: l'Harmattan.

La Cecla, F. 2010. *Modi bruschi: Antropologia del maschio.* Milan: Elèuthera.

Mathieu, N.-C. 1973. "Homme-culture et femme-nature?" *L'Homme* 13 (3): 101–113.

Mitchell, J.P. 1998. "Performances of Masculinity in a Maltese Festa." In *Recasting Ritual, Performance, Media, Identity*, edited by F. Hughes-Freeland and M.M. Crain, 68–94. London: Routledge.

Mitchell, J.P. 2002. "Honour and Shame." In *Encyclopedia of Social and Cultural Anthropology*, edited by A. Barnard and J. Spencer, 424–425. New York and London: Routledge.

Ouzgane, L. 2006. "Islamic Masculinities: an Introduction." In *Masculinities*, edited by L. Ouzgane, 1–7. London, Zed Books.

Peristiany, J.G. 1965. *Honour and Shame: The Values of Mediterranean Society.* London: Weidenfeld & Nicholson.

Piña-Cabral, J. de. 1989. "The Mediterranean as a Category of Regional Comparison: A Critical View." *Current Anthropology* 30 (3): 399–406.

Pitt-Rivers, J.A. 1977. *The Fate of Shechem or the Politics of Sex: Essay in the Anthropology of the Mediterranean.* Cambridge: Cambridge University Press.

Rubin, G. 1975. "The Traffic in Women: Notes on the Political Economy of Sex." In *Toward an Anthropology of Women*, edited by R.R. Reiter, 157–210. New York: Monthly Review Press.

6 Practice Theory and Interactionism

An Integrative Approach to the Sociology of Everyday Sexuality?

Stevi Jackson and Sue Scott

This chapter assesses the value of utilising a 'theory of practice' approach for the sociology of sexuality and whether, and to what extent, this approach can be combined with other theories—for example Interactionism in order to extend our understanding of sexuality in everyday/night life. There has been a growing interest in practice theory in sociology in recent years. In the context of the sociology of sexuality there has been criticism of some theoretical approaches for disembodying what is almost always embodied, but while more recent 'neo' interactionist approaches have attempted to offer an alternative to overly cognitive or discursive analyses of the sexual (Jackson and Scott 2007 and 2010a) a space remains which practice theory might usefully fill. The chapter explores what it means to speak of the practice of sex, how it is we become competent (or otherwise) performers, if and how such practices become 'habitual' and in what ways they are socially and temporarily differentiated.

Introduction

In our previous work we have argued for the continued value of an interactionist approach to sexuality. Utilising George Herbert Mead's theory of the self (1934) and Gagnon and Simon's conceptualisation of sexual scripts (Gagnon and Simon 1974, 2004) we have made the case for a fully sociological account of everyday sexual conduct (Jackson and Scott 2007; 2010a,b). Noting some of the criticisms of interactionism as being overly cognitive, we have attempted to overcome this by developing a more embodied understanding of sexuality. Developing the ideas of Gesa Lindemann (1997) and Tia DeNora (1997) and applying these to the example of orgasm (Jackson and Scott 2007, 2010a), we have paid attention to the ways in which embodied sexual encounters are composed, involving active agency, but are nevertheless often manifested in predictable, even routinised, patterns. In this chapter we will take this further by investigating the possibility of integrating this approach with practice theory.

While we have previously utilised the term sexual practice, and engaged to a limited extent with the work of Bourdieu, we have not until recently begun to fully explore the potential of a practice theoretic approach for further developing the sociology of sexuality. In this chapter we draw particularly on Alan Warde's

(2005) influential sociological elaboration of practice theory, and his development of it (Warde 2016) in relation to consumption, which in turn extends the work of Schatzski (1996) and Reckwitz (2002). We thus bring Warde's account into dialogue with that of Gagnon and Simon in order to explore the contribution that practice theory might make to a sociological understanding of everyday sexual conduct.[1]

Interactionism Revisited

Before considering what practice theory might have to offer, it is worth reprising the key principles of the interactionist approach to sexuality (Gagnon 2004; Gagnon and Simon 1974, 2004, Jackson and Scott 2010a; Simon 1996; Simon and Gagnon 1986). The foundation of the approach pioneered by Gagnon and Simon is that sexual conduct is social and not in any way given by biological drives. It is also seen as meaningful, not in itself but in terms of the significance ascribed to it within a given social context; what makes an act sexual is the meaning attributed to it (before, during and after). Thus while sexual desires and acts are widely seen as 'natural', Gagnon and Simon argue that they are socially ordered and patterned. Scripts are the process through which this ordering and patterning occurs. Gagnon and Simon identify three interconnecting levels of scripting. First, there are cultural scenarios, the knowledge, representations and narratives around sexuality that circulate within any given social milieu. Cultural scenarios provide both general guides for action and the means of making sense of sexual situations, desires and conduct. They do not, however, determine what will happen in any given context; rather they serve as resources that can be drawn on, as and when they are interpreted as relevant, by the social actors involved. Here second and third levels of scripting come into play. Interpersonal scripting occurs in interaction, either between people mutually involved in sexual acts or in the conversations through which we make sense of the sexual in everyday life. Through interpersonal scripting, meanings and guides for action derived from cultural scenarios can be operationalised, negotiated or modified. This process also depends on the intrapsychic scripting of those involved. Intrapsychic scripting refers to conversations with the self, the reflexive capacity to make sense of the social world, our place within it and the expectations of others, as well as of our own desires. It is through intrapsychic scripting that individual desires are constituted, making use of cultural scenarios and experiences of interpersonal relationships. Intrapsychic scripting is thus a "socially based form of mental life" (Gagnon 2004, 276).

The idea of sexual scripts *can* be interpreted as deterministic, as if each and every sexual act happens in terms of a pre-set script, but this is not the intended meaning. Although the scripts available to us set the parameters of what is possible and imaginable, they are more like dramatic improvisations on a theme than the text of a play with explicit stage directions. Scripts 'derive from a complicated set of layered symbolic meanings' (Gagnon and Simon 1974, 23), which are fluid and potentially negotiable. Despite these caveats, the idea of scripting can be seen as overly cognitive because of the emphasis on meaning and reflexive interpretation.

In previous work we have attempted to answer this criticism by giving attention to the embodiment of sexual conduct (Jackson and Scott 2007; 2010a). This is not something we have introduced into interactionism—it is an idea to be found in Mead's (1934) conceptualisation of social selfhood and in Gagnon and Simon's work too. One specific example of an interactionist approach to embodiment is Howard Becker's famous account of becoming a marijuana user (1963), which we have also drawn on in our previous work (Jackson and Scott 2007; 2010a).

Becker (1963) argues that while it is necessary to use marijuana 'properly' in order to get high, this is not sufficient and users must learn to relate their 'symptoms' not only to the action of the drug, but also to deem them comparable to the 'symptoms' experienced by other users and thus appropriate. This process is summed up neatly by one of Becker's respondents: 'I heard little remarks that were made by other people. Somebody said, "my legs are rubbery", I was very attentively listening for all these cues for what I was supposed to feel like' (Becker 1963, 50). What Becker is suggesting is that users must learn to define the effects of drugs as pleasurable. Thus a three-stage process is involved: learning to use the drug, learning to perceive its effects and learning to define them as pleasurable. We would suggest that a similar process is entailed in learning to become a competent sexual actor and to be able to interpret particular sensations as sexual arousal and pleasure—although such learning is less likely to be collective in quite the same sense.

The concept of sexual scripts allows for the complexity, fluidity and diversity of sexual activity through the intrapsychic, interpersonal and cultural dimensions of scripting and thus the interplay between "the agentic individual, the interactional situation and the surrounding sociocultural order" (Gagnon 2004, 276). This approach, however, is less able to explain how patterns of sexual conduct become embodied practices, how cultural resources 'actually "get into" and inform real lines of erotic conduct' (DeNora 1997, 44). It is this idea of sexual practices as embodied practices that suggests to us the relevance of practice theory to the further elaboration of sexual interaction.

The Practice Turn

Since the beginning of the 21st century there has been a trend in some fields, most notably the sociology of consumption, to develop the work of Bourdieu (1990), Schatzki (1996) and Schatzki et al (2001) and the Pragmatists (see Kilpinen 2012) into a theory of practice approach appropriate to sociological research and analysis (Reckwitz 2002; Shove et. al. 2012; Warde 2005, 2016;). The idea of practice has been around for some time in sociological analyses of gender, sexuality and intimate relationships, drawing particularly on Bourdieu. Raewyn Connell (1987) proposed a practice based theory of gender in order to develop theory that "gives some grip on the interweaving of personal life and social structure" (Connell 1987, 61) without being either voluntaristic or deterministic. More recently feminist sociologists have drawn on Bourdieu's concepts of practice and of habitus in relation to gender, sexuality and the body (Skeggs 2004, Witz 2004). There has also been considerable interest in the idea of practice in research and theorising around family life and personal and intimate relations more generally (Finch 2007; Jamieson 2011; Morgan 1996, 2011;), though not always in terms of practice theory as such.[2] Where there has been some feminist development of practice theory is in the sociology of work and organisation (see e.g. Bruni 2006; Yancy Martin 2003, 2006). Nonetheless, there is as yet no fully developed practice theoretic approach to sex and sexuality.

The word 'practice' (praxis) refers simply to human action. A practice (praktik) in the context of a theory of social practices is a routinised type of behaviour made up of a number of interconnected elements. Schatzki (1996) identifies two central aspects of a social practice: practice as a co-ordinated entity and practice as performance. Practices in Schatzki's first sense consist of both doings and sayings which, according to Warde (2005), form a nexus of 'understandings', 'procedures' and 'engagements', through which they are coordinated. This refers to practices as a general level—for example dressing and undressing, which would include a whole set of ideas and actions around appropriate dress and states of dress and undress required or permitted in different social contexts. 'Practice as performance' refers to carrying out practices which both brings them into being and sustains them.[3] In our example it would refer to the actual actions of dressing and undressing, for example what we each put on and take off and the order in which we do so. In both the general sense of practice as a co-ordinated entity and practice as performance it involves both doings and sayings—how things are done and how they are thought about, talked about and, more broadly, represented.

Schatzki (1996) also distinguishes between dispersed and integrative practices. Dispersed practices are those that occur across a range of social arenas and contexts such as describing, explaining or following rules and thus they require understanding. For instance, as Warde (2016) suggests, to perform an act of explanation "entails understanding of how to carry out an appropriate act of 'explaining', an ability to identify explaining when doing it oneself or when someone else does it, and an ability to prompt or respond to an explanation". From a sociological perspective, then, we might regard these as basic social or interactional competences. So, to extend Warde's example, if someone asks us how to do something we know that it is an explanation that is expected and what this explanation should achieve.

Integrative practices, on the other hand, are complex sets of practices that together constitute areas of social practice—Warde's (2005) example being cooking. These may involve specialised forms of dispersed practices so that, for instance, following a guide to spicing up our sex lives could be seen as a particular instance of following instructions. While some branches of sociology, such as ethnomethodology, are interested in dispersed practices—for example how 'accounts' are constructed (Scott and Lyman 1968), here, like Warde, we are more concerned with integrative practices. So, in relation to sexuality, our concern would be with the practices that make sexual conduct 'work' as social practice and that constitute sexuality as a socially meaningful sphere of life.

These distinctions, which define elements of practice, derive from philosophical approaches which, as Warde (2005, 135) points out, "cannot simply be transposed into empirical analysis" because they "tend to be idealized, abstract and insufficiently attentive to the social processes involved in the creation and reproduction of practices". We would add that sociological analysis should also attend to social processes that might disrupt or at least modify practices. Although much of everyday life is habitual, routinised and unreflexive, change is always possible, because social practices are produced by reflexive social actors. As David Morgan makes clear, even the habitual and routine is enacted by knowledgeable agents: "when called upon to do so, by circumstances or by outside intervention, these agents are frequently able to account for these practices and to recognise their taken for granted quality" (Morgan 2011, 26–27). A practice theoretic approach thus seems to us to offer a perspective on social life that recognises the extent to which it is patterned without denying human agency. It challenges both an overly rationalised view of human motivation *and* the idea that we are driven by natural instincts and desires. It thus shifts the analytic focus "from the insatiable wants of the human animal to the instituted conventions of collective culture, from personal expression to social competence, from mildly constrained choice to disciplined participation" (Warde 2005, 146). Thus, as with an interactionist approach, the social is seen as productive, as positively constituting human social action rather than shaping pre-existing wants and needs.

The Practice of Sex

In considering the sense in which sex might be thought of as a practice and what kind of practice it is, we are drawing heavily on Warde's outline of key elements of a practice, which he elaborates in relation to eating. First, there are defining features (albeit some of them historically and culturally variable) which determine what counts as sex. Secondly a sexual encounter is generally recognisable as an event—a period of activity, usually interactive, involving what we generally understand as sexual arousal and conduct. Thirdly there are shared (public) understandings of sex and sexuality entailing embodied procedures and competencies, standards of both good and bad sex. Elaboration of these can be found in discourses circulating within the wider culture, self-help manuals (Jackson and Scott 1997), medical texts, the media and in everyday conversations. In interactionist terms these all contribute to the cultural scenarios that guide sexual conduct.

These elements—the defining features, the recognisable event and the shared understandings—are coordinated through accepted procedures, conventions and meanings or, in other words, in situ 'know how'. This way of understanding social practice emphasises the taken for granted embodied knowledge of how to proceed in a given situation either in a single performance or in repeated sequences. Such procedures and their sequencing are orchestrated via emotion, intuition and embodied memory as well as through interpersonal interaction and negotiation. All of this contributes to practice as performance. Sex is thus a performance constituted through an assemblage of practices by which sex is made to happen.

What is recognisable as sex, then, can be understood in Warde's (2013) terms as a 'compound' practice. Ward (2016) defines eating as such in the following terms:

> It has multiple organizational underpinnings and can be viewed as a complex corollary of the intersection of four, relatively autonomous, integrative practices—the supplying of food, cooking, the organization of meal occasion and aesthetic judgments of taste. The competing injunctions of the four different disciplining practices make the coordination of individual performances and collective institutions difficult. Internal disputation within each of these exacerbates uncertainty about appropriate conduct, making for considerable personal anxiety and collective misunderstanding. Eating may be understood, therefore, as weakly regulated and weakly coordinated when compared with many other more formalized and more authoritatively directed practices like sitting examinations, playing soccer or driving an automobile. At least after early childhood one is unlikely to be punished for eating wrongly, for eating is governed by convention rather than law.

While sex can also be thought of as a compound practice, with some parallels with eating, it is in many ways qualitatively and contextually different, subject to different forms of social regulation and comprised of different elements or integrative practices. There is a tenuous parallel to cooking—the transformation of raw materials into something edible or desirable—in that preparations for the sexual encounter might include preparing oneself to be more sexually desirable. A stronger analogy is that sexual activity can be seen as organised like the meal occasion. Just as a meal might be ordered in terms of a sequence of courses, so conventional heterosexual encounters are also routinely sequenced, as we have noted (Jackson and Scott 1997, 2010a), generally in terms of foreplay, coitus, his orgasm and possibly hers. It is also ordered in terms of its setting, usually in a private space. Whereas we might tidy the house and set the table in preparation for inviting guests for dinner, inviting a lover for sex might involve arranging the bedroom in terms of attractive bed linen, appropriate music and lighting to create the 'right' romantic or erotic ambience. There is also a clear parallel in terms of taste where both moral and aesthetic judgments come into play; what might be seen as erotic by one individual, couple or social group might be seen as disgusting, distasteful or immoral by others.

It is certainly the case that sex, like eating or probably even more so, is the source of "considerable personal anxiety and collective misunderstanding" (Warde 2016). While among adults, sex is now also weakly regulated in many respects, in others, unlike eating, it remains tightly bound by certain rules and conventions. Whereas everyone, in principle, is allowed to eat with whom they like and often wherever they wish, it is not permissible for everyone to engage in sex wherever, whenever and with whom they please. Public sex is still frowned upon almost everywhere in the world, there are restrictions on who one may have sex with—for example laws around incest as well as the outlawing of same-sex activity in many countries—and sex with children is illegal in most. Children themselves, and all those under whatever the local age of consent might be, are not legally permitted to engage in sexual activities, even with each other, that are perfectly acceptable, even conventional, for those deemed adult.

These examples serve to illustrate how sex can be seen as a compound practice in much the same way as eating and thus can be analysed in practice theoretic terms. Having started from interactionism and moved on to practice theory, we now go on to consider the relationship between the two.

Practice and Interaction: Integration or Difference?

Is it the link to practice that is not adequately theorised within interactionism and that practice theory therefore supplements it—or is it that interactionism is itself already an implicit theory of practice?

Both practice theory and the idea of sexual scripts emphasise that behaviour often thought of as individual is socially patterned in particular ways. This is not a popular view of sexuality, where ideas about spontaneity, innovation and diversity are part of everyday and much academic thinking. Gagnon and Simon have consistently stressed the ordinariness of sexual conduct, the way it is embedded in everyday life, the way that improvisation may be little more than an institutionalised variation of an existing scenario (Simon 1996, 41) that it can be routinised and habitual whereby people 'get home from work, have dinner, turn on the television, watch the television, have sex together then go to sleep' (Gagnon 2004, 280).

In that it is both scripted and potentially variable, sex can be seen in terms of Schatzki's two central aspects of practice: it is a co-ordinated entity in that it is recognisable as sex however it is done; it involves performance each time it is enacted and this helps sustain the notion of what sex is, as in an awareness that one has 'had sex'. Complex practices such as sex are not like making a cake; it is not necessary to do the same things in the same order for it to 'work' or at least count *as* sex.

> Complex practices are complex precisely because of their internal variety. Rarely, if ever, is there simply one way to carry out a Practice, or one sole manner of performance that will be acceptable. . . A performance effectively conforms to a template of some kind in order that it can be confirmed to be an instance of the Practice.
>
> (Warde 2016)

The idea of variation of 'doings' within something recognisable as a practice resonates with the idea of scripting. The idea of a template might be too rigid a metaphor here, but it captures the idea of a socially bounded set of activities. Compare with this from William Simon (1996, 46):

> . . . deviations from prevailing cultural scenarios tend to be limited to a universe largely created by such cultural scenarios, the application of

conventional sexual meanings to unconventional sexual objects or the expression of unconventional motives through conventional sexual activities.

While there are obvious parallels here, the use of the terms 'meanings' and 'motives' signals a difference from practice theory in that they refer to subjective processes. However, such subjective processes are not, in scripting theory, regarded as arising from within the individual psyche, but as socially formed through interaction—through interpersonal and intrapsychic scripting both of which are seen as intrinsically and essentially social. Not only is the self, from an interactionist perspective, fully social, but motives are seen as socially situated rather than manifestations of individual psychology. Gagnon and Simon draw on C. Wright Mills' conceptualisation of vocabularies of motive, which explicitly challenges psychological conceptions of motive as subjective "springs" from which actions derive: "rather than fixed elements 'in' an individual, motives are the terms within which interpretation of conduct *by social actors* proceeds" (Mills 1940, 904: *emphasis in original*). Vocabularies of motive delimit what is possible and conceivable in any given social situation, they change over time and are often specific to particular social or institutional contexts. They are always situated. Rather than simply providing accounts for some "real" motive underlying action, vocabularies of motive are a part of purposive action, they "link anticipated consequences and specific actions" and guide our conduct (1940, 906). Vocabularies of motive are learnt along with the norms and rules of action in given situations. The learning of vocabularies of motive happens alongside and as an integral part of acquiring social competences—as Mills points out, instructions to children are often accompanied by motivational accounts—'don't do that, it's rude', or share your toys with your sister, that's a kind thing to do. Normative, habitual conduct is therefore often underpinned by an acceptable vocabulary of motive. This sociological conception of motives "translates the question of 'why' into a 'how' that is answerable in terms of a situation and its typical vocabularies of motive" (Mills 1940, 906).

Both interactionism and practice theory see everyday practices as learnt and embodied. For Gagnon and Simon, embodied and learnt, 'Scripts are involved in learning the meaning of internal states, organizing the sequences of specifically sexual acts, decoding novel situations, setting the limits on sexual responses, and limiting meanings from nonsexual aspects of life to specifically sexual experience' (1974, 19). Here the process of learning is cast in terms of reflexive selfhood, whereas the following, practice theoretic, account focuses more on how learning and teaching are performed as practical activities:

Procedures are embodied and are imparted primarily through practical training, involving enormous amounts of repetition, though not necessarily identical replication nor in identical circumstances. The capacity to act appropriately is thus a product of an individual's specific range of experiences. This is one source of the distinctiveness of performances by different individuals. However, the process of learning is not, usually, a matter of trial and error on the part of autonomous individuals. Rather it occurs in a context of a social imparting of aspects of a shared practice. Sometimes this is by means of verbal instruction alone, sometimes words and practical demonstration, sometimes in the autodidactic mode of reading a manual. However, from the point of first exposure to a practice the novice is influenced by clues and cues about how other people, and particularly how other competent actors, navigate and traverse the sequences of actions that comprise recognisable performances of the Practice.

(Warde 2016)

Learning sexual practices or performances differs from many other practices—in that most, or at least the most socially sanctioned, sexual acts take place in private between two individuals but also, and particularly, because of the specific meanings attributed to sex as a form of intimacy. So, whereas children learn and come to embody locally relevant eating practices through explicit instruction and by example, for instance, to manipulate knives and forks or chopsticks, or whether it is rude or polite to belch during a meal, the same cannot be said for most sexual acts. Parents or teachers offer neither instruction on nor demonstration of how to do sex to young novices, though they often impart moral rules. Sex education may be variable within and across different countries but, as far as we are aware, nowhere are children explicitly instructed on how to do sex. The only source noted by Warde that applies here is auto-didactic—the reading of manuals—or indeed novels—or watching films, including pornography. There is another sense in which we might be said to teach ourselves about sex—through autoerotic activities by which it is possible to discover pleasurable bodily sensations and learn something about our personal sensual preferences. Even this individual learning is shaped by wider cultural scenarios, which offer menus of possibilities, the material for fantasies and normative boundaries. We also learn about sex, crucially, through embodied interaction with sexual partners. Thus we learn through doing, whether alone or with someone else, but always influenced by the wider culture in which this learning occurs. While learnt in different ways, the 'know-how' of sex becomes embodied in much the same way as the know-how of eating.

Although this embodied know-how can become habitual, it is not necessarily fixed for all time. Because much of the learning of sex occurs through doing and through interaction, there is always a potential for re-learning. Not only is it possible to acquire new sexual techniques, from a number of sources, but also sex with a new partner may involve unlearning habituated responses and adapting to new ones. Not everyone enjoys the same range of sexual activities or finds the same sort of touch, for example, pleasurable. Thus negotiating sex with a new partner often involves reaching an accommodation to their tastes and theirs to ours through a process of mutual re-education. This rarely happens explicitly, but through reading subtle (or sometimes not so subtle) bodily cues.

Both practice theory and interactionism emphasise the learnt, acquired basis of human social conduct. They have common ground on which they meet, but there are also differences of focus and emphasis. Interactionism is centrally concerned with the reflexive social self as both constituted through and enabling interaction as well as with the inherent meaningfulness of human conduct. Practice theory, on the other hand is more concerned with the social significance of practice in terms of what is possible, habitual or normative in any given time, place or context. It also allows for a more detailed consideration of actual doing, the performance element of Schatzki's formulation. Interactionism, on the other hand, attributes greater significance to, and provides a better account of, the internal, reflexive processes of the self. It should be noted, though, that if we return to Mead, from whose work interactionism developed, we find that reflexivity is seen as a variable component of human action. While Mead (1934) insisted on reflexivity as a basic social competence, what makes it possible for each individual to interact with others and locate themselves in ongoing interaction he did not consider that we are continually or always consciously self-reflexive: much human social action and interaction is relatively habitual. When we are confronted with novel situations, according to Mead, heightened reflexivity comes into play linking past and future actions to the emergent present. Thus reflexivity increases where there is more opportunity of meeting novel situations and more choices to be made. We can, therefore, act almost automatically when following routine. An example Mead ([1929] 1964, 348) gives in his work on time is that we often do not remember detailed everyday activities: "we must have arisen and eaten our breakfasts and taken the car, to be where we are."

Conclusion

In this chapter we have sought to explore the synergies and differences between practice theory and interactionism. At a more a more empirical level we have taken the practice of eating as a model of how a practice theory of sexuality might be developed. We have shown that where practice theory tends to focus more on the constitutive effects of 'doing', interactionism attends more to reflexive processes and meanings. But all of these things are social. We take it as axiomatic that sexuality is socially constructed; it is produced through doings and sayings (in practice theory terms) through meaning attribution, action and interaction (in interactionist terms). Both focus on the productive effectivity of social life.

Both also provide an alternative to identity based and/or discursive explanations of sex and sexuality and turn our attention towards the everyday. The focus on everyday habits and routines might be seen a move away from the social or sociological. We would strongly argue that this is not the case, because habits and routines are embedded in both biography and social context. Such practices and elements of practices may not be conscious but they are not unconscious in the psychoanalytic sense—they can be recalled to consciousness and be accounted for, either in the form of an explanation (cf. Morgan 2011) or through their results or consequences, as in the example given by G. H. Mead (above).

The practice theoretic analysis of food and eating can, we suggest, be applied to sex. Both eating and sex can be experienced as transformative bodily events, as satisfying—or failing to satisfy—felt needs and desires. Both can be mundane and routine, captured by the terms 'comfort food' and 'vanilla sex'; both can also

be, on occasion, more exotic or adventurous. There are, however, socially constituted limits to variability: even when we think that we are pushing the boundaries
by pursuing unusual tastes, what counts as exotic or adventurous is itself always
socially defined and rarely exceeds the boundaries of what is understood as edible
or sexual. Both of the perspectives we have discussed here would recognise this
paradox.

The difficulties of extending definitions and boundaries of sex can be illustrated by returning to earlier work on attempts to change heterosexual practice
in the context of sexual risk, specifically HIV transmission. From this research
it became clear how certain sexual practices become embodied and embedded
in everyday practice. There exists a certain 'grammar' of sex, an ordering or
sequence of acts that 'doing sex' conventionally involves, thus indicating that
sex is a practice in the sense of being a coordinated entity and also that it is
scripted. The evidence demonstrates how difficult it has been and is to punctuate
the grammar of sex with condoms (see Scott and Freeman 1995; Holland et al.
1990). It is even more difficult, in heterosexual relations, to disrupt the sexual
sentence itself—i.e. the expected sequence of foreplay, coitus and orgasm as the
ultimate goal. Thus both interactionism and practice theory force us to question
the utility of individualised educational materials intended to change behaviour
in order to reduce risk—whether it is to use condoms or eat five portions of fruit
and vegetables a day.

Utilising both of these perspectives together potentially gives us greater purchase on practices that are understood as risky and ways of assessing how they
might be amenable to change other than by simplistic individualistic behavioural
change programmes which continue to fail to change most people's sexual or eating habits. Practice theory and interactionism each have particular strengths: looking at practices in a social sense enables us to avoid overly essentialist, naturalised
notions of habits and routines, while interactionism focuses our attention on a
sexual self that is social and relational without having recourse to the idea of an
unconscious. Both approaches are anti-individualist and anti-essentialist, attending to how social life is ordered and patterned while still allowing for human
agency, not as something existing outside or in opposition to the social but as
itself embedded in social practices and interaction. Together they are conducive
to the further development of a thoroughly social and sociological understanding
of sexuality.

Notes

1 Both interactionism and practice theory can trace their roots back to American pragma-
  tist philosophy, interactionism through G. H. Mead and practice theory through John
  Dewey and William James. This suggests that the congruence between the two is worth
  exploring.
2 David Morgan, however, does include a discussion of practice theoretic approaches in
  his *Rethinking Family Practices* (2011).
3 There are echoes of ethnomethodology here and in some of what follows; Schatzki is
  aware of Garfinkel's work (e.g. Garfinkel 1967).

References

Becker, H. 1963 *Outsiders: Studies in the Sociology of Deviance*. London: Free Press of Glencoe.

Bourdieu, P. 1990. *The Logic of Practice*. Cambridge: Polity.

Bruni, A. 2006. " 'Have you got a boyfriend or are you single?' On the Importance of Being 'straight' in Organizational Research." *Gender, Work and Organization* 13 (3): 299–316.

Connell, R.W. 1987. *Gender and Power*. Cambridge: Polity.

DeNora, T. 1997. "Music and Erotic Agency—Sonic Resources and Socio-Sexual Action." *Body and Society* 3 (2): 43–65.

Finch, J. 2007. "Displaying Families." *Sociology* 41 (1): 65–81.

Gagnon, J. 2004 *An Interpretation of Desire*. Chicago: University of Chicago Press.

Gagnon, J. and W. Simon. [1973] 1974. *Sexual Conduct*. London: Hutchinson.

Gagnon, J. and W. Simon. 2004 *Sexual Conduct*. 2nd ed. New Brunswick: Aldine Transaction.

Garfinkel, H. 1967. *Studies in Ethnomethodology*. Englewood Cliffs: Prentice Hall.

Holland, J., Ramazanoglu, C., Scott, S., Sharpe, S. and R. Thomson. 1990. *"Don't Die of Ignorance"—I Nearly Died of Embarrassment: Condoms in Context*. London: Tufnell Press.

Jackson, S. and S. Scott. 1997. "Gut Reactions to Matters of the Heart: Reflections on Rationality, Irrationality and Sexuality." *Sociological Review* 45 (4): 551–575.

Jackson, S. and S. Scott. 2007. "Faking Like a Woman: Toward an Interpretive Theorization of Sexual Pleasure." *Body and Society* 13 (2): 95–116.

Jackson, S. and S. Scott. 2010a. *Theorizing Sexuality*. Maidenhead: Open University Press.

Jackson, S. and S. Scott. 2010b. "Rehabilitating Interactionism for a Feminist Sociology of Sexuality." *Sociology* 44 (5): 811–826.

Jamieson, L. 2011 "Intimacy as a Concept: Explaining Social Change in the Context of Globalization or Another Form of Ethnocentrism?" *Sociological Research Online* 16 (4). www.socresonline.org.uk/16/4/15.html.

Kilpinen, E. 2012. "Human Beings as Creatures of Habit." In *The Habits of Consumption: COLLeGIUM: Studies Across Disciplines in the Humanities and Social Sciences*, edited by A. Warde and D. Southerton. Helsinki: Helsinki Collegium for Advanced Studies. eScholarID: 213749.

Lindemann, G. 1997. "The Body of Gender Difference." In *Embodied Practices: Feminist Perspectives on the Body*, edited by K. Davis. Pp 73–92. London: Sage.

Mead, G.H. 1929. "The Nature of the Past." In *Essays in Honour of John Dewey*, edited by J. Cross. New York: Henry Holt & Co. Reprinted in Reck, A.J., ed. 1964. *Mead: Selected Writings*. Indianapolis/New York: Bobbs-Merrill.

Mead, G.H. 1934. *Mind, Self and Society*. Chicago: University of Chicago Press.

Mills, C.W. 1940. "Situated Actions and Vocabularies of Motive." *American Sociological Review* 5 (6): 904–13.

Morgan, D.H.J. 1996. *Family Connections*. Cambridge: Polity.

Morgan, D.H.J. 2011. *Rethinking Family Practices*. Basingstoke: Palgrave Macmillan.

Reckwitz, A. 2002. "Toward a Theory of Social Practices: A Development in Culturalist Theorizing." *European Journal of Social Theory*, 5 (2): 243–263.

Schatzki, T. 1996. *Social Practices: A Wittgensteinian Approach to Human Activity and the Social*. Cambridge: Cambridge University Press.

Schatzki, T., Knorr Cetina, K. and E. von Savigny, eds. 2001. *The Practice Turn in Contemporary Theory*. London: Routledge.

Scott, M.B. and S.M. Lyman. 1968. "Accounts." *American Sociological Review* 33 (1): 46–62.

Scott, S. and Freeman, R. 1995. "Prevention as a Problem of Modernity: The Example of HIV and AIDS." In *Medicine, Health and Risk: Sociological Approaches.* Sociology of Health and Illness, Monograph Series, edited by J. Gabe. Pp 151–170. Oxford: Blackwell.

Shove, E., Pantzar, M. and M. Watson. 2012. *The Dynamics of Social Practice: Everyday Life and How It Changes.* London: Sage.

Simon, W. 1996. *Postmodern Sexualities.* New York: Routledge.

Simon, W. and J. Gagnon. 1986. "Sexual Scripts: Permanence and Change." *Archives of Sexual Behavior* 15 (2): 97–120.

Skeggs, B. 2004. "Context and Background: Pierre Bourdieu's Analysis of Class, Gender and Sexuality." *The Sociological Review* 52 (Issue Supplement): 19–33.

Warde, A. 2005. "Consumption and Theories of Practice." *Journal of Consumer Culture,* 5 (2): 131–153.

Warde, A. 2013. "What Sort of Practice is Eating?" in Shove, E and N Spurling (eds) Sustainable Practices: Social Theory and Climate Change. Pp 17–30, London: Routledge

Warde, A. 2016. *The Practice of Eating.* Cambridge: Polity.

Witz, A. 2004. "Anamnesis and Amnesis in Bourdieu's Work: The Case for a Feminist Anamnesis." *The Sociological Review* 52 (Issue Supplement): 211–223.

Yancy Martin, P. 2003 "'Said and done' Versus 'doing and saying': Gendering Practices, Practicing Gender at Work." *Gender and Society* 17 (3): 242–236.

Yancy Martin, P. 2006. "Practising Gender at Work: Further Thoughts on Reflexivity." *Gender, Work and Organization* 13 (3): 254–276.

Part II
Critical Methodologies

7 Making Space at the (Queer) Academic Table?

Yvette Taylor

Reflecting on cross-institutional LGBT Dialogue Day and Exhibition events, emanating from projects about queer-identifying youth, this chapter asks critical questions about how knowledge is communicated and who is, and isn't, included in this process. The chapter asks what could be lost—and what should be gained—as academics make space, are there 'problematic publics' brought into effect as space is made at the academic table? Issues of (dis)engagement cannot be solved simply by an invite to participate; rather, efforts and communications have to be sustained. And there needs to be acknowledgement that sometimes efforts 'fail', compelling honesty about the difficulty with dialogue as well as its collaborative potential. Academics need to listen and respond to the communities they 'invite' in. But there are vulnerabilities in this, where the academic can also be on unfamiliar ground as she takes up space.

Introduction

Where and how to disseminate:

- Offer workshops to bible colleagues
- Via resources to faith schools, and other schools
- Via educational authorities, diocesan educational authorities, teacher training courses, different denominations, Schools Out, Educate & Celebrate, Stonewall.
- Offer presentations/resources to local ecumenical groups
- Through British Sociological Association Teaching Group, specific guidance to A level Belief and Society syllabus.
  (*Making Space for Queer Identifying Religious Youth Exhibition* feedback[1])

Queering Impact

There are long-standing efforts and emphases, particularly from feminist researchers, on working with and making research relevant to plural 'publics' (Armstrong 2010; Browne and Bakshi 2014; Conlon et al. 2014; Santos 2014). Such attention complicates the composition of a holistic or indeed receptive public and makes explicit the private-public pain, workload and (non)promotion, in reaching-out, retreating to and caring in and beyond academia (Back 2007; Taylor 2014). In the above feedback, received following the completion of a research project event *Making Space for Queer Identifying Religious Youth Exhibition* which showcased findings and explored future research avenues, the bullet points arguably orientate the researcher to do more, to extend into—and out of—classrooms, offering presentations, resources and workshops, to diverse audiences. The exhibition dissemination event, open to the general public, came after three years of fieldwork research (only two of which were—prestigiously and gratefully—funded by the Economic and Social Research Council [ESRC]). It came after the production of twelve peer-reviewed publications, four project newsletters, fifteen blogs, twenty presentations, one conference and seven training events. It came in the hope that this 'ticked the box' of impact, as required by the ESRC, and in the hope that other research on sexualities might then also be recognised and funded as publically 'impactful'. It came in the recognition that some of the 'publics'—or 'users'— listed above may be unfamiliar with, sceptical about, or even hostile towards, sexualities subjects.

The 'still to do' list highlights project feedback as necessarily ongoing, rather than a simple tick. It suggests responsiveness to the work 'completed' and the work still-to-do, rightly tasking myself as researcher with a view of where and why the research must continue to resonate. But here I want to pause on such resonance, and the resources and recognition needed to continue to 'make space' at the (queer) academic table. This involves a certain knowingness and mobility, as a responsiveness to new funding regimes, new methods, new audiences; to be everywhere all of the time. And to be on budget. It also involves a certain scepticism and uncertainty, in being 'un-seated' from the academic table (Ahmed 2012; Dillabough and Kenelly 2010).

Of course, it is inviting to map out and consider the possibilities in feeding back, and forward, where the completion of research projects is rarely a neat finishing line. But there is perhaps also something to be said for incomplete research projects, and event research subjects, even if this may challenge the very logic of showcasing research and having labour recognised. Balancing and communicating research projects and subjects in terms of 'what has been done', alongside 'what was not done', is arguably a precarious, rather than celebrated position.

The notion of 'impact' has become increasingly central to the practice of research in the UK[2] (Colosi 2014; Mountford 2014; Taylor 2011, 2014). While many have long stressed the importance of research that has relevance outside the academy, the current drive for impact has triggered a range of questions about the definition of impact, the repercussions of the 'impact agenda' for sexualities research and the effect of the 'impact agenda' on how researchers work with external partners and organisations. Further questions triggered surround issues such as the marginalisation of certain disciplines and particular subjects (Parker 2010; Colosi 2014), as well as issues of promotion, recognition and research report writing (including in formal ESRC 'End of Award' Reports and peer review assessments). In order to 'be recognised' as effective and present at the academic table, funding success and policy-public impact, one has to strategically display and assert impact, something which can be difficult in 'hard to reach' and under-resourced populations, such as lesbian, gay, bisexual and transgender youth.

In making research relevant there is often a problematic imperative to impact upon publics as calculated via a metric calculation of use, value and knowledge transfer (Addison, 2014; Mountford 2014; Paton 2010; Taylor 2014). When considering the *qualitative* experience of marginalised groups, as often structural and embedded, measures of movement and progress can be hard to capture. Despite this, we write our impact reports before *and* after grant submissions and success, evidencing these in UK institutional Research Excellent Framework (REF) submissions for sector assessment/competition. Select institutional 'impact case studies' supposedly convey and substantiate the value of research, pressed into three-page REF submissions, rather devoid of the complexities, labours and challenges of research impact as ongoing and incomplete.

Particular public points and presences are discussed here in relation to the British Academy project *Not All Bright Lives, Big Cities? LGBT Lives in the North East* (Taylor and Falconer 2014) and the Economic and Social Research Council research *Making Space for Queer Identifying Religious Youth* (Taylor, Falconer, and Snowdon 2014a,b). Throughout both projects, there was involvement from marginalised LGBT community and users, extending beyond advising the researcher(s) and extending instead to the decision-making processes. As Browne and Bakshi (2014) have expressed, the goal was not simply to 'transfer' power/resources from the University to 'the community', not least because the very idea of a cohesive community that activists advocate on behalf of, that researchers hypothesis about and that practitioners seek to serve, can be queried (Paton 2010; Santos 2014). Yet, just as the linear direction of transfer is queried, so too is the direction of public points, presences and pressures, as complicated and confusing rather than just the 'bright lights' of celebratory IMPACT.

I focus on these two queerly orientated projects in particular, carried out in parallel and in conversation with a larger body of research (including my own). In situating these legacies and continuations, I hope to be mindful of the longer moments (un)sustained in academic practices, beyond the instant of 'impact' as a summary of what was done in the duration of a particular project. The influence of the 'impact agenda' on the future trajectories of sexualities and queer research, as well as on 'queer researchers' themselves, is a question and dilemma presented in this chapter. The future impact of any research must be located within these embedded, and embodied, 'impacts', which sometimes produce exhaustion as well as public effect. Ultimately, in outlining two projects as ongoing efforts, I hoped to offer some nuanced engagement with both the positionalities and power of the research-researcher-researched, and the possibilities of critical academics who seek to think, theorise and understand, alongside communities.

There is a certain queerness to this, a strange (in)visibility in heightened presences and urgencies, of always proving and maintaining impact for everyone-all-of-the time. I say this not because I am unconvinced of the long-practiced efforts of making research relevant to varied audiences, but rather because I fear that such relevancies, while being required—and desired—are not being effectively resourced and are instead being carried by the researcher. Highly marketised and competitive educational climates are complicit in producing reductive measures of impact, pre-determining and tying project success to policy transmission and public visibility. What is left invisible, exhausted and un-funded in these moments, and what does this mean for being present and on the page? Who will pay attention to and act on (qualitative) bullet points as opposed to metric scores? Certain disciplines and subjects are more precariously located than others in placing worth, value and influence. Arguably, the space that is being 'made' is a normative institutional space-subject as aligned with pre-determined economies of use, value and subject-hood. Sometimes our efforts inside-outside academia 'un-seat' us from being present at the table: "If you lose your seat what happens? Activism is often a matter of seats. . . the dissident is the one would be unseated by taking up a place at the table: your seat is the site of disagreement" (Ahmed 2010, n.p.).

Public Points, Presences and Pressures:
Not All Bright Lights. . . ?

Many academics, who are also activists, like to think of themselves as blurring the boundaries of 'the public' ('community') that is engaged with (Santos 2014). However, being part of academia, also demands consideration of complex power relations, which are not simply one-way; engaging with those outside of academia has the potential to efface or displace academic skills, while non-academics may be rendered as simply technicians, providing technical skills rather than transforming the social relations of knowledge production (Browne and Bakshi 2014). 'Local people'—as those often called on as the fixed and static authentic-in-place subjects who the researcher draws upon and 'out reaches'—may be sceptical about investing their time and may not see the benefit of the research. Participating in a research project also potentially decreases, rather than increases, over time and there are again resource issues to consider here for both the researched and the researcher: the invitation to feedback can itself become a call to action *from* participants.

In further considering that call to action from participants I want to turn to my British Academy funded project '*Not All Bright Lights, Big City*?' which focused upon the diverse and divided lives of lesbians and gay men in three distinct locations in the North East of England: Middlesbrough (8), Newcastle (12) and Northumberland (4). Twenty-four in-depth interviews were conducted with white British individuals identifying as lesbian (n = 8) and gay (n = 16), across the age-range (19–50yrs) and from a range of class backgrounds. In addition, two focus groups were conducted, with a young women's group (n = 10, 16–24yrs) and a young men's group (n = 10, 16–24yrs). Interviews explored a number of issues including: meanings held around the 'North East'; self-identifications; commercial lesbian and gay scene spaces; virtual online spaces and home terrain; and suggested enduring issues of marginalisation and under-resourcing in a context of austerity, voluntary sector cut-backs and retracted welfare provisions (Taylor and Falconer 2014a).

At the end of the project the Weeks Centre for Social and Policy Research, LSBU and Newcastle University recently held a cross-institutional LGBT Dialogue Day event, designed to create an inclusive and open space to foster greater communication between those working *with and in* LGBT communities and *in and beyond* academic communities.[3] Cross-institutional efforts attempt to cross spaces and subjects, to 'reach out' beyond the confines of institutional walls and boundaries, as responsiveness to working collaboratively rather than competitively.

Attending the day were the 'usual suspects' of academics, appearing as Principle Investigators, Co-Investigators, Researchers: capitalised titles generally conveying a presence, appearance and authority. But efforts were made to extend conversations across the career stage and include undergraduate and postgraduate students—often curiously missed out of conversations about impact as part of broader publics, making new knowledges, methods and engagements. Again, the intention was to continually interrogate how presences were constituted in these dialogues, carefully thinking about what and who might be disappeared or dislocated. In other words, to always be asking the question 'how is space claimed and maybe even re-arranged'[4]? Are there *problematic* publics brought into effect as space is made at the academic table?

The feedback from a delegate, outlined below, demonstrates such problematic publics and presences, received as a note of thanks, but also as an invite to rethink some of the dynamics, presentations and performances done by academics:

> Both of you [Principal Investigator and Co-Investigor] were much easier to listen to, and understand, when you were talking about, rather than reading your paper. I understand that there are probably protocols in academic circles on how folk are expected to do this, but I thought that one of the key aims was to reach out beyond the PhD students and colleague researchers.
>
> Would it be possible to give a presentation about the paper and your conclusions in a more relaxed style? Both of you are easy to talk with and have great, warm personalities. For me at least, some of the academic terms you used were unfamiliar, but I didn't like to interrupt your flow by asking you to explain. For example "problematic" seems to have a particular meaning, or a more loaded meaning in the research that Yvette was presenting.
>
> I hope that you will read this in the spirit in which it was sent. I was really glad to be invited to the event, and was very impressed with the diversity of attendees that you had invited. I don't want this to be an opportunity lost. You are both welcome to come and critique my preaching any time you like.
>
> (*Email exchange*, delegate attending cross-institutional
> LGBT Dialogue Day)

By invoking and disputing the boundaries of 'dialogue' and 'community', this event necessarily engaged in thinking through epistemological, theoretical and ethical issues in mobilising 'publics' and engaging as a 'public sociologist'. Being cross-institutional, it also aimed to subvert the competitive logics of institutional authority, success and loyalty, placing the ownership of data, delegates and dissemination as *between* two institutions. But even those terms, and *that language*, sounds academic, disengaging. . . and maybe even 'problematic', as signalled in the quote from one of the delegates. What if efforts, sounds and *different* dialogues collide rather than cohere in these efforts and urges?

Attending the event were policy makers and practitioners working in a number of NGOs and local government posts from across the UK. Between papers the audience was encouraged to break into small informal groups to reflect upon presentations but, arguably more importantly, to also draw from their own research, work and personal experiences. In discussing current LGBT lives, different issues and urgencies (including LBGT youth suicide, hate crime, religiosity, scene spaces. . .) were brought to the table and the diverse lived realities and needs of LGBT communities debated and deliberated. In debating, one attendee stated that it is "hard to find academic research that is actually helpful" and that "academic language is hard to grasp—pretentious, designed for academic papers".

Desperately hoping to move away from 'pretention', questions were posed such as: 'what is dialogue and when do we need it?', 'how can we foster and improve dialogue to ensure it is inclusive?', 'what is the role of academic research in informing NGOs and wider LGBT communities?' These may seem basic questions, instinctive opening points, but even with good intentions it is easy to stumble at these starting blocks, where it can be assumed that 'we' (LGBT researching, presenting, appearing individuals) are on the 'same page'. Such basic questions and understandings need to be clarified over again, rather than solved in entering the (university) room and sitting round the table, even if a shared one.

Different delegates were coming from—and going to—different places; the pain in underfunding for voluntary agencies, in particular, meant that this seat at the table was threatened. The 'table' might have to balance rather sparse offerings in times of funding crisis and cutting back (impacting more on specific vulnerable communities). As resources are cut back the pressure is on the 'innovating', 'enterprising' researcher to perform even more rigorous 'outreach', but how to capture the *absence* and *un-doing* at the table? The drive forward to 'reach out', to other/every non-academic community, also likely misses out the cyclical, returning and reciprocal dialogue of these exchanges (beyond a '*valued*' economic exchange).

Consider these comments voiced at the Dialogue Day in response to the question of 'What is dialogue and when do we need it?':

> It is a circular process, giving, receiving, processing, refining—otherwise there is no benefit to participants. . .

and

> Communication—developing relationships—exchanging ideas—development of thinking—it is a 'vehicle' for bringing the past forward and into the future—moving forward but recognising the sensitivity of the past.

Addressing these responses takes time, consideration and re-visitation as opposed to a snap-shot of 'transfer'. It involves errors, omissions, exchanges and redresses.

Urgencies demand responses and resources—rather than a completed 'transfer'—which was highlighted around changing policies relating to 'queer' lives. The UK, and indeed international context, has seen large-scale political changes impacting on LGBTQ lives.[5] The following issues in particular were discussed, often passionately, at the event, if not resolved:

- "Translating legal frameworks into cultural shifts and positive lived experiences".
- "Better education and educational practices for and about LGBT lives, individuals and families".
- "Identifying geographic gaps in service provision and addressing these gaps".
- "Lack of funding for LGBT services".
- "LGB poverty".
- "Trans poverty".

Lesbian, Gay, Bisexual and Trans categories, and the communities that supposedly represent 'vulnerable' identities may be messy, exclusionary and incomplete (Taylor 2007, 2009, 2012). Such categories are often used expediently in research, both to 'get on the agenda' and to question the 'us' represented. To view 'communities' as heterogeneous collectivities that can be recreated, in particular ways, through research, rather than neutral representations, is to acknowledge tensions and complexities in 'publics' and 'community', as well as the multiple marginalisations 'from within' queer communities, which researchers may well inhabit and embody.

Many of these issues cannot be solved simply by an invite to participate; rather efforts and communications have to be sustained. And there needs to be acknowledgement that sometimes efforts 'fail', compelling honesty about the difficulty with dialogue as well as its collaborative potential ("Openness in research and dialogue is needed"). Having hoped for and experienced an engaging event, I still want to problematise the 'publics' that are brought into effect and to consider what happens tomorrow when the Dialogue Day is over and the Impact Report submitted.

As mentioned, one attendee was quick to follow-up, pulling me up for using the word 'problematic' too many times (how academia re-fuels these 'problematics', as repetitions). She noted that the day was an 'interesting experience' as her first encounter with academic presentation: presenting-academics were ' . . . much easier to listen to and understand when talking about, rather than reading your paper. . .' Academic protocols (' . . . I understand that there are probably protocols in academic circles on how folk are expected to do this. . . ') can and should be adapted. And academics do need to listen and respond to the communities they 'invite in'. There are vulnerabilities in this, where the academic can also be on unfamiliar ground as she takes up space (Colosi 2014; Santos 2014; Taylor 2010). One attendee best reflects this as an *ongoing effort* ' . . . I was really glad to be invited to the event, and was very impressed with the diversity of attendees that you had invited. I don't want this to be an opportunity lost. . .' What is 'lost' in (dis)engaging academia in a heightened moment of cut-backs and educational crisis? What could be lost and what should be gained as the academic travels around the table?

Queer Identifying Religious Youth and the Making of Space

> Perhaps it would be helpful for a paper or multimedia project to be produced as a co-effort from an academic and a member of the LGBT Christian community, as multiple stories. Often, one academic voice is easily mistaken as scientific. The day was a great 'rainbow' of voices and ideas.
>   Collaboration between academics and practitioners/activists is crucial, more events of this kind! Organise dialogues within religious communities and LGBT communities about the relationship between religion and sexuality.
>   *(Making Space for Queer Identifying Religious Youth event feedback)*

Making Space for Queer Religious Youth is a specific case-study exploration of religion and sexuality in young people's lives (n = 38). Adopting an intersectional framework, it asks how religious identity interplays with other forms and contexts of identity, specifically those related to sexual identity. It does this through a detailed investigation of the experiences, choices and identities of queer (lesbian, gay, bisexual) young people involved in Christianity.[6] In the context of a rapidly changing contemporary religious and sexual landscape, this project explores young people's motivations for attending Church, how this shapes their identities, how they manage marginalisation or discrimination associated with religious-sexual practices, and the ways in which their religion might serve as a vehicle for various forms of belonging, identification and political expression. The reasons for Church attendance—and other engagements with religion—are investigated in relation to influences upon senses of belonging and everyday identities (Taylor, Falconer, and Snowdon 2014a). Non-heterosexuality is often associated with secularism, and this study problematises this dominant discourse by exploring the experiences of young people's connections with religion and spirituality. An understanding of how these identities can fit with one another constitutes an urgent response to contemporary social policy issues and campaigns that address equality and human rights for LGBT people, and aim to provide social, cultural and education information and resources.

Popularly, there is a (voiced) pause between what are seen to be clashing categories—'youth', 'religious', 'queer'—that don't normally sit side by side. Some imagine religion, sexuality and youth as 'contradictory', or are apprehensive that these spaces have come to be seen as sites of trouble and struggle, where widely held perceptions have often cast religion as *automatically* negative or harmful to the realisation of LGBTQ identities. This dichotomy is arguably repeated rather than bridged in public commentaries and policy-making, with a previous NatCen

Social Research Report (#28 2011–12) on British Social Attitudes implying a correlation between youth, secularisation and 'liberal' attitudes to non-heterosexuality. In addressing the meaning of a general decline in religion, the report suggests that the UK will continue to see an increase in 'liberal' attitudes to issues such as homosexuality and same-sex marriage. These apparent liberal attitudes to sexuality may, according to the report, ' . . . see an increased reluctance, particularly among the younger age groups, for matters of faith to enter the social and public sphere at all' (NatCen Social Research Report, 173).

Into such a public and policy context, the project aimed to 'make space' to account for, and make visible, young people's experience of being in/out of religious and sexualised spaces. Project findings certainly have implications for practitioners and policy makers working broadly in the fields of youth inclusion, religious participation, citizenship and community cohesion, with similar potential for re-thinking 'public imaginations' in sexual-religious landscapes more generally. This implicates a variety of institutions and individuals and the potential future impact of findings across sectors and for other faith-based groups (and indeed for those without faith) are recognised. Given the vastness of debates—and again the bullet point urges to think across the 'rainbow of voices and ideas'—it is perhaps unsurprising that the project's impacts are still in progress, facilitated by initiation of an international academic user group, and key events with policy, practitioners, non-academics and community user groups (including Metropolitan Community Church, Diverse Church, Equality Network etc.). Such connections take an enormous amount of effort to sustain and develop, involving tangible resources and practices, as well as often intangible feelings, such as trust and confidence.

Multiple consultative processes were enacted throughout the project, with a notable example at St George Church (1/08/2014), including Principal Investigator (PI) and Research Associate presentation, a varied (non)academic panel, performance and exhibition. A key effort has been in building processes that facilitate both short and longer-term impacts through relationships with users and beneficiaries at the levels of consultation and collaboration and which enhance professional practice. In this respect, the *doing* and even *undoing* of the project experienced similar issues as that outlined in the previous sections, with regard to '*Not All Bright Lights, Big City?*'

The policy report *Making Space for Queer Identifying Religious Youth: Politics, Policies and Public Imaginations* (Taylor and Falconer 2014b) attempted to write for different audiences than those who are normally addressed in journal articles, and the report was also disseminated online and linked to multiple blog postings written throughout the project.[7] The policy document engages with key users, and beyond the official duration of the project, such as School Teachers; Health Care Professionals (Counselling services, Psychologists, General practitioners); Relationship counselling and services (Relate, OnePlusOne); Inclusive Churches (e.g. Metropolitan Community Church, Diverse Church); Traditional Churches; MPs working in Religion, Education, Equalities legislation; Equality organisations (Commission for Equality and Human Rights); Inter-faith dialogues/forums; Gender and Leadership organisations; LGBT organisations and activist groups (Stonewall, Queer Youth Network, Equality Network); Specific campaign groups

(No Outsiders, Stonewall's Gay By Degree Poll, Schools OUT); Universities. It has been sent, photocopied, emailed to many of the above organisations and, in turn, they have responded online, by telephone, by email and face-to-face, as exchanges which cannot be captured neatly as impact evidence.

The report highlights the importance of including the voices of queer-identifying religious youth, and how this research can shape implications for politics, policies and public imaginations: it is suggestive of possibilities including further research and, in that regard, acts as an invite for others to continue the dialogue and press for services and supports. The report highlights some key issues that need to be addressed in order to tackle the adverse public, private and institutional experiences of young people who identify as religious and queer. It calls for a greater understanding of how multiple and co-existing identities impact on young people and the services they access. Such understandings can usefully inform and influence individuals, institutions and organisations who work specifically with young people, such as student counselling services, teachers and youth workers, as well as more general practitioners.

Alongside such embedded efforts, is an awareness that the project impacts have yet to be fully achieved and will continue in conversation with key (non)academic groups, taking into account the feedback received, and ongoing conversations. The below statements are notable in 'speaking back' to service providers, and academics, as a series of demands that young people 'should have':

> Young people should have awareness about the public services that can help them with the various issues that they have to deal with. Young people should have more access to resources, information and perhaps through the internet and social media. GPs. Hospitals and health staff have to be more inclusive and non-judgemental achieved through training and seminars.
>
> (Participant feedback from Making Space for
> Queer Identifying Religious Youth event)

The policy document has an appendix with full feedback from a project event. These sentiments constitute substantive outputs in themselves, in making clear the positive personal-professional impact of the event. There is a certain qualitative generosity and appreciation (often absent from academic peer review) present in these pages, motivating and inspiring efforts—not least when the project funds are spent. As with the '*Not All Bright Lights, Big City?*' feedback, it offers areas for future attention and potential impact, and an opportunity for researchers to re-think boundaries of projects, in forming alliances, such as the multi-faith extensions suggested below:

> Maybe forming alliances with other religious and LGBT projects to see what strategies they have for dissemination of information and encouraging inclusion, for example, the Imam project (for LGBT Muslims).
>
> (Participant feedback from *Making Space for*
> *Queer Identifying Religious Youth* event)

I would just like to say thank you for creating this space. I lead a small non-denominational Church in Luton where there is a large Muslim population. I would love for faith groups to have more exposure to research which addresses the relationship between faith/religion and wider society. I think your work and that of those on the panel could make a huge difference to faith communities and how they handle these issues and provide space where people feel accepted and loved. Thank you!

(Participant feedback from *Making Space for Queer Identifying Religious Youth* event)

These *qualitative* experiences of marginalised groups, as often structural and embedded, can be hard to capture and I deliberately showcase these here. The 'making of space' can be generously appreciated and recognised as continuous and done in practice, rather than contained or suppressed as evidence.

Conclusion

Ultimately, in outlining two projects as ongoing efforts, I hope to have offered some nuanced engagement with both the positionalities and power of the research-researcher-researched (and funders), and the possibilities of critical academics who seek to think, theorise and understand, alongside communities. Public sociologists come with the range of skills, expertise and abilities but this does not negate the positions of power that University status brings, and these can be deployed and negotiated in various ways. Public sociologists can and will make mistakes and get things wrong. The 'still to do' post end of award reports, make clear the necessarily ongoing work, rather than a simple completion tick. Reflecting on this is suggestive of a responsiveness to and appreciation of the work 'completed' and the work still-to-do.

'Public sociology' can contribute to processes of inclusion or exclusion (Back 2007; Burawoy 2005; Skeggs 2004), depending on how knowledge is accessed, analysed, interpreted, delivered and used in and beyond the walls of academia. As I have previously argued, the entrepreneurial university—and indeed the 'entrepreneurial' funded researcher—has been tasked with making an impact in responsibilising citizens to come forward and make a difference as conveyed in shifting funding priorities, including for example, of 'changing behaviours' (Taylor and Addison 2009). The strict differentiation of community/public sector, university/community is problematic, suggesting a one-way push—led by academics *into* the public—which effaces the dynamic and changing nature of engagement (and the realities of *dis*engagement). 'The public' or 'the community' can be disruptive, challenging and can stall attempts to 'engage' with 'them' (Browne and Bakshi 2014).

This chapter also raises questions about who becomes the proper subject for (non)academic attention in a time when 'publics' might be positioned as democratising and open or, conversely, as curtailed and shaped through specific and pre-determined economies of value and use. Moves forward, into and through the spaces of access, use, knowledge and value have been troubled but I am cautious not to place trouble with myself, as residing in my own research (in)capacities: as researchers generally, our troubles can act resituate a more sensory, embodied and politicised 'public sociology' which attends to the differences in listening and in measuring and evaluating unequal 'voices'. Having hoped for and experienced an engaging project, events and publics, I still want to problematise the 'publics' that are brought into effect and to publically ask 'what happens tomorrow the Dialogue Day is over and the Impact Report submitted?' *Problematic* publics can be brought into effect, as space is re-made at the academic table, confounding the 'bright lights' of celebratory IMPACT. The completion of the research, and indeed this chapter, sits within the requirement of 'ticking the box' of impact, and in the hope that other research on sexualities might then also be recognised and funded as publically 'impactful'. It sits within a recognition that some 'publics' may be sceptical about, or even hostile towards, sexualities subjects, as a measure confounding a numerical count.

Notes

1 For the End of Award Report see: www.esrc.ac.uk/my-esrc/grants/RES-062-23-2489/outputs/Read/5543d236-42a6-4fe9-8ef1-7e41f13385f5
2 Research councils now expect research to have clearly defined 'pathways to impact', while the Research Excellence Framework (REF) has made the evaluation of impact central to its assessment of the research activity of universities.
3 This was written up as a blog posting 'Problematic Publics? Making Space at the Academic Table', featuring in the British Sociological Association's Network (http:// week scentreforsocialandpolicyresearch.wordpress.com/2012/10/01/problematic-publics-making-space-at-the-academic-table/)
4 I again considered this is relation to recent invitation to participate at an event which asked for 'unconventional input', beyond a stand-and-speak presence. I searched for an object' to bring to the conference, as instructed by the organisers. The chosen object was intended to foster discussion, deliberately deviating from a stand-and-speak format of knowing-feminist speaker versus feminist-in-training audience. These knowledge exchanges, are often bound up with generational positions, and conscious of this I chose to speak about my own retrieved school report cards, marking my own educational trajectory. Which I wouldn't easily describe—or feel—as an 'arrival' (see: www.genderandeducation.com/issues/reporting-feminist-potential-at-the-rebirth-of-feminism-conference-middlesex-university-30th-october-2013-mdxfeminism/)
5 In 2001, the age of consent for sex between males was lowered to sixteen. The Conservative government's infamous Section 2a/28 was repealed in 2001/2003 and in 2004 came the Gender Recognition Act that enabled transgender people to be legally recognised as the gender to which they transitioned. Discrimination based upon both sexual orientation and gender identity in housing, employment and the provision of goods and services was made illegal in 2007. Same-sex attracted people serve openly in the British Armed Forces and same-sex couples have been able to adopt since 2002. In 2005 the UK government introduced the Civil Partnership Act, which enabled same-sex couples to enter into legally recognised relationships. In 2010 Equality Act made it unlawful to discriminate against employees on the basis of sexual orientation.
6 The definition of 'Christian' and indeed 'religious' is contested—and often especially so for youth people generally and queer youth in particular (Yip and Page, 2011; Taylor Falconer and Snowdon 2014a). Various Christian denominations have articulated different perspectives that are enormously complicated and contrary (Gross and Yip

2010). The diversity within Christian organisations and practices as well as between Christian individuals is acknowledged, while this paper focuses on commonalities amongst the sample. Most participants identified with the denomination of their church: Church of England (6 participants), Methodist (3), Catholic (2), Quaker (2), Charismatic (1), Ecumenical (1) and Evangelical (1). Two participants identified as Unitarian but with Pagan and Buddhist leanings. Where churches were non-denominational, like the Metropolitan Community Church (MCC) (15 participants), some participants also identified with the denomination within which they had been brought up (Church of England, 3 participants; Catholic, 2; Greek Orthodox, 1; and Methodist, 1). A substantial body of work on the LGBT population entirely disregards any religious aspect of LGBT lives or refers to such (dis)associations as negative, harmful or superficial (Jordan 2011; Gross and Yip 2010; Kubicek et al. 2009; Yip 1997). There is considerable variety within the category of 'Christianity' and it is the 'queer' stretching, fitting ('sounding' and 'feeling') which the broader research project highlights, also questioning the binary of (non)traditional approaches and backwards versus progressive stances towards religion and sexuality.

7 Research has been publicised and communicated to a range of non-academic users and voluntary organisations and updates have been made available through the project website (www.queerreligiousyouth.wordpress.com).

References

Ahmed, S. 2010. "Polyphonic Feminisms: Acting in Context." *S&F Online*—Issue 8.3: Summer 2010—Polyphonic Feminisms. Accessed December 5, 2014.http://sfonline. barnard.edu/polyphonic/ahmed_01.htm.

Ahmed, S. 2012. "Diversity: Problems and Paradoxes for Black Feminists". In *Educational Diversity: The Subject of Difference and Different Subjects*, edited by Y. Taylor, 203–218. Basingstoke: Palgrave Macmillan.

Armstrong, J. 2010. "Class and Gender at the Intersection: Working-Class Women's Dispositions Towards Employment and Motherhood." In *Classed Intersections: Spaces, Selves, Knowledges*, edited by Y. Taylor, 235–253. Aldershot: Ashgate.

Back, L. 2007. *The Art of Listening*. Oxford and New York: Berg Publishers.

Browne, K. and L. Bakshi. 2014. "Participation Beyond Boundaries? Working as, With and for Lesbian, Gay, Bi and Trans Communities." In *The Entrepreneurial University. Public Engagements, Intersecting Impacts*, edited by Y. Taylor, 43–60. Basingstoke: Palgrave Macmillan.

Burawoy, M. 2005. "Presidential Address: For Public Sociology." *American Sociological Review*, 70: 4–28.

Colosi, R. 2014. "Dancing on the Intersections of (Un)Acceptability: Reflections/Flextions on Disengagement in Higher Education." In *The Entrepreneurial University: Public Engagements, Intersecting Impacts*, edited by Y. Taylor, 27–42. Basingstoke: Palgrave Macmillan.

Conlon, D., Gill, N., Tyler, I. and C. Oppen. 2014. "Going Public: Reflections on Predicaments and Possibilities in Public Research and Scholarship." In *The Entrepreneurial University: Public Engagements, Intersecting Impacts*, edited by Y. Taylor, 185–201. Basingstoke: Palgrave Macmillan.

Dillabough, J.A. and Kennelly, J. 2010. *Lost Youth in the Global City*. New York: Routledge.

Gross, M and Yip, AKT. 2010. "Living Spirituality and Sexuality: A Comparison of Lesbian, Gay and Bisexual Christians in France and Britain." *Social Compass*, 57(1): 40–59

Jordan, MD. 2011. *Recruiting young love. How Christians talk about homosexuality*. University of Chicago Press: Chicago

Kubicek K, McDavitt B, Carpineto J, Weiss G, Iverson EF, Kipke MD. 2009. "God made me gay for a reason: Young men who have sex with men's resiliency in resolving internalized homophobia from religious sources." *Journal of Adolescent Research* 24: 601–633.

Mountford, V. 2014. "Rules of Engagement Beyond the Gates: Negotiating and Capitalising on Student 'Experience'." In *The Entrepreneurial University: Public Engagements, Intersecting Impacts*, edited by Y. Taylor, 61–81. Basingstoke: Palgrave Macmillan.

Parker, S. 2010. "Working Capital: Ownership and (Some) Means of Production". In *Classed Intersections: Spaces, Selves, Knowledge*s, edited by Y. Taylor, 13–34. Aldershot: Ashgate.

Paton, K. 2010. "Making Working-Class Neighbourhoods Posh? Exploring the Effects of Gentrification Strategies on Working-Class Communities." In *Classed Intersections: Spaces, Selves, Knowledge*s, edited by Y. Taylor, 137–157. Aldershot: Ashgate.

Santos, C. 2014. "Academia Without Walls? Multiple Belongings and the Implications of Feminist and LGBT/Queer Political Engagement". In *The Entrepreneurial University. Public Engagements, Intersecting Impacts*, edited by Y. Taylor, 9–26. Basingstoke: Palgrave Macmillan.

Skeggs, B. 2004. *Class, self, culture*. London: Routledge.

Taylor, Y. 2007. *Working-Class Lesbian Life: Classed Outsiders*. Basingstoke: Palgrave Macmillan.

Taylor, Y. 2009. *Lesbian and Gay Parenting: Securing Social and Educational Capital*. London: Palgrave Macmillan.

Taylor, Y. 2010. "Stories to Tell? (De)legitimised Selves." *Qualitative Inquiry* 16 (8): 633–641.

Taylor, Y. 2011. "Accessions: Researching, Designing Higher Education." *Gender and Education* 23 (6): 777–782.

Taylor, Y. 2012. *Fitting Into Place? Class and Gender Geographies and Temporalities*. Farnham: Ashgate.

Taylor, Y., ed. 2014. *The Entrepreneurial University: Public Engagements, Intersecting Impacts*. Basingstoke: Palgrave Macmillan.

Taylor, Y. and M. Addison. 2009. "(Re) constituting the Past, (Re)branding the Present and (Re)imagining the Future: Young Women's Spatial Negotiation of Gender and Class'" *Journal of Youth Studies*, Special Issue Young People, Class and Space 12 (5): 563–578.

Taylor, Y. and E. Falconer. 2014a. " 'Seedy Bars and Grotty Pints': Close Encounters in Queer Leisure Spaces." *Social and Cultural Geography* 16 (1): 43–57.

Taylor, Y. and E. Falconer. 2014b. "Making Space for Queer Identifying Religious Youth: Politics, Policies and Public imaginations" https://weekscentreforsocialandpolicyresearch. files.wordpress.com/2014/09/final-policy-doc.pdf [accessed 5th March 2015].

Taylor, Y., Falconer, E. and R. Snowdon. 2014a. "Queer Youth, Facebook, and Faith: Facebook Methodologies and Online Identities." *New Media and Society* 16 (7): 1138–1153.

Taylor, Y., Falconer, E. and R. Snowdon. 2014b: "Sounding Religious, Sounding Queer." *Journal of Ecclesial Practices* 1 (2): 229–249.

Yip, A.K.T. 1997. *Gay Male Christian Couples: Life Stories*. Westport: Praeger.

8 Challenges in Reflexive Research into Loneliness and Isolation in Older Lesbians

Jill Wilkens

This chapter explores some of the methodological challenges of researching older lesbians that arose during the author's MA research. It reflects on the complicated ethics where friendship exists or develops with and between participants. It also considers the benefit and limitations of shared sexual identity, or 'insider' status, to the participants and to the researcher and discusses the personal cost to the researcher when emotions such as empathy or guilt are provoked. The chapter draws on extracts from the author's research diary to illustrate the complexity of the research process to illustrate how she became drawn into her participants' social world.

Introduction

This chapter explores the context and the methods utilised in a study of older lesbians, examining how feminist methodology and a qualitative research design, incorporating a focus group and in-depth interviews, were used in an attempt to empower participants, encourage them to feel part of the research process and apprise them of the research outcomes. The chapter also reflects on the complex ethics of research where friendship with participants exists or develops during the life course of the research, exploring the need for self-reflexivity and awareness of the personal and professional challenges that can arise. While being mindful of the dangers of assuming commonality with participants (Almack 2008), I consider the benefits and limitations of 'insider' status (Archibald 2010; Traies 2012; Woodward 2008), and acknowledge the personal cost to the researcher when emotions such as empathy, sadness or guilt are provoked.

In 2011, I conducted a small-scale study with ten older lesbians for my dissertation on lesbians and loneliness, whilst I was a student on a Women's Studies MA course at the University of York, UK. My participants attended a fortnightly social group for lesbians and bisexual women aged 55 plus at a dedicated lesbian, gay, bisexual and transgender (hereafter LGBT) centre in West Yorkshire. Lesbian and bisexual elders are noticeably absent from much LGB research and, by focussing exclusively on the female experience, I offer a contribution towards more balance. One of my research aims was to ascertain whether being part of a same-sex, same-sexuality, same-generation group benefited the lives of the women who attended.

I also explored the significance of the group being only for older lesbian and bisexual women. While 'elders' are frequently regarded as a homogenous group for research and advocacy purposes, within this category are distinct populations with different histories and needs. The lives of older individuals are shaped by factors including ethnicity, class, gender, marital status and sexual identity (Arber 2006; Cruikshank 2013; Estes, Biggs, and Phillipson 2003) which, in turn, intersect to create unique positionings generating both advantages and inequalities (Cronin and King 2010; Krekula 2007). My research was motivated by the fact that several studies suggest that sexual identity is an important influence on the ageing experience, with many lesbians and gay men suffering disproportionately from loneliness and isolation as they grow older (Kuyper and Fokkema 2010; Musingarimi 2008). There is also evidence that group membership has benefits and may afford some protection against isolation and depression (Grossman 2006; Jacobs, Rasmussen, and Hohman 1999).

I do not subscribe to a 'deficit model' of inevitably solitary and mostly unhappy lesbian ageing, indeed my research revealed great joys, showing that participants valued independence and the fact that they could 'be themselves' above all else. However, it also demonstrated that many women in my study were lonely or feared loneliness and often found these feelings exacerbated by 'mainstream' groups. It was evident that the group offered some respite from loneliness and was highly valued by its members as an opportunity to meet in a safe place, with people with whom they could 'be themselves'. The fact that the group was organised on the basis of sexual identity and age was seen as crucial to its success; its 'private' nature was perceived as critical. The group and the centre offered many members a sense of 'belonging' and the strength of feeling expressed by all participants suggests that this model is a highly positive one offering social and emotional benefits (Wilkens 2015).

Creating a 'Respectful' Methodology

From the outset I wanted to create a feminist methodology, which would feel respectful to the participants and acknowledge their deeply ingrained, often necessary, life-long habits of privacy and concealment (illustrated here by Cathy):

> I am a very private person and believe I would be even if I weren't lesbian. . . I've never felt the need to confide my feelings to people. Having said that, when I was a teenager, I did tell a couple of friends about my sexuality [. . .] and that was the end of the friendship, so perhaps I've learned to keep myself private—that's the difficult bit. Am I as private as I think I am or would I be different in other circumstances?

> (Cathy, aged 63)

In the early 1980s as an under-graduate sociology student I, like Renzetti (1997), had been schooled into an 'objective' social science where the researcher remained outside the research, unbiased, value-free and definitely never disclosing opinions or personal circumstances. To be introduced as a postgraduate to feminist theories that challenged these positivist ideas, offering an opportunity, "to dismantle the smokescreen" (England 1994, 243) was in turn unsettling and liberating and, as my studies progressed, I became increasingly drawn to the idea of feminist methodologies that addressed women's lives and focused on the inequalities of marginalised groups with the aim not merely of reporting but of changing them. The challenge of developing a holistic reflexivity that spans the whole research process is discussed by Hesse-Biber and Piatelli (2012) and I aimed to adopt some of their ideas by being aware of my own positioning and relationships with participants, as well as the wider political and structural environment.

Many sexuality studies are based on quantitative methods (Boyle and Omoto 2014; Gabrielson et al. 2014). While these are useful for highlighting associations between certain factors, they lack a reflexive dimension and cannot offer a nuanced analysis of relationships between variables such as ageing, sexual identity and loneliness. I felt that using quantitative methods would not sufficiently capture the participants' subjective experience or allow me to 'hear' the silences and spaces in the narratives. I also rejected digital research techniques, knowing that several women were not technologically confident and might feel unable to participate, although email interviews and Internet recruitment have both been used to good effect in previous research with a similar cohort (Cronin 2006). My sense was that using face-to-face qualitative methods and a 'partially participative' approach were essential for a 'community' which had previously been marginalised and rendered invisible.

There is no space within this chapter to explore the debates surrounding the term 'community' and I use it with the awareness that it conflates a diversity of experiences and hides tensions and conflicts within groups intersected by factors—including class and capital—which impact a sense of 'belongingness'. The use of language and acronyms to describe sexual minority communities is another complex and contested area. Like Weston's (2004) sample, my participants were more likely to describe themselves as lesbians, reserving "gay" as a male descriptor, particularly if they had come out in association with the Women's Liberation Movement. Formby's (2012) participants and Cronin and King (2010) acknowledge the advantages of acronyms for promoting visibility and 'strength' but raise questions about the LGB/T acronym and whether it acknowledges the diversity within the communities it is tasked with representing. Whilst recognising these concerns, in conducting and reporting this research I have used the terms lesbian and bisexual and the abbreviation LGB, feeling that they are the most appropriate to describe my sample and ones that my participants also understood and related to.

The Research Process and My Commitment to the Participants

I wanted participants to feel part of the research and stay connected to it throughout the study. To these ends, I set out to use qualitative methods in as participative a way as possible holding a preliminary focus group followed by individual,

face-to-face interviews to elicit the subjective experiences of loneliness and isolation amongst my participants. I aimed to engage the participants, create trust and
reduce potential power imbalance by offering 'member checks' for participant
validation of the interview transcript and holding a feedback and discussion session at the end of the project. I also facilitated a number of sessions for the group
in an attempt at reciprocity.

My research is far from what Renzetti (1997) or Riessman (2008) would
describe as participatory and I acknowledge that an imbalance of power exists
that no amount of reflexivity on my part could change. Furthermore, fully-partici-
patory research would impose demands on the interviewees and myself that could
not realistically have been met within the scope of this type of project. Kirsch
(2005, 2169) notes that time constraints, along with conflicting values and differ-
ing levels of commitment, have the potential to "restrict the collaborative level
we hope to achieve". However, I hope that the small gestures of involvement and
connection ensured that the women experienced the process as engaged participants rather than 'subjects'. Certainly, if I take Renzetti's (1997, 142) view that,
in participatory research, the study "becomes truly an educational process for the
researcher" then I have, at least partially, succeeded.

I chose my methods carefully, seeing them as the most appropriate to empower
my participants and uncover their unique subjective experience within my time
frame and skill set. As a feminist, I believe my work should be inclusive and give
participants their own 'voice', as far as possible. However, this desire is fraught
with complications. In McDermott's (2004) study of class and power relations in
lesbian interviews, women who identified as middle-class spoke for around 40
minutes longer than those saw themselves as working-class although Roseneil
(2012, 130) report that depth interviews using the biographical narrative interpretive method (BNIM) produces "rich complex narratives [. . .] across classes
and educational backgrounds". My own study revealed no obvious correlation
between self-defined social class and length of narrative, while interview location
did exert some influence, as can be seen later in this chapter.

My 'participative' approach was designed to lessen the potential power imbalance with my participants. In an open letter to the group members prior to the
focus group I was explicit about my intentions, my desire to demonstrate respect
and establish the benefit of the centre, although I remained aware that equity
between 'researcher' and 'researched' is not easily achieved. Using a focus group
at the start of the research showed me what issues the group members considered to be most important and this discussion guided the choice of questions and
themes for the in-depth interviews. All ten focus group participants volunteered to
be interviewed and so my sample was formed. Liamputtong (2011) suggests that,
in focus groups, self-disclosure and positionality may be critical in determining
the quality of the discussion and degree of disclosure. In my study, several factors
may have promoted disclosure: a short piece on the centre's website outlined my
gender, sexual identity and motivations prior to the meeting; the women were in a
safe environment and most people already knew each other, some for many years;

and I had also met several women either socially or from living locally. I feel these factors positioned me more positively than if I had been a complete stranger although, as Weston (2004, 182) suggests, "presumptions of a common frame of reference and shared identity" can also complicate the process of research. This was evidenced in these and subsequent interviews where women have assumed my familiarity with a range of lesbian and feminist activists and events and been disappointed—perhaps dismayed—by my lack of knowledge.

The interviews were transcribed in full and emailed back to the participants for amendments and changes. There were very rarely either. Knowing I was returning the transcripts meant the transcription process was thorough and necessarily slow, but the labour at this end of the research paid dividends when I came to the analysis stage as I was familiar with the narratives and their narrators. The checking stage was designed to keep participants involved in the project and confirm that I had not misinterpreted their words or intentions. In taking their words back to the participants I aimed to strengthen trustworthiness and several participants, whilst making no corrections, returned a 'friendly' email that indicated a certain level of trust. Riessman (2008) warns however, that while ethical factors render it important to find out what participants think, the notion that this process establishes a 'corroboration' is by no means straightforward and may even be 'illusory'.

I was mindful of the issue of potential exploitation of women participants through even the most well-intentioned feminist interviewing. The end of research feedback lunch and the facilitation of group sessions were designed not only to keep participants engaged but also demonstrate my desire that the research be of mutual benefit. I was keen to 'give something back' and in the course of the year I ran film and book groups, a session on confidence building and a 'My Pride' lunch for the women's group. I subsequently wrote a short paper detailing the outcomes of the research that I hoped might prove useful as the centre is forced to compete for ever-diminishing funds.

Confidentiality and Anonymity

There is much debate about anonymity in the research of marginalised or sensitive communities (Kaiser 2009; Saunders, Kitzinger, and Kitzinger 2015). Given the private nature of many of the participants and the fact that they had lived their lives so very carefully, often existing 'under the radar' at work and within their family of origin, I was surprised and humbled by their concern not to protect themselves but to conceal the identity of others. Ultimately, four of the women chose to use a pseudonym. In writing subsequent articles, unplanned at the time of the research, I have anonymised all participants, the centre and the group, aiming to find aliases that reflect commonality with the participants' given names. My own identities are however, exposed. As Ryan-Flood (2009, 223) discusses, "this openness both within and beyond the Academy can make the researcher potentially vulnerable".

Interview as 'Communion'

For me, face-to-face methods were the best way to respect and honour the courage and resilience of this group of elders at the same time affording them space and time to tell their stories to an interested insider/outsider and thus a wider audience. I was drawn to Ezzey's (2010) description of interviews as 'communion' and tried to adopt his ideas of 'emotional framing' when preparing for my own interviews, quietly reflecting on what I knew about the person or remembered from the focus group and re-connecting with their issues en route to the interview. Ezzey's (2010) analysis of over 30 qualitative interviews reveals that he spoke for approximately 16% of the time.

> Good interviews are not dominated by either the voice of the interviewer or the agendas of the interviewee. Rather, they feel like communion, where the tension between the research question and the experience of the interviewee is explored.
>
> (p. 164)

Combined, my interviews yielded over 100,000 words. An analysis of two interviews (selected randomly) suggests that my participants spoke for approximately 85% of the time. My focus was on 'being present' and listening attentively, allowing the participant to talk without interrupting or mentally framing the next question. Although some of the questions evoked painful memories and difficult emotions—even some tears—when the transcript was returned for checking, several women commented on the positive experience they'd had. Comments such as these from Valerie and Nancy were very welcome and mitigated my sense of unease at probing these emotive issues:

> Well it's been good for me to get it all out because there's nobody I can talk to about it you see, so it's been very, very productive getting it out. So thank you for that."
>
> (Valerie, aged 64)

> Thanks for doing this project. It was nice to be able to talk to you about these things. They are my life and we don't get asked these things very often.
>
> (Nancy, aged 62)

Location, Location, Location

In addition to emotional preparedness and reflexivity, the interview location also seemed to make a difference to the participants' experience:

> Originally I thought [name of centre] would be the ideal venue for the interviews—neutral, safe space. Actually, the three interviews conducted in the centre have all been much more 'business like' than the ones conducted in

people's homes. They have lacked the warmth and intimacy that the other interviews have had. I may also want to look at the length of the interviews to see if there is a difference. [There was. . .]

Research diary 23 November 2011

The three interviews conducted at the centre were shorter and less intimately detailed than the rest, one significantly so. This may have been a consequence of the location, personality differences or pure chance. Finch (1984, 74) suggests that if woman-to-woman interviews are conducted in the participant's home they can 'easily take on the character of an intimate conversation' resulting in participants talking (and revealing) more than they expected. Several interviews, conducted in participants' homes, often over a cup of tea in the fading light of a winter's afternoon, took on this level of intimacy; a fact I became aware of and, somewhat uneasily, exploited:

Joan text and asked where I wanted to interview her. I deliberately chose her house as I want her to be surrounded by her things [. . .] so that she feels relaxed and at ease to open up. This disturbs me and I feel it is somewhat unethical.

Research diary 1 December 2011

It's Complicated: Friendship With and Between Participants

Research techniques that encourage friendship in order to explore private/personal issues may be potentially damaging (Cotterill 1992), although it is suggested that researchers can avoid compromising trust and confidentiality by setting clear boundaries (Kirsch 2005). In my research, as the process evolved, it became increasingly difficult and artificial to separate my social interactions from my research interests. Many of the participants already knew each other fairly well, some having friendships of many years. My relationship with the women deepened to a point where at least one significant friendship developed alongside several social relationships and I was frequently invited to (and attended) other social events. As Claassen (2005, 9) observed in her investigation into the lives of American lesbians aged 59 and over: "widening my social circle and in many respects transferring my social life to women sixty and older has been the joy of this project for me".

I facilitated several group sessions to offer something in return for the time and generosity afforded me by the participants and staff at the Centre. These meetings also afforded me great privilege and enjoyment and have thus proved mutually beneficial. Ettore (1980) shared her work with her lesbian participants, becoming actively involved in their community. She believed this demonstration of her commitment and serious intent had benefits:

Since I had become a trusted member of the lesbian community, my contact with other lesbians expanded into social contexts outside of my initial weekly meetings. [. . .] A "promotion process" through the lesbian ghetto gave me acceptability. . . as well as validity in terms of my research role.

(1980, 12)

At the start of the research process I had planned to negotiate the emotionally charged area of interviewing friends or acquaintances carefully. In June 2011, after the focus group but before the interviews, I wrote in my field notes:

> The fact that I have a personal friendship with one of the participants, and a social relationship with another four, requires me to find mechanisms by which to navigate what could become increasingly muddy waters. Oakley (1981) recommends reciprocity and adaptability and the fact that I have facilitated a number of [name of group] sessions feels like the beginnings of reciprocity.
>
> Research diary 11 June 2011

However, as the research progressed, I was increasingly drawn into the older lesbian community, creating an ethical minefield, which I traversed hesitantly and with trepidation. My ethical concerns can be seen in this diary extract, knowing that both Nancy and Joan were feeling unhappy and lonely, yet both perceiving each other and other group members to be confident, happy and self-sufficient:

> I felt in a real dilemma today. In her interview, Nancy was talking about how very lonely she is and then talked about Joan being 'happy' to go to the pictures on her own. . . I know that Joan is also desperately lonely. Both women tell similar stories of sitting alone night after night. . .
>
> Research diary 3 November 2011

The relationships that developed during the life course of the research gave me access to feelings, thoughts and situations, which would otherwise have been inaccessible. The ethics of using these and potentially exploiting those friendships still makes me uneasy despite participants' assurances that they were happy to contribute and felt the research to be worthwhile. It is likely that these friendships have impacted on the research in many ways, some of which are not straightforward or even known. While interviewing friends (or participants who become friends) increases the likelihood of rapport and trust, conversely some may be reluctant to reveal too much. Some researchers avoid this pitfall altogether by taking the decision not to interview friends or acquaintances (Crowhurst et al. 2013) but as O'Connell-Davidson (2008, 63) suggests, neither researchers or participants have any way of knowing that such deep friendships will emerge:

> [. . .] nobody can fully predict at the outset all the possible outcomes of engaging in a social and emotional relationship with another human being, and nobody can completely control the way in which such a relationship develops.

O'Connell Davidson, who documents the close friendship with a sex worker which emerged as she conducted an ethnographic study, argues that we must question the meaning and validity of informed consent in research that explores intimacies. Some of the risks and tensions created by trying to strike this balance between research that is good and produces rich data and research that is ethical and mindful of friendship are revealed in this email exchange with my 'participant-turned-friend', Joan:

> I have been thinking about the interview that you have said you will do with me. While I am very keen to have you in the research project, I would not like the interview to compromise a friendship that I value a lot. [. . .] I just want to say that I wonder if you really want to do it or will find it too difficult? If so, please say because our friendship is actually more important to me. Jill

> Re the interview, my only thoughts on it have been that I maybe somewhat at odds with what others might have said & I think this is more to do with me rather than the group & may mean me revealing aspects of my psyche I might not always reveal. However it had not occurred to me that it could harm our friendship (I trust you) which I greatly value too. Have you thought of something I have not!? Joan

> No I am not that perceptive! Just didn't want to put you 'on the spot' because I know that you are a very private person. If you are out of kilter with the others that is beneficial because it shows that there is another aspect. (Also the other participants have not all agreed by any means). Jill

Shared Characteristics

> It does take a lesbian to understand a lesbian.
>
> —Heather (aged 58)

Heather's words capture what many participants felt. Years of concealment, harassment and heteronormative oppression meant that, for some, psychological safety lay with other lesbians. There is much debate about the value of shared characteristics in research. Woodward (2008, 547) suggests that the insider/outsider dichotomy is "too crude a polarisation", whereas others see shared sexual identity as essential for access, recruitment and trust in lesbian research (Archibald 2010; Traies 2012). Almack (2008, 2.4) points out "there are many other facets of identity which may have an impact on aspects of the research project". It is often impossible to ascertain the full impact of the researcher's characteristics, self-presentation and how she positions herself within the research but my gender and same-sex relationship have generally been received positively in my research with older lesbians and bisexual women.

Although there were many points of difference between myself and members of the group, I felt that my personal characteristics of sexual identity and gender combined with my frequent presence at the centre and social events positioned me as an 'insider outside' of the group, an important consideration when conducting research on loneliness, a sensitive and potentially distressing issue. I have no way of knowing how my shared characteristics, choice of methods and attempts at reciprocity and participatory research impacted on the participants, but I was overwhelmed by the length and richness of the interviews. Sitting with someone, often in their home, for an hour or more, sometimes felt, to continue with the religious theme offered by Ezzey (2010), more than communion—almost confessional; the particular circumstances of confidentiality and a known, 'insider interviewer' liberating the participants to share their lives, give voice to their joys and offer up the bared bones of their loneliness, hopes and fears of future isolation as they aged. Kirsch (2005) explores the intimacy created in depth interviews, citing the interviewer's attention and sincere interest, the interviewee's enjoyment of the process and desire to 'help' the researcher. Whatever the underlying reasons, I experienced these interviews as a gift; a 100,000 word donation from a brave, honourable group of women whose courage has shaped the future and made the life journey of people like me so much easier. They gave their stories generously and with spirit and humour—pretty much the way they have lived their lives. Sometimes these stories were raw and mostly unheard; others were polished and rehearsed, told and retold in different circumstances, often over different decades.

The Impact of Research: Interviewer Guilt

The very richness and emotion of the narratives made their transcription a traumatic and uncomfortable experience. I listened over and over to these women's outpourings of loss, grief and isolation, knowing that I was responsible for prompting them to share these emotions, feeling that my questions had forced them to focus on loneliness, bringing it to the forefront of their awareness whilst offering no solutions. Although I had embarked on this research with the best of intentions—a feminist woman interviewing women, keen to 'give voice' to a marginalized group—during this period of transcription, England's (1994, 249) words came back to me repeatedly: "fieldwork is inherently confrontational in that it is the purposeful disruption of other people's lives".

Duncombe and Jessop (2002) reflect on the use of rapport in interviews and the ethical tensions between the satisfaction of gaining rich, revealing data and guilt that their 'power of persuasion' as interviewers had created relationship conflicts between couples. Listening to my interviews sometimes made me cry and I was frequently left feeling sad for the rest of the day. This sadness was induced by the guilty knowledge that the interviews—and the rapport I had created with the participants—had prompted them to expose their own emotions. Bowtell et al. (2013) call for a protocol around researchers' emotional safety when working with participants on sensitive issues, noting that while participants' well-being is paramount, researchers must also be mindful of their own emotional health: listening repeatedly to stories with emotional content can result in an emotional toll on the researcher that might lead to burnout.

The Emotional Impact of Research: Interviewer Empathy

Listening to stories of loneliness and abandonment, at times felt like holding a mirror up to a potential future, and some days I was aware of a feeling of huge sadness as I transcribed the interviews. The women's honesty and wry humour was often painful to witness and impacted on a deeply emotional level as I imagined my own older age mirroring theirs. Scott's (1998, 5:14) description of the interview as "a personal encounter that I relived in slow replay in the course of transcription" resonates with my feelings at this time. I tried to use my research diary more reflexively to capture how the participants (and many issues emerging from the research) were spilling into my own life, blurring the precarious boundaries between myself and the research:

> As an 'ageing' lesbian with a significantly younger partner, many of these women's narratives of widowhood or being left (by younger partner) and loneliness chime, if not with my experience, then at least with my fears.
>
> Research diary 8 November 2011

Approaching the End of an Era

In 30 years or so, this generation of LGBT elders will no longer be around to bear witness to the lives they have led. The current proliferation of research into older LGBT populations and the unique needs and challenges facing them in health, care and end of life settings is both welcome and deeply ironic. Unrecognised for most of their lives, this generation have lived on the margins and in the shadows. Now, researchers are quite rightly mindful of the imperative to be focused on their needs; striving for the attention of this small, and soon to be dwindling, generational group. This is a timely awakening; their history is both precious and precarious:

> How often do we tell our own life story? How often do we adjust, embellish, make sly cuts? And the longer life goes on, the fewer are those around to challenge our account, to remind us that our life is not our life, merely the story we have told about our life.
>
> (Barnes 2011, 95)

I hope this chapter has illustrated some of the joys, difficulties, tensions and contradictions inherent when researching marginalised groups with whom one has some kind of affiliation. My work continues to explore the lives of older lesbians and bisexual women and I hope I have learned to protect them and myself more effectively from the emotional demands of this sensitive but necessary research. If this study revealed anything, it was the resilience and bravery of the women who shared their stories. My journey as a lesbian has been immeasurably easier because they refused to be silenced.

References

Almack, K. 2008. "Women Parenting Together: A Reflexive Account of the Ways in Which the Researcher's Identity and Experiences May Impact on the Processes of Doing Research." *Sociological Research Online* 13 (1).

Arber, S. 2006. "Gender Trajectories: How Age and Marital Status Influence Patterns of Gender Inequality in Later Life." In *Ageing and Diversity: A Critical Introduction*, edited by S. Daatland and S. Briggs, 61–76. Bristol: Policy Press.

Archibald, C. 2010. "A Path Less Travelled: Hearing the Voices of Older Lesbians: A Pilot Study Researching Residential Care and Other Needs." In *LGBT Issues: Looking Beyond Categories*, edited by R. Jones and R. Ward, 30–41. Edinburgh: Dunedin Academic Press Ltd.

Barnes, J. 2011. *The Sense of an Ending*. London: Vintage Books.

Bowtell, E.C., Sawyer, S.M., Aroni, R.A., Green, J.B. and R.E. Duncan. 2013. "Should I Send a Condolence Card? Promoting Emotional Safety in Qualitative Health Research Through Reflexivity and Ethical Mindfulness." *Qualitative Inquiry* 19 (9): 652–663.

Boyle, S.C. and A.M. Omoto. 2014. "Lesbian Community Oughts and Ideals: Normative Fit, Depression, and Anxiety Among Young Sexual Minority Women." *Psychology of Women Quarterly* 38 (1): 33–45.

Claassen, C. 2005. *Whistling Women: A Study of the Lives of Older Lesbians*. London: The Haworth Press.

Cotterill, P. 1992. "Interviewing Women: Issues of Friendship, Vulnerability and Power." *Women's Studies International Forum* 15 (5–6): 593–606.

Cronin, A. 2006. "Sexuality in Gerontology: A Heteronormative Presence, a Queer Absence." In *Ageing and Diversity: A Critical Introduction*, edited by S. Daatland and S. Briggs, 107–122. Bristol: Policy Press.

Cronin, A. and A. King. 2010. "Power, Inequality and Identification: Exploring Diversity and Intersectionality Amongst Older LGB Adults." *Sociology* 44 (876): 876–892.

Crowhurst, I., Roseneil, S., Hellesund, T., Santos, A.C. and M. Stoilova. 2013. "Close Encounters: Researching Intimate Lives in Europe." *International Journal of Social Research Methodology* 16 (6): 525–533.

Cruikshank, M. 2013. *Learning to Be Old: Gender, Culture and Aging*. Plymouth: Rowman & Littlefield Publishers, Inc.

Duncombe, J. and J. Jessop. 2002. "'Doing rapport' and the Ethics of 'faking friendship'." In *Ethics in Qualitative Research*, edited by M. Mauthner, M. Birch, J. Jessop and T. Miller, 107–122. London: Sage Publications.

Estes, C., Biggs, S. and C. Phillipson. 2003. *Social Theory, Social Policy and Ageing: A Critical Introduction*. Maidenhead: Open University Press.

Ettore, E.M. 1980. *Lesbians, Women and Society*. London: Routledge & Kegan Paul.

Ezzey, D. 2010. "Qualitative Interviewing as an Embodied Emotional Performance." *Qualitative Inquiry* 16 (3): 163–170.

Finch, J. 1984. "'It's great to have someone to talk to': The Ethics and Politics of Interviewing Women." In *Social Researching: Politics, Problems, Practice*, edited by C. Bell and H. Roberts, 70–87. London: Routledge and Kegan Paul.

Formby, E. 2012. *Solidarity But Not Similarity? LGBT Communities in the Twenty-First Century*. Sheffield: Sheffield Hallam University.

Gabrielson, M.L., Holston, E.C. and M.J. Dyck. 2014. "Are They Family or Friends? Social Support Instrument Reliability in Studying Older Lesbians," *Journal of Homosexuality* 61 (11): 1589–1604.

Grossman, A.H. 2006. "Physical and Mental Health of Older Lesbian, Gay and Bisexual Adults." In *Lesbian, Gay, Bisexual and Transgender Aging: Research and Clinical Perspectives*, edited by D. Kimmel, T. Rose and S. David, 53–69. New York: Columbia University Press.

Hesse-Biber, S.N. and Piatelli, D. 2012. "Holistic Reflexivity: The Feminist Practice of Reflexivity." In *Handbook of Feminist Research: Theory and Praxis*, edited by S.N. Hesse-Biber, 557–582. 2nd ed. Thousand Oaks, CA: Sage Publications.

Jacobs, R.J., Rasmussen, L.A. and M.H. Hohman. 1999. "The Social Support Needs of Older Lesbians, Gay Men, and Bisexuals." *Journal of Gay and Lesbian Social Services* 9 (1): 1–30.

Kaiser, K. 2009. "Protecting Respondent Confidentiality in Qualitative Research." In *Qualitative Health Research*, 19 (11). 1632–1641.

Kirsch, G. 2005. "Friendship, Friendliness and Feminist Fieldwork." *Signs: Journal of Women in Culture and Society* 30 (4): 2163–2172.

Krekula, C. 2007. "The Intersection of Age and Gender: Reworking Gender Theory and Social Gerontology." *Current Sociology* 55 (2): 155–71.

Kuyper, L. and T. Fokkema. 2010. "Loneliness Among Older Lesbian, Gay and Bisexual Adults: The Role of Minority Stress." *Archives of Sexual Behaviour* 39: 1171–1180.

Liamputtong, P. 2011. *Focus Group Methodology: Principles and Practice*. Los Angeles: Sage.

McDermott, E. 2004. "Telling Lesbian Stories: Interviewing and the Class Dynamic of 'talk'." *Women's Studies International Forum* 27: 177–187.

Musingarimi, P. 2008. *Older Gay, Lesbian and Bisexual People in the UK: A Policy Brief.* London: International Longevity Centre—UK.

Oakley, A. 1981. "Interviewing Women: A Contradiction in Terms." In *Doing Feminist Research*, edited by H. Roberts, 30–61. London: Routledge.

O' Connell Davidson, J. 2008. "If No Means No, Does Yes Mean Yes? Consenting to Research Intimacies." *History of the Human Sciences* 21 (4): 49–67.

Renzetti, C.M. 1997. "Confessions of a Reformed Positivist: Feminist Participatory Research as Good Social Science." In *Researching Sexual Violence Against Women: Methodological and Personal Perspectives*, edited by M.D. Schwartz, 131–143. Thousand Oaks: Sage Publications.

Riessman, C.K. 2008. *Narrative Methods for the Social Sciences*. Los Angeles: Sage Publications.

Roseneil, S. 2012. "Using Biographical Narrative and Life Story Methods to Research Women's Movements: FEMCIT." *Women's Studies International Forum* 35 (3): 129–131.

Ryan-Flood, R. 2009. "Queering Representation: Ethics and Visibility in Research." *Journal of Lesbian Studies* 13 (2): 216–228.

Saunders, B., Kitzinger, J. and C. Kitzinger. 2015. "Participant Anonymity in the Internet Age: From Theory to Practice." *Qualitative Research in Psychology* 12 (2): 125–137.

Scott, S. 1998. "Here Be Dragons: Researching the Unbelievable, Hearing the Unthinkable. A Feminist Sociologist in Uncharted Territory." *Sociological Research Online*, 3 (3). www.socresonline.org.uk/3/3/1.html.

Traies, J. 2012. "Women Like That: Older Lesbians in the UK." In *Lesbian, Gay, Bisexual and Transgender Ageing: Providing Effective Support Through Biographical Practice*, edited by R. Ward, I. Rivers and M. Sutherland, 67–85. London and Philadelphia: Jessica Kingsley Publishers.

Weston, K. 2004. "Fieldwork in Lesbian and Gay Communities." In *Approaches to Qualitative Research: A Reader on Theory and Practice*, edited by S.N. Hesse-Biber and P. Leavy, 177–184. Oxford: Oxford University Press.

Wilkens, J. 2015. "Loneliness and Belongingness in Older Lesbians: The Role of Social Groups as 'community'." *Journal of Lesbian Studies* 19 (1): 90–101.

Woodward, K. 2008. "Hanging Out and Hanging About: Insider/Outsider Research in the Sport of Boxing." *Ethnography* 9 (4): 536–561.

9   Reading Texts and Their Silences

Sexuality and the Autobiographical Method

Roma Dey

Drawing from the interpretative approaches of phenomenology and symbolic interactionism, this chapter advocates for the use of autobiographical accounts to study gender and sexualities. It is premised upon the notion that autobiographical accounts are enmeshed within the social context and the experiences of individuals born out of social interactions. It uses constructive grounded theory to interpret the autobiographical accounts of four Indian women from different socio-economic and geographical locations published from 1970s to 2000s. From these accounts it teases out the changing notions of gender, gender roles and sexualities. The chapter demonstrates the use of autobiographical accounts as viable sociological data for the possibilities of building multiple histories of sexualities.

Introduction

Building upon phenomenology and symbolic interactionism, this chapter suggests the use of autobiographies as relevant sociological data within studies of gender and sexualities. More specifically, it utilises constructive grounded theory to interpret autobiographical accounts of four Indian women and their perspectives on their lives and work, gendered social roles and relations, emotions and sexuality. This work is premised within the interpretative approach of social constructivism. Social constructivism draws from symbolic interactionism and phenomenology, two interpretative approaches of sociology that developed, simultaneously in North America and Europe, respectively. They grew as critique to structural-functionalism and insist on human agency in social action. Social constructivist approaches highlighted the socially constructed character of sexual identities and sexualities (Gagnon and Simon 1974; Jackson 1978; Kessler and McKenna 1978; Plummer 1975) and helped in dismantling the biological notion of sexuality (Weeks 1986).

According to Ken Plummer (1995, 16) the stories people tell about their intimate lives are "socially produced in social contexts by embodied concrete people experiencing the thoughts and feelings of everyday life". He argues that such stories are symbolic interactions and identifies three sets of actors in story telling—producers; the coaxers, coachers and coercers; and consumers, readers, audiences. The focus is not on the story teller or the story but on the "interaction which emerge around story telling" (ibid., 20) and the political process involved in telling it.

Here, instead of sexual stories I am using autobiographical accounts of women from different socio-economic backgrounds and over different periods. Like Plummer (1995), I am concerned with the interactions around the production of these autobiographies: why do these women want to tell their stories; what is it that they chose to speak about and what is it that they remain silent about, and what are the political processes involved in these choices? There is another angle of politics to the sociology of stories, the politics at the end of the consumer. Given a choice, which are the stories that the consumers choose to hear, interact and engage with and why? This requires me to speak of my location of a university-educated lower-middle class, backward caste feminist from a small town, researching on the notions of gender, caste and sexuality contingent on women's experience in a complexly stratified society. My interest in these aspects began from my observations on the differentially gendered and caste-loaded interactions played out in rural Bihar (where I worked as a social worker). Subsequently, as part of my university MA dissertation in philosophy I collected and worked on published autobiographical accounts of Dalit women.

In the context of the Indian subcontinent, caste has a special significance in the way dominant ideas of 'womanhood', gender and sexuality have come to play. Uma Chakravarti (2006) terms the caste/class and gender intersectionalities as 'brahminical patriarchy', a structure unique to Hinduism and caste order based on historical processes of economic production, social reproduction and social status. "It is a set of rules and institutions in which caste and gender are linked, each shaping the other and where woman are crucial in maintaining the boundaries between castes" (Chakravarti 2006, 34, *emphasis added*). Historically, Dalits have been kept dependent on upper castes by religious sanctions on occupational choice, land and property ownership and education. In pre-colonial and colonial periods, there have been Dalit movements in several parts of the country, notably, in Tamil Nadu, Kerela and Maharastra. Not surprisingly, rich Dalit and autobiographical accounts thrive in the native language in these states. The autobiographies used here are from these three states. Two of these are by Dalit women.

Dalit women had remained marginalised within the Dalit's and the women's movements and cultural spaces (Rege 2006, 33). The 1980s saw as increasing Dalit and other backward caste self-assertion in economics and politics from which resulted more violence on the lower castes and the 1990s anti-Mandal agitations (by upper caste young men and women against the implementation of reservation against other backward caste). This made visible the rifts in the notion of 'sisterhood' on caste and class lines (Tharu and Niranjana 1994). Within this socio-historic context, Dalit women have organised and asserted their difference within the women's struggle.

An important aspect of the politics of hearing the story in the context of autobiographies from the 'Third World' is their publication and translation. The 1990s economic liberalisation that ushered globalisation and opened the markets to global forces led to an increase in translation of Dalit and other subaltern writings (Rege 2006). There were speculations that this was a newer form of colonisation, albeit a cultural one (Niranjana 1992). Translation of vernacular texts to English (or other dominant language) made them more accessible and, in this way, translation became a political process (Spivak 1993). Translation is also a politics of cultural transmission where the translator and translation perpetuate or contest values of a particular culture (Bose 2002). The possibilities of homogenisation and hegemonisation can be offset by the translator "surrendering" to the text to become the "intimate reader" (Spivak 1993, 180). Translation is closely linked to feminist politics and "offer an opportunity to interrogate our misrecognition of the world and transform our feminist politics" through a 'translation praxis' with a concurrent engagement with 'translation' of a Dalit feminist [Third World Feminist] standpoint towards "more emancipatory modernity" (Rege 2006, 77).

In the next section, I briefly introduce the constructionist grounded theory which is used to interpret the autobiographies. This is followed by a detailed interpretation of the autobiographies.

Interpretation of the Autobiographies

In this chapter I use what Kathy Charmaz (2006) terms constructionist grounded theory, which borrows from the grounded theory developed by Glaser B and Strauss A (1967) and social constructionism. According to Charmaz (2006), grounded theory that lies within the ambit of positivism sees data as real in themselves and is not concerned with the process of production of the data, whereas constructivist grounded theory lies within the interpretive traditions and assume that both data and analyses are social constructions and contextually situated. While positivist theories are deterministic and rest upon causal relationships, generalisation and universality, interpretative theories are contextually situated and assume emergent and multiple realities (Charmaz 2006).

I now present a detailed interpretation of the four autobiographies, which consist of a brief socio-economic location of each of the women, the reason they cite to tell their stories and an interpretation of their autobiographical accounts around the axes of gender and sexuality.

Kamala Das's *My Story* (1977)

Kamala Das (1934–2009), a poet and author in Malayalam and English, wrote her autobiography as a serialised account in a popular Malayali weekly, while she was hospitalised and considered terminally ill. Doctors suspected she had leukaemia. Her autobiography was later published in Malayalam in 1973 as *Ente Katha* and in English as *My Story* in the year 1977.

Kamala was born in the year 1934. Her father belonged to the landlord class. He was educated and worked in Calcutta. Her mother belonged to the matrilinear Nair community[1] and was a Malayalam writer. The closest revelation of Kamala's intentions to write can be found in these lines (195):

> With words I had destroyed my life. I had used them like a sword in what was meant to be a purification dance, but blood was unwittingly shed.

There are two major urges in her autobiography: to tell the story of a woman caught in a web of relations and an unhappy marriage desperately seeking love, and a critique of social practices and institutions that led to human sufferings.

Married to a man of her father's choice, she was unhappy and felt trapped in her marriage while she had to keep up the image of it being successful. She hoped 'for a more tranquil relationship with a hand on my hair and a voice in my ear, telling me that everything was going to be all right for me'. This portrays the pathos in the lives of women (and men) who had been entrapped in the culture of love and its promises (which are gendered and hetero-normative, where the man is supposed to say or make everything all right), while the existing social institutions such as marriage and the gender relations are not in consonance with these. At the same time, she was not able to shed her shyness with her husband except under medically prescribed sedatives. As has often been the case with women, her resistance is pathologised (Showalter 1987). This is also evident in the way her maid claims she is going mad when she questions her regarding her role in letting in a man in her house who, eventually, rapes her.

Kamala does not move out of her marriage fearing a rift between hers and her husband's families. Prospect of another marriage seemed low to her as she felt she was not beautiful and was a mother to a two-year-old son. She claims she had no qualification for a job and did not have the aptitude for sex work. Her narration elucidates how the hetero-normative ideal had limited her options and her inability to adhere to it had demoralised her.

Kamala talks about her relationships—a sexual relationship with an older girl at college (everyone had asked her not to be friends with her as she was lesbian); a long-time platonic relationship with Carlo, a pen-friend who loved her and wanted to marry her but she did not; a woman friend who took care of her when she was hospitalised; her art teacher with whom she was infatuated and a family friend she met just before marriage, who made her feel beautiful and wanted. She mentions instances of sexual longing for some unknown men. However, Kamala does not find this ideal lover in any of the human relations and believes the mythic figure of Krishna to be her ideal lover.

She criticises her community. Even though it is matrilineal, decisions are made by the male relatives (husband, father and uncles) and in the past women were forced to keep their torso uncovered. She points out hypocritical moralities that impinge upon women's sexuality and how gender and class play out in the favour of upper class male. Rich male relatives who lured and sexually exploited maids would not be questioned. In one such incident, a cook who loved a maid was beaten up and probably killed, whereas a rich relative who also had feelings for the maid, simply stopped seeing her. The next kitchen maid conducted an abortion on herself in her living quarters and was thrown out by Kamala's grandmother. In the meantime, the rich relative married a cousin who quarrelled and cried every night. Kamala relates this to the sexual obligations in marriage. Sex, Kamala says, is attached with violence and bloodshed. Young women are introduced to it by their much older husbands, like in her case where he gives her 'a rude shock by his haste in the first night'. In her view it was only Radha, a mythic figure who had an 'untumultuous' sex life with her lover Krishna, although their love was considered adultery.

Kamala felt that she was misunderstood as a 'nymphomaniac' by men of her community because she wrote about love in her poems and articles. They approached her and on being turned down spread scandals about her. She hits out at society for treating sex, in general, and women's sexuality, in particular, as scandalous.

Kamala's bold writing is perceived by her relatives as a threat to their respectability and they tried to pressurise her to stop writing. But she realised that she would rather give up all that she had, her identity as a daughter, wife, mother, to be able to write.

Baby Kamble's *The Prisons We Broke* (2009)

Baby Kamble is a Mahar-Buddhist woman from Phaltan, Maharashtra. After independence, with constitutional safeguards, some Dalit communities have been able to overcome socio-economic constraints to a certain extent, the Mahar community being one of them. Baby's father was a contractor for government building work and earned depending on the availability of work. As he never saved or allowed his wife to work, their family would often go through economic hardships. After her marriage, Baby along with her husband opened up a small grocery shop in her own locality. They reasoned that no one would give them work owing to their caste and incomplete education.

Baby shares the story of her people, their sufferings and their experiences as Dalit in a historical moment under the leadership of Dr. B. R. Ambedkar, a Dalit leader of national repute from the Mahar community. His role was pivotal in shaping and safeguarding the rights of the Dalits and other non-dominant communities in India, as the Chairperson of the Drafting Committee of the Constitution of India. In her autobiography, Baby upholds Ambedkar's advices to fellow Dalits and his influence in changing their lives. These advices are on the 'public-political arena', such as temple entry, acceptance of Buddhism, claiming education and the more contested arena of the 'private-cultural' life, such as giving up on superstitions, giving up eating dead meat or involving women in the political activities.

Baby calls superstitions a prison for her community. For her community, their poverty, ill-health, want and squalor resulting in violence and resentment is caused by the wrath of gods and goddesses.[2] She listened to Ambedkar, whom she calls Baba (as he was popularly known), and his teachings to decide about her life. She starts a small business within her own community, and sends her children to school even while facing difficulty in paying fees. As a result, she is well placed and all her seven surviving children are successful.

Baby's narrative focuses on the vulnerability of women from the Dalit communities. She brings out the subtle gendered obligations as well as the brutal oppression that women (and often men) of her caste undergo. She calls the bondages of caste 'slavery'. Dalits bonded to other villagers have to depend on them for work, money, and food. It is worse for daughter-in-laws who are made to work as 'slaves' by their in-laws.

In her childhood, girls as young as eight years old were married off and had to endure verbal and physical abuses from their husbands and in-laws for their inability to cook properly, cover themselves properly, or behave in a way deemed improper for girls of good breeding. Suspecting husband or in-laws would question every action and gesture of young unsuspecting brides as sexually provocative. On the slightest pretext, the woman had to undergo brutal physical abuse and psychological pain. Under such brutalities if a woman tried to flee, she was flogged and her feet tied with a heavy wooden load. She would have to drag the load with her feet wherever she went.

Daughter-in-laws had to bear the burden of their sexuality. They would be easily labelled 'slut' by their husbands and in-laws and tortured. She accounts that at least one out of a thousand Mahar women would have the tips of their noses cut off by their husbands and driven away for suspected adultery. This was in vogue until the 1940s. It was generally done under the instigation of husbands' parents to safeguard their family's name. Even as the girl is mutilated and is in pain, she is driven away and no 'good' homes in the community give her entry. The husband is then remarried to a woman his mother would have already found for him.

Her childhood, apart from the time spent with her maternal grandparents, is full of want and struggle. Her family would often go hungry but her father will not allow her mother to go out to work. This would lead to fights and eventually her mother would be beaten up. This was almost a daily routine.

Baby mentions few details of her personal life: how she was married at thirteen, how started a grocery shop, how her children fared and her social work for the community. She is silent about her home and married life. This silence is potent, almost impossible to ignore.

In an interview with the translator that is part of the book form, she explains that her life's story is enmeshed with that of her community; it is difficult to think of herself outside the community. Eventually she reveals that she, like women in her community, has been beaten up by her husband on slightest pretext or suspicion of promiscuity. It was not possible to make him see reason or to move out and marry another man as this 'husbandness' was the same with everyman. She never complained to her brothers or father, as women were expected to bear all this (her father used to beat her mother too). Young girls were told stories of pativrata[3] women, sons learnt from their fathers to treat their wives as footwear. The root cause, according to her, was male ego, men considering themselves as superior and tortured their wives as did other men. Within the caste hierarchy Mahars have to face discrimination and humiliation at the hands of upper castes.

Nalini Jameela's *The Autobiography of a Sex Worker* (2005)

Nalini Jameela is an Ezhava woman from the state of Kerela. She worked as a labourer in clay mine and as a domestic worker before starting sex work. She joined a sex-workers' collective and becomes an activist fighting against police atrocities on sex workers. She also ventured into short-film making. She is coaxed by her activist colleagues and friends to write her autobiography.

For Jameela writing her autobiography was a struggle as she is not used to writing. She spoke about her life and the recording was used by a biographer to write down the autobiography. However, part of the recording was lost and the biographer had to rely on his memory. The first version was published in Malayalam titled *Oru Laingikatozhilaliyute Atmakatha* (literally, Autobiography of a Sex Worker) in 2005. The present version is a translation of a revised version. In the preface Jameela acknowledges that she does not know if there are rules about making revisions to one's own biography but she is not concerned about being the first to change those rules, for she wants her autobiography to match her standards and style (Jameela 2005, viii-ix). There is a rebellious streak in her, someone who Is not ready to accept the social rules and challenges these.

Jameela's father would not go to work and they would have to depend on relatives for food. As a child Nalini saw that her mother, owing to her poor monetary conditions, was a scared and trembling figure, wearing ill-fitted dress compared to her aunt Valyamma, who looked dignified with her clothes accentuating her sensual figure. This impressed upon Nalini that pride and dignity came from possessing money. An adolescent Jameela walks in a political march and becomes aware of the power that her body had over the onlookers. She realises that her body gives her power over others and she manipulates the objectification of her body as power.

Jameela's relationship with her father was difficult as he tried to control whatever she earned as a labourer. Eventually, he told her to get out of the house when she supported her elder brother's marriage with an older woman. Homeless, that night while she was looking out for the person who had proposed marriage to her, she came across another acquaintance who took her to his uncle's place to stay. She stayed there for a week and went to his home, where people considered her as his wife, while there was no customary marriage. She decides not to marry him but pretended to be his wife. She had children with him and worked with him in selling local liquor until his death due to alcoholism.

Her 'mother-in-law' would take care of the children only if she paid a fixed amount every day, but the labouring jobs she could get did not earn her that amount. These circumstances led her to engage in sex work. In her words, sex work entails 'using the woman the way the husband does'.

Nalini learnt that men could be both tender and cruel from her very first client, an upper caste policeman. As a lover he was tender like the lover of her fantasies, however, the next morning he handed her over to the police for indulging in sex work. This made her realise that laws were partial. The laws criminalise sex workers; the client is let off while the burden of crime falls on the sex worker.

In her narrative there is a constant struggle to find a home, literally, a place to stay and be safe. There are men with false promises of marriage and the status of wife, a relationship where she was deemed wife socially, but as it turned bad Jameela moved out.

In her third relationship, she lived some years in a home she built with a man and managed a business with him. Eventually, he got interested in another woman and Jameela had to move from mosque to mosque with her daughter, living in the courtyards and on the streets. By this time, she had taken up a Muslim identity and the name Jameela. She comes back to sex work eventually and this time she joins the trade union movement of sex workers and comes out publicly as a sex worker. This gives her the platform to speak about and demand the rights of dignity, decriminalisation of sex-work and protection from police atrocities for sex workers. She raises some pertinent questions such as why sex cannot be seen as any other commodity; why all sexual relations should end in family ties; why not accept lesbianism as family planning? Jameela also raises issues of police apathy towards sexual abuse of sex workers by criminal gangs and incidences of murders by drug dealers. She questions why society does not question when sex workers are gang raped or killed.

Bama's *Karrukku* (2000)

Bama (1958-) is the pen name of a Tamil Dalit woman from a Roman Catholic family. She does not reveal much about her identity. She is a Paraya, one of the most socially and economically backward community in Tamil Nadu. She belongs to a rural village close to Madurai. The village has people belonging to a number of castes and they live in segregated colonies.

Bama writes about her first understanding of caste, through a fight of her community with another in her village over a disputed land. In her village and school she, along with others of her community, faced discrimination because they were Paraya. She later came across regional discrimination in the course of her teaching life when she was placed in a school where people from another region worked. She joins a church order and becomes a nun but she realises that the sisters were equally caste-minded. She felt removed from her people as she taught children of elite families. She writes about practices of discrimination, beating up children, disciplining them to be faithful Christians, creating and administering a religion that discriminates on caste, is more like a painful bondage, it kills the individuality, the uniqueness of a child and promotes subservience, order and a forced sameness.

Her autobiography is a protest statement against such a religion, which does not allow questioning, is blind to the conditions of the poor and struggling masses and discriminates against them in ways which are against the very foundation of the religion—Christ's sacrifice for the powerless.

Coming from a working-class Dalit family, she grew up seeing hard-working men and working hard herself. She was enthusiastic about her studies but at home she had to work as an agricultural labourer which she did not have to do when she went to a boarding school attached to a convent. She is critical of the fact that it would be girls who would be doing household chores and labour work but not boys, who would only be let off with looking after some cattle. She also questions unequal wages for men and women for the same work.

In her childhood, they would play games such as shop keeping where boys would take up the roles of the shop keepers (more powerful caste). It was again boys who would playact as the upper caste land lords and humiliate them and girls would act as the over-worked labourer. There were games of being married off, which depicted girls setting off on a bus, husbands coming home drunk and hitting his wife and the police arriving and beating him up. While young men would go to the cinema, women were not allowed in the fear that men from other communities will grab them. There were men who would beat up their wives but no one would interfere.

In the description of the fight over the disputed land, she brings out how entrenched patriarchy is, as even an old woman is shown to instigate people of her community to prove their masculinity by killing ten people for the one attacked. The police are shown in an equally bad light, using obscene language and harassing the women of the community once the men had fled.

Bama at the very end mentions that because she lives alone by herself, without family, husband and children she faces many challenges, yet it is this very position as an independent woman that gives her the opportunity to work for the liberation of Dalits. Bama does not specify the problems she faces as a single woman but from the other autobiographies we get an idea of the society as a hetero-normative patriarchal caste based stratified society. We do not have any data as to what these problems are or why she chose not to join the order against the advice of her family and friends, deviating from what was expected of her as a young woman (marriage, motherhood). But we are aware that these silences are meaningful, they are very much a part of her narrative and we have to acknowledge them.

Discussion

In this final section, I try to weave together the autobiographical accounts, comparing and contrasting the perspectives and concepts presented in the previous section. At the very onset I lay bare two important conditions of interpretive method—to read the text within the larger social context and their social situatedness.

The women belong to three different states. Kamala's autobiography (1973 in Malayalam) appeared in public almost a decade ahead of Baby's (1986 in Marathi) and a couple of decades ahead of Bama's (in 1992 in Tamil). Jameela's autobiography (2005 in Malayalam) is a post-liberalisation account. These decades mark an important period for gender and sexuality in India. In this period, issues of gender and sexuality have gained considerable visibility owing to the opening of the media to Western and global corporate houses (1990s) and interventions by international NGOs in HIV/AIDS prevention programs beginning in the 1980s (Menon 2009). Thus, Jameela's account has an inflection in its openness and engagement with sexualities. Her taking up a Muslim identity or pretence of a married life mark the fluidity of identity and a heightened sense of performativity which is much subtle in the three other women.

As we move through each of the autobiographical accounts, and from one to another, the notions and practices of gender and sexuality shift. Over time, the women evolve and their notions towards themselves, their bodies and sexuality change. Jameela remains aware of the way her body changes from that of a young girl to a sick dying women in hospital. Kamala reflects upon the way sickness and age have taken away the glow from her face. Her narrative also points towards sexual fluidity, from homoeroticism to fear and pain in heterosexuality to a longing for the mythical lover Krishna.

The women use creative strategies to rework straight-jacketed roles and accepted notions of gender and sexual behaviours. Baby successfully manages a shop along with the duties of child rearing and household chores while her mother was prohibited to work. Kamala escapes the institution of marriage through her writing. Jameela risks moving out of her father's house into a gendered patriarchal world and sex work. Bama joins the Church order and later comes out of it when she is disenchanted.

They write about the ways in which notions of masculinity are practiced through control over women and their sexuality, through coercion, false accusation and physical violence (Baby); using gendered abuse and inciting men to physical violence in the name of valour and family honour (Baby and Bama). An opposing and binary notion of desirable femininity is built and maintained through social norms that envisage the masculine as powerful and the decision maker and the feminine accepting and following them. Jameela's father tells her to leave the house when she goes against him and supports her brother. Baby's father beats her mother to make his point and keep her away from working and inside the house; Bama feels it when she decides to study further and her father tells her he will not support her monetarily anymore. Women are not supposed to take independent decisions. Sometimes they hide from others important choices, as Baby does when she decides to join a library or write her autobiography. Some decisions could lead to danger and stigma, for example, Kamala finds herself in the midst of scandal for writing about love.

Bama joins the Dalit movement after she leaves the Church. Jameela joins the sex workers' collective Jwala. Kamala's openness and boldness endears her to the youth in her home state and finds support in them for her call for change in the value system of their society. Baby Kamble engages in Dalit political activism from a young age and it gives her the ideology and support system to continue working for her own independence and that of other Dalit women from the prisons of patriarchy and casteism. Their different experiences of discrimination based on gender, caste and their unconventional work motivate them to be part of collectives and movements to resist them. Thus, they are able to read their 'private troubles' as 'public matter' which helps to locate and rework the crisis in the institutional arrangements (Mills 1959, 3).

A comparison of the autobiographies is possible when contextualised within the caste/class and gender intersectionalities. As discussed earlier, due to caste-based access to land and property, generations of Dalit men and women had to work for upper caste/class landlords. This dependency had imposed "upper caste male privileges over lower caste women's bodies, which in turn constructs the lower caste men as effete" (Anandhi, Jeyaranjan and Krishnan 2002, 4399). Baby touches on this issue, referring to the violence women in her community faced if their in-laws suspicion was raised by a caste man. In this single interaction, the Dalit woman is rendered sexualised and available and the Dalit man is emasculated in his inability to "protect" his woman within the patriarchal frame. This notion of competing masculinities is at the basis of intimate partner violence that Dalit women undergo as mentioned in both the Dalit autobiographies. In Bama's narrative the upper caste male is replaced by police men (part of state machinery) who harass women of her community when the men of her community fled fearing arrest. Such incidences of misuse of state machinery on caste lines show the resilience and adaptability of brahminical patriarchy (Chakravarti 2002).

In the colonial period, the middle class increasingly tried to have control over women's sexuality. This went on to create the lower caste/class women as "licentious" and saturated the middle-class women with virtue and purity (Tharu and Niranjana 1994, 101). It appears that this logic has somehow inhibited both the Dalit women to speak on issues of sexuality. As if they have chosen to remain silent on issues of sexuality to break free of this hegemonic image. On the other hand, Kamala (writing in the 1970s) transgresses the boundaries of her upper caste/class virtue and breaks the silence around marital sexual abuse (which is still not recognized in India as sex is seen as an obligation in marriage). She goes on to question the base of social sanctity and obligation of sex in marriage when it is not pleasurable for women.

In conclusion, the reading of autobiographies as social interactions requires one to go beyond what is said and observing the patterns of silences and recognising them as potent, meaningful. When read with other autobiographies and within the socio-political context, there are possibilities of unpacking these silences.

Notes

1 According to G. Arunima, Nairs in Kerala followed matrilineal inheritance and entered into Sambandham or sexual unions which needed not be lifelong, and both men and women could have more than one such relationships and continue to stay in their own natal households. This became an issue of administration difficulty for the colonial administrators in the early 19th century. In the late 19th century, Nair men were increasingly getting education and moving away from agriculture. They now wanted a share of their family property and attacked their own marriage customs as "immoral" and attacked Nair women as "promiscuous, adulterous and lacking in morals" (2002, 222–223). Eventually, in 1930s matrilineality was abolished by the colonial government (229).
2 These goddesses such as Kalubai and Margi Mai and Gods such a Laman Pathan and Yetal Sahib are not part of the dominant Hindu mythologies and are shown to belong to different regions and people come to be possessed by them when they visit these places.
3 Pativrata is an upper caste Hindu ideological construct aimed at controlling women's sexuality which idealises "chastity and wifely fidelity as the highest expression of their selfhood" (Chakravarti 2006, 74).

References

Anandhi,, S. Jeyaranjan, J. and R. Krishnan. 2002. "Work, Caste and Competing Maculinities: Notes From a Tamil Village." *Economic and Political Weekly* 37 (43): 4397–4406.

Arunima, G. 2002. "Some Issues in an Analysis of Caste and Gender in Modern India." *Translating Caste*, edited by T. Basu, 219–233. New Delhi: Katha.

Bama. 2000. *Karukku*. Translated by L. Holmstrom. Chennai: Macmillan India.

Bose, B. 2002. "'The Most Intimate Act': The Politics of Gender, Culture and Translation." In *Translating Desire: The Politics of Gender and Culture in India*, edited by B. Bose, 256–281. New Delhi: Katha.

Chakravarti, U. 2002."Through Another Lens: Men,Women and Caste." In *Translating Caste*, edited by T. Basu, 198–218. New Delhi: Katha.

Chakravarti, U. 2006. *Gendering Caste: Through a Feminist Lens*. Calcutta: Stree.

Charmaz, K. 2006. *Constructing Grounded Theory: A Practical Guide Through Qualitative Analysis*. London: Sage.

Das, K. 2009. *My Story*. Noida: HarperCollins Publishers India. Originally published in 1977.

Gagnon, J. and W. Simon. 1974. *Sexual Conduct*. London: Hutchinson.

Glaser, B. and A. Strauss. 1967. *The Discovery of Grounded Theory: Strategies for Qualitative Research*. Chicago: Aldine.

Jackson, Stevi. 1978. *On the social construction of female sexuality*. London: WRRC.

Jameela, N. 2005. *The Autobiography of a Sex Worker*. Translated by J. Devika. Chennai: Westland ltd.

Kessler, S.J. and W. McKenna. 1978. *Gender: An Ethnomethodological Approach*. Chicago: University of Chicago Press.

Menon, N. 2009. "Sexuality, Caste, Governmentality: Contests Over Gender in India." *Feminist Review*, 91: 94–112.

Niranjana, T. 1992. *Siting Translation: History, Post-Structuralism, and the Colonial Context*. Berkeley: University of California Press.

Plummer, K. 1975. *Sexual Stigma: An Interactionist Account*. London: Routledge & Kegan Paul.

Plummer, K. 1995. *Telling Sexual Stories: Power, Change and Social Worlds*. London: Routledge.

Rege, S. 2006. *Writing Caste/Writing Gender: Reading Dalit Women's Testimonies*. Delhi: Zubaan.

Tharu, S. and T. Niranjana. 1994. "Problems for a Contemporary Theory of Gender." *Social Scientist* 22 (3/4): 93–117.

Showalter, E. 1987. *The Female Malady: Women, Madness and English Culture, 1830–1980*. New York: Penguin Books.

Spivak, G.C. 1993. *Outside in the Teaching Machine*. New York: Routledge.

Weeks, J. 1986. *Sexuality*. London: Routledge.

Wright Mills, C. 1959. *The Sociological Imagination*. London: Oxford University Press.

10 Intimate Partner Violence in Lesbian Relationships

An Interactional-Structural Analysis

Alžběta Možíšová

The focus of this chapter is intersections of gender and sexuality in the context of intimate partner violence in lesbian relationships. The first part discusses discourse of domestic violence based on feminist theory with its emphases on the gendered context of domestic violence and the system of male domination. It critically reflects upon the limits of the gender-based approach towards domestic violence based on gender inequality and power imbalance in heterosexual relationships, and points to the heteronormativity of the domestic violence discourse. The chapter argues that the assumption of male perpetrator and female victim universalises heterosexual experience and binary categories and excludes people who have experienced abuse in a non-heterosexual relationship, as well as those who do not fit into these categories.

Introduction

Academic debates on domestic violence have shifted over the decades from the initial need to address it as an important social and theoretical issue—in particular through the discussion of gender a/symmetry in the perpetuation of domestic violence (Kimmel 2002)—to addressing violence in various types of relationships, including same-sex relationships (McHugh and Frieze 2006). The concepts that have been used traditionally in studies of domestic violence in heterosexual relationships can be expanded when researching intimate partner violence (IPV) in same-sex relationships. This chapter focuses in particular on the concept of gender and on the ways in which it can be applied to understand IPV in same-sex relationships, thus opening up new perspectives on the broader understanding of this issue.

The first part of the chapter discusses and critically reflects on how, despite the limits of the gender-based approach to IPV, this can be adopted fruitfully in addressing same-sex IPV. The second part presents preliminary results from a pioneering mixed method (quantitative and qualitative) study on IPV in lesbian relationships in the Czech Republic; here I stress the importance of taking gender as an analytical tool to expand the understandings of the interactional-structural context of violence.

Domestic Violence and Gender in and Beyond Feminist Discourses

Much feminist theory has established gender as the central concept through which we can understand violence in intimate relationships, thus pointing out the systemic inequalities that lead to the discrimination of women as a group, and creating a strong argument in the criticism of patriarchy. Itzin (2000, 360) argues that "one of feminism's major contributions to domestic violence policy and practice has been to identify men as the primary perpetrators of domestic violence. . . gendered in terms of male dominance and female subordination." In this understanding, violence is analysed as the effect of gender inequality and of the powers and structures which maintain women's subordination, for example the patriarchal family (Maynard and Winn 1997). From this perspective, violence in the family is seen as one of the means of subordination of women who have been oppressed by techniques of control, including physical, economic and emotional violence, along with intimidation and isolation (McPhail et al. 2007). Violence is thus regarded as the abuse of power that is unevenly distributed in intimate relationships reflecting gender inequalities present in the broader society.

This basis of the feminist approach to domestic violence is depicted in the "power-control wheel" model, which describes the multiplicity of forms of violence and a pattern of violent behavior that is used to control another person through intimidation, blame, coercion, isolation, emotional and economic violence, and abuse of male privilege (Yllö 2005). The original intent of this model was to highlight the variety of forms of violence and their context, but it gradually became the most influential explanatory tool for understanding domestic violence. Although it succeeded in addressing various forms of violence and linking them to the structural inequalities reflected in heterosexual relationships, this model represents a rather generalising view on domestic violence which fails to capture the specific dynamics of power among individual couples, and the ways in which power is distributed when gender intersects with other categories.

The gender imbalance in the perpetration of domestic violence (DeKeseredy and Schwartz 1998) is illustrated mostly by criminal statistics or data—the majority of which are found in studies carried out in the USA—from domestic violence intervention centers and shelters which show that 90–95% of people seeking help in cases of domestic violence are women (Belknap and Melton 2005; Dobash et al. 1992; Johnson 1995). Some see violence against men as a marginal topic which is incomparable to violence against women (Straton 1994). Others have even questioned its very existence (Dobash et al. 1992).

However, understanding gender as a homogeneous category, where men and women are grouped in two homogeneous clusters, each of which share a particular role—either that of the perpetrator, or that of the passive victim—has been criticised by anti-essentialist feminists who reject using such universal and rigid gender categories (Flax 1987; Segal 1993). Poon (2011) questions the concept of violence as a manifestation of power in order to gain control over one's partner, as well as the clearly defined roles of innocent victim (female) and an evil aggressor (male), which is often present in feminist discourses of domestic violence. Opponents of this gender asymmetry approach argue that studies which show that most victims of domestic violence and those with the most serious injuries are women, are exaggerated and misleading (Dutton 1994). Findings of quantitative studies based on Conflict Tactics Scale (CTS) have repeatedly reported similar levels of violence in intimate relationships perpetuated by both women and men (Moffitt, Robins, and Caspi 2001; Straus and Gelles 1986). However, CTS has met with a great amount of criticism, especially for its narrow definition of violence, which only focuses on the physical forms (Loseke and Kurz 2005). It has also been criticised for its sampling limits (telephone interviewing, examining only cohabiting couples, etc.), which fail to address many cases of violence that do not meet the criteria established in the methodology (DeKeseredy and Schwartz 1998; Kimmel 2002). Critics thus accuse the gender symmetry approach of ignoring the cultural, social and institutional context in which violence takes place (Belknap and Melton 2005). These ongoing disputes about gender symmetry or asymmetry in domestic violence have resulted in attempts to critically examine the concepts that have been used in research on the subject.

The discourse of gender binary and inequality of power between men and women is challenged when a woman is in the role of the perpetrator or a man is in the role of the victim. This is especially the case of violence in same-sex relationships, where power dynamics are influenced not only by gender, but also by the effects of heteronormativity (Renzetti 1998; VanNatta 2005) and other intersecting factors. The universalisation of the heterosexual experience and of gendered binary categories obscures the experiences of people who have lived in an abusive non-heterosexual relationship, as well as those who do not fit into the categories (e.g. trans* people and intersex people). Heteronormative assumptions underlying dominant theoretical approaches to domestic violence are inapplicable to the non-heterosexual experience. Davis and Glass (2011, 13) for example criticize "the disjunction between feminist rhetoric and the lived experiences of lesbians." They argue that the feminist discourse has created a "grand narrative" of domestic violence, with a predominant association of violence with gender inequality which fails to address the ways in which power operates in lesbian relationships.

Giorgio (2002) also expands this perspective with her study on the ways in which the language used in mainstream domestic violence discourse (with terms such as "battered women" "male violence") is exclusionary and contributes to further isolation and silencing of the victims, especially when they do not conform or identify with this normative language.

Ristock (2002) also criticizes models adopted in explaining violence—she argues that not all aggressors use violence to exercise control, not all victims experience fear and isolation, and not all cases of violence have the same dynamics. In her research of violence in lesbian relationships, the dynamics of power prove to be more complex, with some women using violence in self-defense, others as a form of revenge, or in retaliation.

Some authors therefore reject the feminist discourse as a whole. Among the most vocal critics are Island and Letellier (1991) who studied violence in gay relationships and refused to use feminist theory as heterosexist and inappropriate for the context of same-sex relationships. The existence of violence in same-sex relationships and violence against men has also been used as an argument against the feminist perspective by researchers who question the relevance of the concept of gender in theory and research on domestic violence altogether (Dutton 1994).

The core issue which underlies debates on gender a/symmetry is not whether men and women are violent to the same extent. Rather it is about the ways in which violence is defined and understood *through* gender. Stanko (2006, 551) argues that in the context of domestic violence, "gender, quite simply, still matters and influences the way we speak, conceptualize, and challenge violence." DeKeseredy and Dragiewicz (2007, 875) claim that the perspective of gender symmetry is preoccupied with the sex category, not gender, because "discussions of prevalence that rely on the variables 'male' and 'female' cannot tell us much about gender, the socially constructed and normative set of meanings attached to these categories." According to Anderson (2005), the problem lies in the understanding and definition of gender. Most researches use the category of gender as interchangeable for sex, which is interpreted as a predictor of violent behavior, thus reifying essentialist notions of gender difference (or a lack thereof). Gender is understood as a characteristic belonging to individuals and reduced to the statistical category 'male' or 'female'. The discussion of gender is thus reduced to the question of whether individuals of both sexes perpetuate domestic violence equally, making gender as a concept in the context of domestic violence irrelevant. Anderson moves away from this reductive perspective to a conceptualisation of gender in the context of interactionism and structuralism. The interactionist concept of gender refers to the construction of gender within social meanings and expectations. Anderson's argument corresponds to West and Zimmerman's (2002) conceptualisation of gender as not static, fixed or given, but as repeatedly performed and accomplished in social interactions. This conceptualisation of gender allows us to see how the same behavior (in this case violence) is understood and which meanings are attached to it in terms of construction of masculinity and femininity. While an individualistic perspective assumes that gender determines violence, in the interactionist perspective violence is an instrument of construction and reaffirmation of gender. The question is not whether masculinity leads to violence, but rather how masculinity is reaffirmed through violence.

The interactionist approach has important implications in the explanation of the context in which violence takes place, as it highlights the role of gender expectations in both heterosexual and non-heterosexual relationships. The construction of masculinity in relation to dominance and its association with violence substantially influences the perception of violence perpetrated by women. Either such violence is downplayed, or it is framed as unfeminine. The association of masculinity with violence leads to the assumption that among same-sex couples, it will be the more masculine partner who is violent, which is particularly problematic in the context of lesbian relationships with butch and femme identities (Townley 2001). Gendered interpretations of violence also shape the self-reflection and experience of survivors of violence—men who are victims are reluctant to talk about their situation, as well as lesbian survivors (Giorgio 2002).

The structuralist approach views gender as a social framework that organises institutions, identities, interactions and attitudes. Anderson (2005, 858) refers to Risman (2004) who sees the potential of this perspective in the examination of the construction of inequalities at various levels of social existence and the relationship between structures of power. It focuses on the gendered context of violence, manifested for example in the unequal distribution of resources and gender socialisation. Within this understanding, Loseke and Kurz (2005) argue that exploring the role of gender in violence does not simply mean to compare how men and women use violence against their partners, but refers to the fact that the violence happens in a context which reflects the structural position of men and women in society. Gender as a basic principle is present in the functioning of social institutions and the distribution of resources. The institutional impact of gender manifests itself in the structure of the labor market. The gender pay gap, for example, leads to greater economical dependency of women on their male partner, which may be an important factor that also establishes inequality within a relationship, and for the women who become victims, it limits the possibilities of leaving the relationship.

These arguments explain how a structuralist conceptualisation of gender can be useful when examining violence in heterosexual relationships. The above-mentioned examples, however, cannot be used to explain violence in same-sex relationships, simply because the effects of gender socialisation or gendered labor market are not reflected in same-sex relationship in the same way. With regard to this, Sokoloff and Dupont (2005) suggest that gender should not be the only model for understanding domestic violence. The link between gender and other power structures means that not all women experience gender as the primary source of oppression; and not all women experience gender in the same way (McLaughlin and Rozee 2001). Nevertheless, the structuralist perspective offers also a reflection of other power structures, such as heteronormativity, that can account for the intersections of gender and sexuality. Heteronormativity, as a power structure, is crucial for understanding same-sex IPV, because it highlights how experiences of violence tend to be viewed within hetero-norm assumptions which affect, for example, help-seeking strategies and opportunities for exit, as the availability of services for victims (and perpetrators) is limited due to the heteronormative framework of domestic violence.

Risman (2004) proposes combining interactionist and structuralist perspectives, thus allowing to describe the social framework as well as personal strategies and actions of the actors involved. This approach reflects on how the social structures shape actors' perceptions of the situations they encounter and constrain their choices, while considering their agency and possibilities of resistance. In the following section, I explore how the structural-interactional approach can be used in understanding the specifics of violence in lesbian relationships.

Researching Violence in Lesbian Relationships

This part of the chapter discusses the preliminary results of an ongoing doctoral research which aims to describe the characteristics, dynamics and context of violence in lesbian relationships through the experience and attitudes of lesbian, bisexual and queer women in the Czech Republic.

The research combines survey and in-depth interviews. Participants who took part in the study were recruited at the Czech pride parade festival in 2012 and 2013, or online through LGBT organizations' e-mail lists, websites and social media. The sample consists of 275 questionnaires from LBTQ women from different parts of the country. The age range of participants was 15 to 55, the most frequent (53.5%) was the age category of 18–25. The majority (73.9%; N = 203) of participants identified as lesbian, 23.2% (N = 64) as bisexual, and 2.9% (N = 8) as queer. There were only three transgender participants in the study and three participants who identified their gender outside the pre-established categories (one "genderfluid", another as "half man-half woman", one refused to answer). Experience with same-sex IPV was reported by 22.6% (N = 61) participants; 11 participants have experienced violence in more than one relationship.

Qualitative data are based on six interviews with women aged 20 to 45 who filled in the questionnaire and self-reported to have experienced violence in a same-sex relationship.

Interviews were semi-structured; covering the following areas: the relationship context in which the violence occurred, the characteristics of violence, seeking help and attitudes to domestic violence issues.

Research on the attitudes of lesbians to violence in heterosexual and lesbian relationships showed that the respondents were more able to recognise and name the violence in heterosexual relationships than in lesbian relationships. I suggest this is due to the heteronormativity of the domestic violence discourse and heteronormative gender norms (McLaughlin and Rozee 2001). The same situation is also apparent in the answers to two open questions in the survey I carried out that ask about the understanding of the term 'domestic violence' and 'domestic violence in lesbian relationships'. With the term "domestic violence", only seven respondents (2.5%) did not respond as to what the term means to them. 24% (N = 66) listed specific acts and types of violence; 16% (N = 43) connected the term domestic violence directly to the notion of male aggressor and female victim. When asked about 'domestic violence in lesbian relationships', 36% (N = 99) argued that it is the same as domestic violence in general or in heterosexual relationships. However, other answers reveal uncertainty about the meaning of the term: 42 women reported that they do not know or had never heard of it or could not imagine it, and 12 replied that simply nothing comes to their mind with this term.

Merlis and Linville (2006, 131) described the most common attitudes to violence in lesbian community as "denial, minimization and silence". Hassouneh and Glass (2008) identified the four basic myths—women do not commit violence, the myth of lesbian utopia, violence among women cannot be serious and the feminine victim—which are present in the lesbian community and demonstrate the impact of gendered expectations on the perception of violence. The common denominator of these ideas is the dissociation of femininity and violence and the reproduction of the idea of non-violence, love and femininity in relationships among women. These myths appeared in the responses that expressed the view that violence in lesbian relationships does not occur or that women are simply not violent (7%, N = 20). One responded commented: "We are the gentle sex, whether we are lesbians, or not, and who lays a hand on a woman is pathetic" [Survey #80].

The idea of female non-violence is closely tied to the "myth of lesbian utopia" (Barnes 2011)—the ideal image of lesbian relationships as equal, loving and non-violent which is maintained often as a defense against the stigma of deviant relationships and sexuality. Some respondents for example claimed: "It doesn't happen. Everything is dealt with, without any violence" [Survey #166]; "I think it occurs minimally, maybe rather [with] those 'male' lesbians" [Survey #120]; "They are not women if they can do this" [Survey #112].

These opinions reproduce a binary framework of gender where masculinity, understood through gender expression or physical appearance, is connected to aggressiveness and violence. Behavior is judged according to gender roles which shape the understanding of violence in lesbian relationships. 64.4% (N = 177) agreed that violence among women is mostly psychological or emotional. One interviewee expressed the same opinion when she described her understanding of the difference between violence in heterosexual and in same-sex partnership as follows:

I think that girls can hurt each other the most by some psychological abuse. . . a guy just hits the woman, and he hits her so much that she can't get up afterwards. But girls hurt each other much more by what they say. . . . It's like a dagger through your heart, and I think that's much worse than one slap each night.

[Iva]

There is a notion that violence in lesbian relationships is distributed accordingly in butch-femme roles (Renzetti 1992). The gender expression or physical appearance is interpreted as a determinant of violence in the relationship, assuming that a violent person is the masculine partner, while the feminine partner is a victim. 18% (N = 50) of respondents expressed agreement with the statement that "the bigger, stronger or more masculine partner is the one who uses violence in a relationship." "Butchness" or assuming a masculine gender expression was addressed by participants in the interviews as a factor in the power dynamics of the relationship. Participants in the interviews often reflected upon the concept of dominance, linking it to various sources of power within the relationship, including the effect of gender norms. As Iva put it:

The way our patriarchal society works, dominance equals a man. And that's how society views homosexual relationships and some lesbians see them the same way. They talk about themselves as 'I am the daddy, I am the man' . . . because [they] have short hair and would never wear high heels and this and that—but I disagree with it. I think that. . . this 'dominance equals a man' is the problem. (. . .) And my girlfriend tried to behave like a man. Literally, like a man! (. . .) She just tried to be a man, but I didn't want to be with a man. And that was the source of the other problems, too.

[Iva]

What Iva described here is performance of gender through violence, as addressed by the interactionist approach (Anderson 2005). Here, violence is not situational, but it is a constitutive aspect of gender performance, defined within a gender binary framework. Iva talked about her partner suffering from low self-esteem and insecurities about her body and education as compared to her, while at the same time her partner had more economical power and greater physical strength, which she used to perpetuate dominance. The effect of physical dominance is reflected in Iva's experience: "She weighted over 100 kilos, and I am such a 'lightweight', so then she would simply push me to the wall and hold me down so I couldn't get away" [Iva].

However, being butch and physically stronger can affect the dynamics of the abuse in an opposite way. Monika described her experience of abuse by a feminine and physically weaker partner in the following way:

Interviewer: Did you fight back in defense?

Monika: Not at all. Because I was afraid I would hurt her. She was very slim, a tiny blond girl. I was boxing at that time, and it seemed very funny to her that I wouldn't defend myself.

The power dynamics of embodiment was addressed also by Veronika, who was physically assaulted by her disabled partner.

Interviewer: You didn't tell anybody?

Veronika: No. (. . .) I was afraid they would say: 'A disabled person hit you like that? Why didn't you fight back?

The experiences of Monika and Veronika show that the link between physical attributes or between constructions of masculinity and the perpetuation of violence is much more complex in reality. Their greater strength actually prevented both from defending themselves, and caused them additional feelings of shame and inability to speak about the abuse they suffered, because of the normative assumptions about physical power and violence.

The Structural Context of Heteronormativity

If we look at the characteristics of violence, as reported by women with the experience of violence in a lesbian relationship (N = 61), 34% (N = 21) had experienced violence in their first lesbian relationship. This resonates with research findings of Ristock (2002) where 49% participants experienced violence in their first same-sex relationship, most often with a partner who had come out a long time ago.

In the first same-sex relationship, it may be difficult to identify the situation of violence due to the lack of relationship experience. Differences in social or information capital related to the experience of lesbian identity and ties to the community could be some of the sources of power imbalance leading to isolation and dependence on the partner, especially if other factors (such as difference in age or income) are present.

> I was married 20 years to a man. (. . .) I think she used [the fact] that it was my first experience. She really was my first experience with a woman, a relationship. So I was madly in love with her.
>
> [Eliska]

The aspect of coming out was present in four of the six stories in my research. Coming out represents a crucial structural factor—within the context of heteronormativity—which impacts the context of violence. The first relationship in particular may be complicated by rejection from the family, which strengthens the isolation and lack of support for the survivor when violence appears. Rejection from the family of origin creates a specific context of power imbalance and isolation and puts emotional and economic pressure on the relationship, resulting in conflict and psychological and material dependency between the partners. The combination of the pressure with isolation creates conditions for the development of violence that remains behind the closed door, and is hard to escape, because of economic factors (shared housing and finances) and lack of support.

The consequences of negative family reactions are illustrated in the story of Veronika, whose mother kicked her out of the house in response to her coming out and the relationship with her girlfriend.

> We were living together early on in the relationship, and I think it was one of the mistakes, but somehow we had no choice. . . We started living together out of necessity.
>
> [Veronika]

A similar situation may occur when it is the family of the violent partner who does not accept the relationship. The dynamics of the impact of coming out and the age difference may also work in reverse. Monika was in a relationship with a partner seven years younger than her and who came out at the time of their relationship and her family rejected her.

> Actually, she left her parents because of me. They resented the fact that she was with a woman. And it was one of the reasons why I'd always stayed with her. I thought, 'Who else would be with her, when she's gay and seriously ill?'
>
> [Monika]

In this case, the dominant position of "older and more experienced" Monika manifested itself in her sense of responsibility for the relationship and her partner. Monika was staying in the relationship despite numerous brutal physical and psychological attacks from her partner. The story shows that the simplistic notion of power dynamics distributed on the basis of age, economic status or relationship experience, is much more complex in reality.

Participants in the research showed high level of openness about their sexual orientation. Of those who had experienced abuse in lesbian relationship, only 1.6% had not revealed their sexual orientation to anybody in the family. On a 10-point scale (1-no one knows; 10-everybody knows), the median level of "being out" was 8 within family, and 10 among friends.

However, being out does not erase the effects of heteronormativity. As Balsam (2001, 32) points out, the silence surrounding abuse in lesbian relationships is present at all levels of coming out. Those who are closeted cannot talk about the abuse which makes them even more isolated (the threat of being "outed" can be used as an additional form of violence and control). Those who are partially out but do not speak about their relationships also remain silent about problems in their relationships. And those who are out and active in the community feel as if they have an image to uphold—being the role models and keeping alive the 'myth of lesbian utopia'.

Violence in same-sex relationships is different in certain respects from heterosexual relationships due to the heteronormative context within which it takes place. Gays and lesbians are more reluctant to talk about violence in their relationships and remain in a violent relationship for fear of homophobia and ignorance of the subject from society and the community (Island and Letellier 1991). Giorgio (2002) considers silence to be the constitutive aspect of the experience of violence in lesbian relationships. 44.3% of women (N = 27) in the study did not talk to anyone about the violence during the duration of the relationship; 13 of them (48%) remained silent even after the relationship had ended.

Silence is the typical reaction of victims of domestic violence, mostly because of shame or fear; but in case of violence in lesbian relationships, it is maintained also by heteronormative assumptions about violence which further affect help-seeking strategies. Victims face isolation, lack of rights and services (Rohrbaugh 2006). And sometimes even institutional homophobia of the police or the criminal and justice system (Renzetti 1998). Fear of not being taken seriously and of the secondary victimisation maintains the silence surrounding the topic and prevents victims from seeking help, especially institutionalised forms of help (e.g. the police, courts or organisations).

> Take these help-lines—imagine calling there and telling them my partner is a woman. I would be afraid they would laugh at me or they wouldn't believe me or take it seriously, because 'how could a woman hurt another woman?'
>
> [Daniela]

The fear of negative reactions because of the sexual orientation sometimes proves to be justified. Monika sought out a psychiatrist after the relationship had ended and she received a homophobic reaction.

> My therapist obviously had a problem with it [that it was a lesbian relationship]. She even told me something like 'if you were with a boy, it wouldn't have happened to you.'
>
> [Monika]

These two aspects—silence and heteronormativity—are interrelated and reinforcing each other. Lack of information and fear of homophobia lead to silence, which keeps the problem hidden and not spoken about. Victims in my research were aware of this, as they named silence (N = 42, 69%) and social attitudes towards LGBT people (N = 39, 64%) as the two biggest problems associated with violence in lesbian relationships. As Balsam (2001, 25) concisely put it, "the context of homophobia in society, in addition to sexism, creates some unique dynamics, issues and barriers to change."

Conclusion

Intimate partner violence is experienced in many different ways by women in same-sex relationships, and the characteristics and dynamics of these experiences do not necessarily comply with the dominant assumptions about domestic violence. Same-sex violence lies within a specific context that can be grasped by the structural-interactional approach to gender. Gender itself may not be the only explanatory tool, but when conceptualised in relation to other categories, such as sexuality, it allows us to understand the specifics of violence in lesbian or gay relationships, shaped not only by the gender binary and the notions of femininity and masculinity, but also by its intersections with other power structures, such as heteronormativity.

The effects of heteronormativity and gender binary create a distinct framework that shapes the dynamics of the relationship, the forms and characteristics of the violence, and the ability to name it and seek help. The association of violence with masculinity influences and defines the ways in which LBTQ women understand and experience violence in same-sex relationships.

In the Czech Republic, IPV has only been addressed since 1990s, and solely in the context of heterosexual relationships. Violence in same-sex relationships has been largely ignored—within and outside LGBT community, including services for IPV survivors. Although Czech society is said to be the most tolerant towards LGBT from the post-Soviet countries, the levels of support and visibility of same-sex relationships are still limited, including awareness of LGBT identities and experiences. Institutionalised heteronormativity along with everyday experience of marginalisation create a specific context for violence in same-sex relationships.

These aspects of domestic violence in same-sex relationships reveal the limits of the current theoretical models which are reflected in the ways in which the issue is addressed in public discourse, everyday practice and services for the survivors. It calls for reconceptualisation of current practices to embrace the diversity of experiences of domestic violence, without ignoring the wider framework of intersecting structures of power. The existence of same-sex IPV does not challenge the relevance of gender as a concept in the theory of domestic violence. Rather, it casts light on how gender can be further understood and analytically used, moving on from the limited debates about gender a/symmetry towards a more reflexive approach which focuses on the ways in which gender and sexuality intersect.

References

Anderson, K.L. 2005. "Theorizing Gender in Intimate Partner Violence Research." *Sex Roles* 52 (11/12): 853–865.

Balsam, K. 2001. "Nowhere to Hide: Lesbian Battering, Homophobia, and Minority Stress." In *Intimate Betrayal: Domestic Violence in Lesbian Relationships*, edited by E. Kashak, 25–38. New York: The Haworth Press.

Barnes, R. 2011. "'Suffering in a silent vacuum': Woman-to-Woman Partner Abuse as a Challenge to the Lesbian Feminist Vision." *Feminism and Psychology* 21 (2): 233–239.

Belknap, J. and H. Melton. 2005. "Are Heterosexual Men Also Victims of Intimate Partner Abuse?" *VAWNet.org* online. Accessed August 21, 2015. www.ncdsv.org/images/VAWnet_AreHeterosexualMenAlsoVictimsIPV_3-2005.pdf.

Davis, K. and Glass, N. 2011. "Reframing the Heteronormative Constructions of Lesbian Partner Violence: An Australian Case Study." In *Intimate Partner Violence in LGBTQ Lives*, edited by J.L. Ristock, 13–36. New York: Routledge.

DeKeseredy, W.S. and M. Dragiewicz. 2007. "Understanding the Complexities of Feminist Perspectives on Woman Abuse: A Commentary on Donald G. Dutton's Rethinking Domestic Violence." *Violence Against Women* 13 (8): 874–884.

DeKeseredy, W.S. and M.D. Schwartz. 1998. "Measuring the Extent of Woman Abuse in Intimate Heterosexual Relationships: A Critique of the Conflict Tactics Scales." Accessed August 20, 2015. www.vawnet.org/Assoc_Files_VAWnet/AR_ctscrit.pdf.

Dobash, R.P., Emerson Dobash, R., M. Wilson and M. Daly. 1992. "The Myth of Sexual Symmetry in Marital Violence." *Social Problems* 39 (1): 71–91.

Dutton, D.G. 1994. "Patriarchy and Wife Assault: The Ecological Fallacy." *Violence and Victims* 9 (2): 167–182.

Flax, J. 1987 "Postmodernism and Gender Relations in Feminist Theory." *Signs* 12 (4): 621–643.

Giorgio, G. 2002. "Speaking Silence: Definitional Dialogues in Abusive Lesbian Relationships." *Violence Against Women* 8 (10): 1233–1259.

Hassouneh, D. and N. Glass. 2008. "The Influence of Gender Role Stereotyping on Women's Experiences of Female Same Sex Intimate Partner Violence." *Violence Against Women* 14 (3): 310–325.

Island, D. and Letellier, P. 1991. *Men Who Beat the Men Who Love Them: Battered Gay Men and Domestic Violence*. New York: Harrington Park Press.

Itzin, C. 2000. "Gendering Domestic Violence: The Influence of Feminism on Policy and Practice." In *Home Truths About Domestic Violence: Feminist Influences on Policy and Practice a Reader*, edited by J. Hanmer and C. Itzin, 356–380. London: Routledge.

Johnson, M.P. 1995. "Patriarchal Terrorism and Common Couple Violence: Two Forms of Violence Against Women." *Journal of Marriage and the Family* 57 (2): 283–294.

Kimmel, M.S. 2002. "'Gender Symmetry' in Domestic Violence: A Substantive and Methodological Research Review." *Violence Against Women* 8 (11): 1332–1363.

Loseke, D.R. and Kurz, D. 2005. "Men's Violence Toward Women Is the Serious Social Problem." In *Current Controversies on Family Violence* (2nd ed.), edited by D.R. Loseke, R.J. Gelles and M.M. Cavanaugh, 79–96. Thousand Oaks, CA: Sage.

Maynard, M. and J. Winn. 1997. "Women, Violence and Male Power." In *Introducing Women's Studies: Feminist Theory and Practice*, edited by V. Robinson and D. Richardson, 175–197. New York: New York University Press.

McHugh, M.C. and I.H. Frieze. 2006. "Intimate Partner Violence: New Directions." *Annals New York Academy of Sciences* 1087. 121 141.

McLaughlin, E.M. and P.D. Rozee. 2001. "Knowledge About Heterosexual Versus Lesbian Battering Among Lesbians." In *Intimate Betrayal: Domestic Violence in Lesbian Relationships*, edited by E. Kashak, 25–37. Chicago: The Haworth Press.

McPhail, B.A., Busch, N.B., S. Kulkarni and G. Rice. 2007. "An Integrative Feminist Model: The Evolving Feminist Perspective on Intimate Partner Violence." *Violence Against Women* 13 (8): 817–841.

Moffitt, T.E., Robins, R.W. and A. Caspi. 2001. "A Couples Analysis of Partner Abuse With Implications for Abuse-Prevention Policy." *Criminology and Public Policy* 1: 5–36.

Poon, M.K-L. 2011. "Beyond Good and Evil: The Social Construction of Violence in Intimate Gay Relationships." In *Intimate Partner Violence in LGBTQ Lives*, edited by J.L. Ristock, 102–130. New York: Routledge.

Renzetti, C.M. 1992. *Violent Betrayal: Partner Abuse in Lesbian Relationships*. Thousand Oaks, CA: Sage Publications.

Renzetti, C.M. 1998. "Violence and Abuse in Lesbian Relationships: Theoretical Perspectives and Empirical Issues." In *Issues in Intimate Violence*, edited by R.K. Bergen, 117–127. Thousand Oaks, CA: Sage Publications.

Risman, B.J. 2004. "Gender as a Social Structure: Theory Wrestling With Activism." *Gender and Society* 18 (4): 429–450.

Ristock, J.L. 2002. *No More Secrets: Violence in Lesbian Relationships*. New York: Routledge.

Rohrbaugh, J.B. 2006. "Domestic Violence in Same-Gender Relationships." *Family Court Review* 44 (2): 287–299.

Segal, L. 1993. "False Promises: Anti-Pornography Feminism." *Socialist Register* online, Accessed August 20, 2015. http://socialistregister.com/index.php/srv/article/viewFile/5624/2522.

Sokoloff, N.J. and I. Dupont. 2005. "Domestic Violence at the Intersections of Race, Class, and Gender: Challenges and Contributions to Understanding Violence Against Marginalized Women in Diverse Communities." *Violence Against Women* 11 (1): 38–64.

Stanko, E.A. 2006. "Theorizing About Violence: Observations From the Economic and Social Research Council's Violence Research Program." *Violence Against Women* 12 (6): 543–555.

Straton, J.C. 1994. "The Myth of the Battered Husband Syndrome." *Masculinities* 2: 79–82.

Straus, M.A. and R.J. Gelles. 1986. "Societal Changes and Change in Family Violence From 1975 to 1985 as Revealed by Two National Surveys." *Journal of Marriage and the Family* 48: 465–479.

Townley, K. 2001. *Domestic Violence Within Lesbian Relationships*. MSc thesis, Loughborough University. Accessed January 6, 2015. http://lgbt-dv.org/html/lesbian_dissertation.pdf.

VanNatta, M. 2005. "Constructing the Battered Woman," *Feminist Studies* 31 (2): 416–52.

West, C. and D.H. Zimmerman. 2002. "Doing Gender." In *Doing Gender, Doing Difference: Inequality, Power, and Institutional Change*, edited by S. Fenstermaker and C. West, 3–23. New York: Routledge.

Yllö, K.A. 2005. "Through a Feminist Lens: Gender, Power, and Violence." *Current Controversies on Family Violence*, edited by D.R. Loseke, R.J. Gelles, and M.M. Cavanaugh, 19–34. Thousand Oaks, CA: Sage.

11 "Inside/Out"

Researching Young Adults' Sexuality in a(n) (Un)Familiar Space. A Reflexive Approach

Ana Cristina Marques

This chapter analyses, reflexively, the process of researching young adults' sexuality in a(n) (un)familiar space: the author's home town and its surroundings. It addresses the issue of being both an 'insider' and an 'outsider'. The chapter focuses on this "inside/out" position and its articulations with the research process, especially when the research is concerned with sexual representations and practices. The chapter considers key axes of similarity and difference between the researcher and participants, particularly in terms of space, time, gender and sexual orientation, and how this affects the interview process and wider aspects of research in the field of sexualities, arguing that the research process is a dynamic and dialectic interrelationship.

Introduction

In this chapter, my aim is to analyze, reflexively, the process of researching young adult's sexuality in a(n) (un)familiar place, my home town and its surroundings. I argue that being a "young" heterosexual woman at the time of the interviews, and having grown up in the same geographical space as some of the young interviewees, meant I was positioned as both an insider and as an outsider, when considering the geographical space, time, gender and sexual orientation of my participants. I will focus on this "inside/out" position and its articulations with the research process, especially when research is concerned with sexual representations and practices.

The chapter begins with a discussion of the insider/outsider debate and the use of reflexivity. Then, after some methodological considerations related to my study, I will introduce the research location: my hometown, Leiria (Portugal). I will reflect on the implications of being from the same geographical area as my young interviewees, even if from a slightly different 'generational' time. Subsequently, I will move on to consider an unfamiliar space, where I felt an outsider, especially at the beginning of my research: the Lesbian, Gay, Bisexual and Trans* (LGBT) Bar. I reflect on my previous lack of knowledge about LGBT issues; how that was evident in the design of the interview guide and in some situations while interviewing young people who identified as LGB. I conclude with some final notes on the insider/outsider position and on the importance of reflexivity, especially in the field of sociology of sexualities.[1]

The Insider/Outsider Debate and the Use of Reflexivity

The insider/outsider position of the researcher has been much discussed in sociological literature. Merton (1972) gave us a summary of conflicts between those researchers that defend an insider position, where knowledge should be acquired by those people who are part of the same (social and/or cultural) contexts that are being studied, so that they can understand what is happening to the subjects of the study, and, thus, get valid information. He contrasted this to researchers that defend an outsider position, where the opposite is apparent; that is, only a researcher who does not belong to the same context as the research subjects can obtain legitimate knowledge about it. However, Merton positions himself neither on one side or the other in the insider/outsider debate. Instead, he asks for a serious examination of both positions, where their strengths and weaknesses are evaluated and emphasized.

Patricia Hill Collins (1986) underlines the potential that the status of an 'outsider within' can have. They "occupy a special place" (Hill Collins 1986, 29) because their differences sensitize them to aspects of the social world that others may not see. Moreover, 'outsiders within' use "their own personal and cultural biographies as significant sources of knowledge", bringing them "back into the research process" (ibid.).

In my own case, as I grew up in the region where I subsequently conducted my research I had a particular insider's view, but not to the extent that I had a complete insider perspective. As soon as the fieldwork started, and the first interviewees were contacted, interesting aspects of my relationship with them emerged. For example, for some, I was a young woman, of about the same age as they were. They had seen me in the same public places that we used to frequent. For them—and for me—I was "Cristina". I was similar to them. For others, I was different. I was different because I was older; because of my heterosexuality; because I am a woman. I could then be called "você" (a pronoun that in Portuguese corresponds to the 3rd person of the plural and is a more formal way of addressing others). I was perceived as a researcher and as a heterosexual person without any knowledge of LGBT people or of what "really" happens within LGBT spaces. In the role of researcher, I sometimes felt an insider, whereas, at other times, I was an outsider. Most surprisingly, or maybe not, I could feel like both an insider and an outsider at the same time.

It was then important for me to acknowledge and to analyze what could be the strengths and the weaknesses of this positioning. By doing so, I was also recognizing the importance of situating knowledge, of considering it as "partial, locatable and critical" (Haraway 1988, 584); I was calling on a reflexive approach to my research.

According to Riach (2009), reflexivity requires a (re)questioning of what individuals know in a specific context; a (re)questioning that conditions current and subsequent practices. Borrowing from Rahmam and Jackson (2010, 156) I define reflexivity, as "the ability to think about, act upon and engage in internal conversation with ourselves". For the purposes of this chapter, I use the concept of reflexivity as a door into and a (re)construction of, a more or less recent past on my part, my youth and the years when I was undertaking doctoral research, and on the part of the young adults, their own reconstructed biographies and the moment of the interview.

However, I also recognize that this definition does not fully account for the potential, complexities and limitations that this concept can have. According to Holmes (2010, 140) reflexivity is more than just a reflection; it also includes "bodies, practices and [a complexity of] emotions" Therefore, it can be difficult to interpret and individuals might have problems explaining their emotions or be unaware of their own complexities (Holmes 2010). As McNay (1999, 111) noted, reflexivity is a "capacity of the agent that is unevenly realized".

Even if the idea of a "do-it-yourself biography" (Beck and Beck-Gernsheim 2001), or a "reflexive project of the self" (Giddens 1991) was present in the stories of some of my interviewees; for others, reflecting on concepts, that were so much taken for granted within their day to day lives, was more difficult. Many of them told me how they were thinking about the meanings of concepts such as love and/ or sexuality for the first time in their lives. Others, had difficulties reflecting on their intimate lives, attributing to chance the reason for events such as their first sexual intercourse or living in conjugality (Marques 2014).

Yet being reflexive is also a way of being critical; of thinking about what one is doing and considering the motives which lie behind that (Mason 2002). It involves confronting and challenging one's assumptions and "recognizing the extent to which your thoughts, actions and decisions shape how you research and how you see" (Mason 2002, 5). It is, quite simply, a way of doing qualitative research (Mason 2002).

Methodological Considerations

The data presented in this chapter was part of my doctoral research,[2] which concerned questions of intimacy during young people's transitions to adulthood. The main purpose of the research was to analyze the influence of structural factors, like gender, level of education, age, sexual orientation, religiosity and socialization contexts (namely, family, peers and school) on young people's representations and practices of intimacy. It focused, especially, on sexuality during their transitions into adulthood, particularly where conjugality and parenthood were concerned.

Taking into account the objectives of the research, I used qualitative methods, especially in depth interviews. Two interview guides were developed, one for heterosexual young people and the other one for LGB young people. Though the interview guides are almost alike, the one concerning non-heterosexual interviewees had a few more questions related to their sexual identities and experiences.[3]

The interviews were conducted between 2008 and 2009, in the region of Leiria, with 60 young adults, aged between 18 and 29. I recruited participants in two ways. Firstly, through health centers and the Portuguese Youth Institute, where family planning for young people existed, and where either I or a doctor explained the purpose of my research. Secondly, I recruited through convenience and snowball sampling (Mason 2002) from my personal networks and previous interviewees. The interviews were conducted face-to-face, in places chosen by the interviewees, mostly public places, such as cafes or bars. Interviews lasted, on average, between one and a half to two hours. All interviews were recorded and transcribed. The research adhered to the ethics guidelines of the Portuguese Sociological Association, to ensure anonymity, confidentiality and avoiding emotional distress. Therefore, the names that appear throughout the text are pseudonyms.

I considered the social context of the interview as important and specifically acknowledged the implications of the relationship between researcher and interviewee in the data produced in the interview context (Robinson, Meah, and Hockey 2007). In addition, I paid attention to the conditions and the possibilities of researching and/or talking about sexuality, because several studies (see for example, Holland et al. 2004 [1998], or Robinson, Meah, and Hockey 2007) mention the difficulties, uneasiness and omissions in (young) people's stories about sexuality. In this sense, following Holland et al. (2004), Robinson, Meah and Hockey (2007, 187) state that: "interviewees may not feel able to use their customary slang and colloquialisms without the interviewer's 'permission'". Furthermore, interviewees might reflect on their language use and on "the degree of openness" (Robinson, Meah and Hockey 2007, 189) in relation to the researcher's social position, namely their gender, but also their age, sexual orientation, level of education and social class, among other aspects of self and social division.

However, authors like Plummer (1995) and Attwood (2006) consider that, recently, there has been an increase in public "stories" about sexuality. For instance, Plummer (1995) argues that in contemporary western societies, people are compelled to talk about sexuality, not only in terms of their sexual practices, but also about their identities, dreams, desires, fantasies and fears. They have become storytellers in a society permeated by sexual stories (Plummer 1995).

Researching Young Adults in (Un)Familiar Spaces

In this section, I will explore my own personal experience of researching young people's stories about sexuality, gender and intimacy. I will start with an account of some familiar spaces, in my hometown—Leiria and its surroundings. I will then move to one particular unfamiliar space—the LGBT Bar, where I met most of my young LGB interviewees. However, it is firstly important to consider what happened in Portugal in terms of the social organization and regulation of sexuality,[4] in the last decades of the 20th century and first decade of the 21st century, in order to contextualize the stories I was told by my interviewees.

Portugal: Changing Intimate Scenarios

In Portugal, several changes have occurred in the domain of sexuality and intimacy in the past few decades. Whilst some of these changes might have started many years earlier, they accelerated in 1974, with the end of the period of dictatorship, and again when Portugal joined the European Union, in 1986. Since then Portugal has been through a rapid process of transformation in the fields of gender, family and sexuality (Roseneil et al,. 2013; Torres 2010).

During the 1950s and 1960s there was a rigid and conservative sexual moral, framed by the political, religious and moral ideology of the "Estado Novo", that imposed a view of sexuality that indicated it should be heterosexual, monogamous and restricted to marriage and reproduction. It also condemned any form of same-sex sexuality (Policarpo 2011). After the Carnation Revolution of 1974, new values of democratization and freedom spread throughout Portuguese society, which established new models and practices regarding family life, gender and sexuality (Policarpo 2011). Indeed, since the 1980s, the Portuguese government has debated and passed several legal measures with the aim of promoting sexual health and sexual education; and of protecting equality based on sexual orientation and gender. Nowadays, there is a notion that people are entitled to express their sexuality freely and that heterosexuality is no longer the only social accepted norm, because there has been a diversification of sexual experiences and identities (Policarpo 2011). For example, according to the 2010 survey concerning the attitudes and behaviors of the Portuguese in relation to sexuality (Ferreira and Cabral 2010), there has been a decrease in women's age of first sexual intercourse (which, for them, ceases to coincide with conjugality), a convergence in women's and men's sexual behavior and a lessening of the sexual 'double standard' (without implying its disappearance). Furthermore, in 2001 the União de Facto Law for couples of the same gender was approved, in 2004 discrimination based on sexual orientation was forbidden, and in 2010, the Parliament approved the legalization of civil marriage to same-gender couples. However, concurrently, a strong heteronormativity, based on the idea of the heterosexual nuclear couple with children, remains predominant in Portuguese society (Santos 2012). The coexistence of different attitudes towards gender and sexuality, existing in Portuguese society, could be seen in the stories of my young interviewees.

Revisiting Leiria: Familiar Spaces

Leiria is small city, the capital of a district that is situated in the central coast of Portugal. Its main economic activities are composed of small and medium sized enterprises (predominantly within the plastic and glass industries), and commerce. The Leiria region is characterized by a complex, continuous, urban and industrial space, where several urbanized and industrialized villages coexist with small cities (Silvano 2001).

I was born in Leiria and lived there until the age of 18, after which I went to university in Lisbon. After completing my degree, I returned to my parents' home, like many other students (Jones 1995).

I started my empirical research in 2008, when I was 29 years old, and used to socialize with my own group of friends in some of the same spaces that many of my interviewees frequented. Indeed, it was through the owners of some of those spaces, and/or through people I used to see in them, that I first made contact with some of the interviewees. There had been changes in the 11 years since I first left the city, compared to when I conducted my research. Many of the places where I used to socialize were still there, but some were not. While some bars and nightclubs remained, others were closed, or had been transformed into other businesses. The Street, which had been full of bars, and where we would gather at nighttime to drink and socialize, was almost entirely disused. Even so, some of my youngest female interviewees still referenced that place as one that they used to go to or that their parents would warm them about or forbid them going there. In this sense, Cristina (aged 18), when talking about how her parents used to control her nights out, said:

> There is always preconceptions: "oh don't go here, because . . ." I remember a few years ago the [Street] was totally "um papão" [a bogeyman] for my parents. Oh, and the nightclubs as well.

For some of the older interviewees, that Street was, as it had once been for me, a meeting point: a place to socialize, drink and talk, until it was time to go home or to a nightclub. Matilde (25), for example, whose mother tended to have a more liberal attitude towards her sociability, not interfering with her choices of boyfriend(s), group of friends or nights out (Marques 2014), used to spend a lot of time there as a young teenage girl.

But it was not only the spaces of Leiria that had been familiar to me. The interviewees told me many things I could also relate to; things I had experienced myself.[5] Their accounts made me remember my own past and my own representations and expectations of intimacy, creating a sense of self-reflexivity for me. When I was talking with my interviewees, especially with some of the young women, usually the more educated ones (attending university or with a degree), who were older than 20 years of age, I thought so many times: "I've done that. I've been through it". It was like I knew exactly what they were talking about, because so many of my experiences were similar, so much of the way I used to think, and still do in some aspects, were alike. My own representations and experiences of sexuality were, like most of the young people I interviewed, inter mediate (Marques 2014). That is, like many of them, I had had my own sexual relationships and some casual sex, but not nearly as much as appears to be implied in contemporary discourses about sexualization (Attwood 2006). These express an overall concern for the existence of a hyper-sexualized society, wherein children are supposed to became sexualized at younger ages and young people are said to be engaging more often in "risky", casual, sex, with more partners and in

relationships disconnected with some kind of intimacy. Like many of the interviewees, I tended to accept that others should do whatever they wanted to do in
the field of sexuality. However, many of my interviewees refused the possibility of
engaging in sporadic sexual intercourse themselves.[6] For them, the idea of having
sexual intercourse with another person without having at least some knowledge of
that person, some trust in her/him, some intimacy with him/her, was rejected, not
only because it could be "dangerous" for themselves, but also because it was not
something they idealized. Like Clara (28) said:

> I don't understand the part of not knowing the person and having sexual inter-
> course with him/her [. . .] I respect people who do that, they are free to do it.
> But it doesn't seem ok to me. At least in my mind I'm not able to do it.

The ideal of a relational sexuality was incorporated in most of my young interviewees' ideas about sexuality, independently of their social positionings. For
most of them, sexual intercourse in the context of a loving relationship tended
to be more valued than hook ups. But, more than love, trust, communication and
respect between partners, disclosing intimacy (Jamieson, 2005 [1998]), were the
aspects considered as essential to having a sexual relationship.

> I think one person shouldn't have sex with the other in the instant she or he
> meet the other person. They should mainly know each other, like each other
> and feel at ease with each other. [. . .] There is more intimacy with the person.
> (Cristiano, 21)

Still, significantly, both love and pleasure were part of these young people's
sexual stories, as expressed by Catarina's (22) example: "There are several ways
of doing sex: making love; doing it for the sake of doing it; doing it for pleasure". As many authors (for example, Jackson and Scott [2010] and Jamieson
[2005 (1998)]) have concluded before me, the representations and practices of
sexuality tended to be, among my young interviewees, often complex, ambiguous
and contradictory, denoting both signs of change and continuity with previous
generations.

In this section I have predominantly reflected upon my experiences within
familiar spaces. Familiar spaces that, notwithstanding, were also permeated by
differences (for example, in terms of attitudes towards sexuality). However, doing
research in a location where a person has spent much of their life, does not imply
that there are not unfamiliar spaces. And this is what I will move to consider now:
the LGBT spaces, which at that time, were so unfamiliar to me.

Moving in an Unfamiliar LGBT Space

Whilst living in Leiria, I had not really considered LGBT issues. I was a heterosexual, cisgender, young woman, having heterosexual relationships and did
not know a single person (close to me or otherwise) that identified (publicly or

privately) as LGBT. I was an "outsider" in issues related to sexual orientations and gender identity.

However, by this time, LGBT issues had started to become more and more prevalent in the Portuguese media, particularly due to the movement for the inclusion of same sex people in the "União de Facto" law. That was when I started to pay more attention to them. As a "daughter of the revolution"[7] I already believed in (class and gender) equality, and I started believing in equality for all individuals, regardless of their sexual orientation and/or gender identity.

When I started my doctoral research, I mainly focused on the more familiar space of heterosexuality. But I become aware of the fact that I was replicating heteronormativity and wanted to be inclusive. I wanted to acknowledge the sexual diversity of young adults and so, after reading some LGBT studies, I designed two different interview guides: one for heterosexual young people and one for LGB ones. The guides were mainly the same, but the one for self-identified LGB youth had a set of questions related to sexual identity. I was not questioning the young people I assumed as heterosexual if they identified as it or not; if their sexual orientation had any impact on their lives; or how did they feel about it. Basically I was just following the rules of heteronormativity, where heterosexuality is often rendered invisible, due to the fact that it remains deeply rooted, in contemporary Western societies, as the most correct and superior form of sexuality (Weeks, 2006). In spite of the changes that occurred in the regulation of heterosexuality, it remains as the "natural" and "normative" form, not only in the domain of sexuality, but in other domains of life as well,[8] being taken for granted in everyday life (Jackson and Scott 2010; Seidman 2002; Weeks 2006). Heteronormativity still defines a normal way of life (Jackson and Scott 2010), having an important part on the organization of "mundane", day-to-day life, in different areas of the social world, such as family, work or education (Hockey, Meah, and Robinson 2007).

Furthermore, in the interviews with the young people who identified as lesbian, gay or bisexual, it was clear that I lacked knowledge about sexual practices between same sex couples, as can be evidenced by Vanessa's (29) comment: "I bet you have no idea about what two women do, do you?!".

Another important point, relating to the young people who identified as LGB, was the means by which I met them. As noted earlier, I did not know any (young) people who identified as LGB. But I had heard about a LGBT Bar in the region, and though I had never been, it seemed to me that the easiest way to contact LGB identified young people would be through this Bar. The problem was I did not know anyone there and my friends were reluctant to go with me. I did not want to go alone. I found it (and still do) very strange and uncomfortable to attend certain public spaces, like restaurants, bars or nightclubs, by myself, first because I consider them mainly places where you go with others and second because "women aren't supposed to go alone" to these places. In spite of the existence, in contemporary public discourses, of what McRobbie (2009) calls the new sexual contract, in which young women are now allowed in public, nighttime, leisure spaces, I was still restraining myself to the rules of heteronormativity. Once again I was 'thinking straight' (Ingraham 2005), without even realizing it. I was doing 'normative' heterosexuality and gender in my daily life, without reflecting critically about it (Jackson 2005).

After a while I persuaded someone to go with me, but it took a while longer to ask for the owner's help. But once I had, I was introduced to, and started to talk with some (although not many), of the LGB people that attended the place regularly. Soon after, I began to go to the Bar on my own. I could see how full the place was on Friday and Saturday nights, especially after one or two o'clock in the morning. I saw how people had fun, drank, danced and "made out", as in any heterosexual nightclub I had ever been to. It was the kind of place in which you feel comfortable. In the Bar you could see that a considerable amount of people not only knew each other (or at least recognized each other), they also knew the owner and all the staff. Furthermore, the data from the interviews gave me the sense that this was actually an important space—a 'community' (Weeks 1995), for most of my LGB interviewees. For them, the Bar was a place where they could meet other people with the same sexual orientation. The Bar appeared to work as place of identity recognition, a place where these young people did not need to hide, an environment where they could find the support they felt was lacking in heterosexual dominated spaces. In this sense Mariana (24) said:

> It's our space. We can be at ease and express our feelings [. . .] [and] our relationships as we wish [. . .] I think it ends up being our community.

Being a space where these young people could be "themselves", where they felt respected and at "home", the community of the Bar gave these young people a sense of belonging (Seidman 2002).

Although several authors consider that, in Western Contemporary Societies, there is a tendency for more tolerance and a certain normalization of non-heterosexualities, they also recognize that much prejudice and discrimination towards them still remains (see, among others, Roseneil et al. [2013] and Seidman [2002]). In this sense, Roseneil et al. (2013, 186) argue that, in Europe, there has been "a legal displacement and partial dis-establishment of heteronormativity", associated with "a new legal norm of 'homotolerance'". However the authors (Roseneil et al. 2013, 187) also emphasize that the recognition of the existence of this new norm does not mean that heteronormativity has ceased to exist, because people who live "outside normative heterosexuality" are often denied "their intimate citizenship rights" and often, in their everyday lives, experience "moments of misrecognition and social exclusion".

In this context, it does not look surprising that the "community" of the Bar represented a "safe haven" to these young people; a place where they could be "themselves" and where they could feel comfortable. And after a while, so could I. I felt comfortable in the Bar. I liked the people and had fun there. In the end, I was not an insider, but I also did not feel that I was an outsider anymore.

Conclusion

Writing this chapter some months after concluding my doctorate, I wanted to reflect on some of the issues I had started to discuss there, but, which I felt, were unfinished. These issues were raised by my specific positioning as both an 'insider' and an 'outsider' in several ways. I was born and lived for many years in the Leiria region, both before and after leaving for university, but I also lived in Lisbon and experienced academic life there. I was about the same age as my older interviewees, but around ten years older than the youngest ones. I also identified as heterosexual, lived most my youth questioning some aspects of heteronormativity that related with gender, family and sexuality, although as I noted earlier, LGBT issues were not something I considered before my early twenties. I interviewed mostly heterosexual young people, but also incorporated LGB issues into my research. Thus, in terms of space, age and sexual orientation (I could add gender, class and educational level as well), I began to view myself as sometimes an 'insider', sometimes an 'outsider' and at other times, simultaneously both. Moreover, in some of the familiar "spaces" where I could feel mostly as an insider, such as with the older young women, there were also differences, for example, in terms of attitudes towards sexuality; whereas in unfamiliar spaces, like the LGBT "Bar" I ended up feeling welcomed and comfortable—that is I felt accepted, even if I wasn't truly an 'insider'.

Through this process, I have realized the importance of reflexivity, especially when researching sexualities. Often, it is difficult to recognize the specific factors that might affect the social context of the interview and that can interfere with the data being produced. Yet our interpretation of data cannot be removed from our own, individual and social contexts. In my specific case, I have reflected on my own knowledge of the spaces that many young people were talking about and my lack of knowledge in relation to other ones; the similarities, and also the differences, of my own sexual experiences and representations when compared to those of my young interviewees; and my naturalization of heterosexuality and initial lack of knowledge of LGBT issues.

To conclude this reflexive approach, I want to reiterate the importance of reflecting on the weaknesses and strengths of our positions as researchers (Hill Collins 1986; Merton 1972), in relation to our being insiders, outsiders, or outsiders within. Thus, admitting the limits of our own possibilities, but also the strengths that we bring into play can help make sexualities research more transparent and highlight the context of the interview as a social situation. In turn, the recognition of the interview as such forces researchers to consider the biographies of both interviewers and interviewees, the way they negotiate what is said, and the (re)construction of (sexual) stories that need to be contextualized.

In a field where, in spite of all the contemporary pressures to talk about sexuality, some (young) people may still have difficulties to talk about their intimate (sexual) lives, being ethical, reflexive and situating one's research, can create a safer ground for claims of a partial and locatable knowledge, that can help us better understand everyday sexualities.

Notes

1 Following Jackson and Scott (2010), I consider sexuality as a domain of social life that encompasses several aspects, like multiple sexual practices, orientations and representations.

2 The Doctoral research had the institutional frame of CIES-IUL, Lisbon, Portugal, and was funded by FCT (Portuguese Foundation for science and technology).

3 The reasoning behind having two different interviews guides for heterosexual and homosexual young people is explained in the section: "Moving in an unfamiliar LGBT space".

4 For a better understanding of what happened in Portugal, for the last decades, in the domain of sexuality, see, among others, Policarpo (2011) and Santos (2012).

5 There were also things that I could not relate to the interviewees. Even in the case of some of the older young women, which could be more familiar to me, there were still some differences. The example of Clara illustrates one difference, between myself and some of my interviewees, independently of their age, gender or level of education, in terms of attitudes towards sexuality.

6 In terms of casual sex, I tend to have a general acceptance of people engaging in consensual sexual practices, whereas some of my young interviewees tended to defend an ideal of individual liberty, where people can do whatever they want to in terms of sexual practices, but they tend to be more restrictive in their personal case, by conflating sexuality and intimacy. Some other young interviews refuse the idea of casual sex not only for themselves, but also for people in general, either they are men or women, devaluing the existence of sexual practices without intimacy. There was also a small group of, usually, more qualified young people that engaged in casual sexual relations(hips). Lastly, there was a minority of young men who replicated the idea of the sexual double standard, by saying that they wouldn't trust a woman that had several sexual partners, and not making the same statement for men.

7 Torres and Lapa (2010) note that the Portuguese younger generations, being born after the period of dictatorship, and being socialized in the midst of processes of individualization and differentiation of life-styles' options, tend to defend an ideal of individual liberty and to be are more flexible and tolerant regarding the norms associated with the life course.

8 As Roseneil et al. (2013, 166) note, the concept of heteronormativity highlights: "The multitudinous (social, legal, political, cultural) ways in which heterosexuality is normalized, naturalized and privileged as an institution, and to the ways in which homosexual practices and relationships are excluded, stigmatized, marginalized and minoritized."

References

Attwood, F. 2006. "Sexed Up: Theorizing the Sexualization of Culture." *Sexualities* 9: 77–94.

Beck, U., and Beck-Gernsheim, E. 2001. *Individualization: Institutionalized Individualism and its Social and Political Consequences*. London: Sage.

Ferreira, P.M. and M.V. Cabral. 2010. *Sexualidades em Portugal: Comportamentos e Riscos*. Lisboa: Bizâncio.

Giddens, A. 1991. *Modernity and Self-Identity: Self and Society in the Late Modern Age*. Oxford: Polity Press.

Haraway, D. 1988. "Situated Knowledges: The Science Question in Feminism and the Privilege of Partial Perspective." *Feminist Studies* 14: 575–599.

Hill Collins, P. 1986. "Learning From the Outsider Within: The Sociological Significance of Black Feminist Thought." *Social Problems* 33: 14–32.

Hockey, J., Meah, A. and V. Robinson. 2007. *Mundane Heterosexualities: From Theory to Practices*. London: Palgrave Macmillan.

Holland, J., Ramazanoglu, C., Sharpe, S. and R. Thomson. 2004 (1998). *The Male in the Head: Young People, Heterosexuality and Power*. London: The Tufnell Press.

Holmes, M. 2010. "The Emotionalization of Reflexivity." *Sociology* 44: 139–154.

Ingraham, C. 2005. *Thinking Straight: The Power, the Promise, and the Paradox of hetero-sexuality*. New York: Routledge.

Jackson, S. 2005. "Sexuality, Heterosexuality and Gender Hierarchy: Getting Our Priorities Straight." In *Thinking Straight: The Power, the Promise, and the Paradox of Hetero-sexuality*, edited by C. Ingraham, 15–37. New York: Routledge.

Jackson, S. and S. Scott. 2010. *Theorizing Sexuality*. Maidenhead: Open University Press, McGraw-Hill.

Jamieson, L. 2005 (1998). *Intimacy: Personal Relationships in Modern Societies*. Cambridge: Polity Press.

Jones, G. 1995. *Leaving Home*. Philadelphia: Open University Press.

Marques, A.C. 2014. *Amor, Sexo e Género: Trajetórias íntimas dos/as jovens para a vida adulta*. Libson, Portugal: PhD diss. ISCTE-IUL.

Mason, J. 2002. *Qualitative Researching*. 2nd ed. London: Sage.

McNay, L. 1999. "Gender, Habitus and the Field: Pierre Bourdieu and the Limits of Reflexivity." *Theory, Culture and Society* 16: 95–117.

McRobbie, A. 2009. *The Aftermath of Feminism: Gender, Culture and Social Change*. London: Sage.

Merton, R. 1972. "Insiders and Outsiders: A Chapter in the Sociology of Knowledge." *American Journal of Sociology* 78: 9–47.

Plummer, K. 1995. *Telling Sexual Stories: Power, Change and Social Worlds*. New York: Routledge.

Policarpo, V. 2011. "Sexualidades em construção, entre o privado e o publico." In *História da vida privada em Portugal*, coordinated by A.N. Almeida, 48–79. Maia: Círculo de Leitores.

Rahman, M. and S. Jackson. 2010. *Gender and Sexuality: Sociological Approaches*. Cambridge: Polity Press.

Riach, K. 2009. "Exploring Participant-Centered Reflexivity in the Research Interview." *Sociology* 42: 356–370.

Robinson, V., Meah, A. and J. Hockey. 2007. "Representing 'Sex' in the Research Process." *International Journal of Social Research Methodology* 10: 181–194.

Roseneil, S., Crowhurst, I., Hellesund, T., Santos, A.C. and M. Stoilova. 2013. "Changing Landscapes of Heteronormativity: The Regulation and Normalization of Same-Sex Sexualities in Europe." *Social Politics: International Studies in Gender, State and Society* 20: 165–199.

Santos, A.C. 2012. "The Politics of Sexuality in Portugal." In *Sexualities: Past Reflections, Future Directions*, edited by S. Hines and Y. Taylor, 168–185. London: Palgrave Macmillan.

Seidman, S. 2002. *Beyond the Closet: The Transformation of Gay and Lesbian Life*. New York: Routledge.

Silvano, F. 2001. *Antropologia do espaço: uma introdução*. Oeiras: Celta Editora.

Torres, A. 2010. "Lição de Síntese: Mudanças na Família: O privado na agenda pública." Apresentação no âmbito das Provas de Agregação em Sociologia, ISCTE—IUL.

Torres, A. and T. Lapa. 2010. *Familia y jóvenes en Europa. Convergencia y diversidad*. Revista de Estudio de Juventud. Madrid, Spain: Instituto de la Juventud, España: 11–32.

Weeks, J. 1995. *Invented Moralities: Sexual Values in an Age of Uncertainty*. New York: Columbia University Press.

Weeks, J. 2006. *Sexuality*. New York: Routledge.

Part III
Critical Practices

12 Uncomfortable Bargains?

Networking Between Local Authorities and LGBT Associations in the Context of Neoliberalism

Beatrice Gusmano

This chapter examines the relationship between research, activism and politics. It explores how LGBT issues are translated into policies or demands, to understand if queerness can still escape from the politically sedative articulation of a homonormative sexual citizenship. Hence, the chapter asks critical questions about the relationship between sexual politics, social structure and collective action. In so doing, it draws on research gathered from in-depth interviews and focus groups with LGBT activists, the LGBT Office of the Turin City Council and its local, regional and national network in Italy.

Introduction[1]

In the neoliberal context of welfare cuts and governance overload, networking between local authorities and Lesbian, Gay, Bisexual and Trans (LGBT) associations is playing a core role in the development of policies addressing sexual orientation and gender identity. This is the case in Italy, where the central state appears to be stuck in a legislative standstill over LGBT rights, lacking a national framework of formal rights provision. Despite a substantial absence of civil rights recognition, national anti-discrimination policies for non-heterosexual people are starting to be introduced with the promise of improved sexual citizenship for victimized lesbian and gay individuals (the 'T' and 'B' of the LGBT acronym are not even contemplated in these developments).

This chapter looks at how LGBT issues and national-level politics related to them are translated into local policies, asking whether queerness can escape the politically sedative articulation of a homonormative sexual citizenship (Duggan 2003). It asks critical questions about the relationship between social structure, collective action and sexual politics in a neoliberal regime of governance. In order to grasp the importance of the local-level impact of these dynamics, I present a case study of Turin,[2] where the only example in Italy of the long-term institutionalization of LGBT policies through the local LGBT Office can be found. This case study is drawn from the research project AHEAD (*Against Homophobia. European local Administration Devices*)[3] which focused on identifying strategies implemented by local administrations and associations to foster LGBT equality. More specifically, I examine the networking developed in Piedmont, the region where Turin's LGBT Office is located and where it coordinates its activities with other institutions at various levels of governance, in addition to the local board of LGBT associations. The analysis builds upon data gathered in 2010 through documentary analysis, 12 in-depth interviews and five focus groups with representatives of local LGBT associations, public administration employees and city councillors who had supported the activities of the LGBT Office in Turin since its foundation.

The first section of the chapter will address key theoretical perspectives, which draw from observations of other Western European contexts to shed light on the specificities of LGBT politics and how they have been operationalized in the Italian neoliberal framework. I will then highlight the process of governance, through networking, which has been put in place by the LGBT Office since 2001, when the Office was built and when more power was given to local authorities through Italian Constitutional Reform.

The case study of the LGBT Office in Turin will then be explored in conjunction with different legitimizing discourses arising in the Italian public arena on LGBT social and civil rights, thus showing how the politics of inclusion pursued by the Turin LGBT Office stretches the hegemonic discourse of LG victimization, driven by its committed mission to achieving full sexual citizenship through the pursuit of both civil and social rights. However, I will argue that some uncomfortable bargains within the context of neoliberalism have had to be made. In this landscape, the LGBT Office uses its institutional power to accommodate grassroots associations' demands through the means of mainstreaming, networking and training, challenging the neoliberal framework of welfare cuts, privatization of responsibilities and assimilation for victimized LG subjects.

Shifting LGBT Demands in the Context of Neoliberalism

Shaped by the expansion of neoliberalism[4] in the last 40 years, LGBT policies in Western Europe have moved from a focus on the fight for civil and social rights to a defence of personal security, thus changing the subject of policies from an active agent of change to a consumer citizen (Cooper 2006; Richardson and Monro 2012; Richardson 2005). As I advance in this chapter, this shift can be understood by looking at the processes whereby social rights are being dismantled through the withdrawal of social policies, while at the same time residual civil rights that do not question unequal social structures are granted. The Italian translation of this shift can be observed in the contemporary focus on upholding the civil right to personal security, which in turn creates a new subject of policies: namely, a victimized subject (Bertone and Gusmano 2013).

As far as local authorities are concerned, some features of the neoliberal agenda in Italy operate by reinforcing structural conditions of inequality such as: the austerity-led reduction of public funding to social services; the dismantling of concepts such as 'the public good' or 'community', in favour of 'individual responsibility'; and the precarious job and life conditions in an increasingly privatized labour market lacking social protections.

Much of the above can apply to LGBT politics in Western Europe more generally: in the 1970s LGBT claims went beyond political recognition in the public
arena, fighting for "the reformulation of the (positive) self" (Richardson 2000,
35). It was a period in which visibility and embodied differences were considered
concepts to be proud of: demands were framed as the right to be different, not as
a request to fit in. In Italy, this approach was fostered by the 1969 riots that took
place through students' and workers' protests against conservative powers in the
realms of family, education and work.[5] This was the context in which the launch
of the first homosexual movement in Turin took place in 1972: *FUORI* (*Fronte
Unitario Omosessuale Rivoluzionario Italiano*) which positioned itself as part of
the leftist revolutionary movement of the time, similar to other LG movements in
other European countries.[6] Its first action was on April, 5th 1972, supported by
its international allies, when FUORI protested against the Italian Centre for Sexology's international conference on sexual deviations. As repressive tolerance,
more than legal banning, has characterized the condemnation of homosexuality in
Italy (Dall'Orto 1988), medical discourse has been used to criminalize it through
pathologization. *FUORI*'s demonstration was aimed at publicly condemning how
homosexual people *did not* recognize themselves in medical discourse, and how
they could speak for themselves as political subjects. This protest is considered
the 'Italian Stonewall', as it gave rise to the national LGBT movement. However,
from this very beginning, the Italian LGBT movement split between *FUORI*,
which became part of the Radical Party[7] in 1976, and autonomous collectives
convinced of the need for a revolutionary approach to politics. The latter groups
were able to exist as political entities in the social and political context of Italy
until 1977, when differences between the Communist Party, on one hand, and the
working class and radical students, on the other, eventually led to an irreconcila-
ble rupture. Once this conflict had waned, the re-emergence of radical claims was
accompanied by the affirmation of the need to establish effective collaborations
with local authorities in Milan, Rome and Bologna. At the same time, this new
approach to dialogue with public institutions was visible in the LGBT politics of
other Western European countries in the 1980s, as Richardson explains:

> Unlike earlier social movements that sought to transform key institutions,
> contemporary struggles for "equality" help to reaffirm the regulatory power
> of the state by reinforcing the authority of the institutions appealed to which
> confer rights and responsibilities [. . .] and through which sexualities are
> regulated.
>
> (2005, 532)

In Italy, the creation of the first gay association *Arcigay* in 1985 opened space
for this type of less provocative, more pragmatic new politics. *Arcigay*'s political commitment was to civil rights, cultural education, dialogue with institutions,
political participation in elections and fighting AIDS—which was presented in
mainstream discourse as a 'gay disease'. Despite a lack of information on AIDS
prevention at the national level, local councils started to invite gay associations

as experts in preventing the diffusion of AIDS stressing their expertise in safe sex practices, the destigmatization of (homo)sexual acts, solidarity with HIV-positive people and access to healthcare. *Arcigay*'s citizenship agenda of the 1990s consisted of three points: anti-discrimination law; fighting AIDS; and recognizing same-sex unions. This corresponded with developments in other Western European countries in the 1990s, when a 'third way' of doing politics was pursued as a viable strategy between the conservative right and the progressive left—what Santos calls "a politics of containment, whereby controversial issues are negotiated amongst liberal and conservative sectors of society. The aim is to achieve a wider consensus through the suspension of radical strategies or arguments" (2013a, 56–57). In both Italy and beyond, this led to a shift in demands and political discourses: from transformation to reformation of society; from liberation to equality (Richardson and Monro 2012), focusing solely on civil rights and giving up on the aim of fostering social rights as a way of fighting inequalities.

This political landscape changed slightly in 2001, after September, 11th, when security and safety became the new common ground of right and left politics, making the buzzwords 'property' and 'safeness' more prominent than the concepts of 'freedom' and 'equality'. This change emerged due to another shift that characterizes the 21th century, namely the rise of a new enigmatic figure that crystalized politics on diversity, shifting the focus from inequality (due to structural conditions) to discrimination (linked with individual responsibility): the victim subject. The prominence of this subject is evident in the issue of violence against women, as explained by Ratna Kapur:

> The focus on the victim subject has led to a proliferation of rights for women, but it has not resolved the problem of gender subordination [. . .]. This subject risks denying women the agency [. . .]. This category is disempowering and does not translate into an emancipatory politics.
>
> (2005, 134–135)

This argument can be applied to illuminate the process of LGBT subjects' inclusion: the latter are neglected in their access to agency and empowerment by a dominant discourse on security that focuses on their condition as victims. In order to be protected by a paternalistic state, these newly designated 'victims' have to comply with the role designed for them. Only once they agree not to deconstruct the 'victim' subjecthood they are ascribed, can they easily be assimilated.

Given the silencing of the homosexual subject in Italy (Bertone and Gusmano 2013; Rossi Barilli 1999), victimization's power lies in the ability to protect homosexual people from discrimination, without changing the negative imaginary associated with them. Indeed, the victim subject, thus constructed, paves the way to represent LGBT people as weak and helpless. Given the lack of positive imaginaries concerning LGBT people emerging out of state rhetoric and politics, non-heterosexual and gender non-conforming people remain relegated to the lower levels of the hierarchy of citizenship, respectability and agency.

Moreover, since the economic crisis of 2008, European governments have asked citizens to collaborate in the name of austerity, such that issues of access to education, services, healthcare and employment have become dimensions of personal responsibility—a private, primarily economic matter. Through the containment of all social rights, one of the main objectives of neoliberalism has therefore been reached: "privatization, and withdrawal of the state from many areas of social provision" (Harvey 2005, 3).

In the Italian context of state withdrawal, local networking has become an essential strategy to cope with privatization. As a result of the 2001 Italian Constitutional reform of local authorities, the State has handed down some of its responsibilities to local administrations, while outsourcing other services. This has led to the diminishing of the universalist, public nature of the welfare state (Brenner and Theodore 2002). In order to cope with the scarcity of resources, local councils have established networks with civil society, pursuing a bottom-up approach that stresses their social duty to comply with citizens' claims (Bertone and Gusmano 2013). As far as LGBT claims are concerned, these can be analytically divided into what Santos (2013b) defines as 'individual claims' (focusing on individual rights such as employment law, protection from violence, welfare benefits) and 'relational claims' (addressing rights stemming from relationships such as parenting, partnering, friendship). In Italy, LGBT relational claims are still contested, because the only socially respectable and legally sanctioned relationships are heteronormative ones.[8] Therefore, the last decade has seen active lobbying by lawyers from LGBT associations, aimed at shaking the national standstill over relational claims, while some local authorities have exercised their power to grant equality to same-sex cohabiting couples. Concerning individual rights, the age of consent is 14 years old for both homosexual and heterosexual people, while the only Italian anti-homophobic law regards protection from discrimination in the workplace as a response to the binding EU Employment Equality Directive (2000/78/EC).

The empirical data presented in the next section will show how the Turin LGBT Office continues to resist the containment of LGBT rights by constant networking with the board of LGBT associations. The following empirical sections therefore start by exploring LGBT associations' claims and how these are translated by administrators in public institutions by applying the 'continuum of five institutional approaches to LGBT equalities' developed by Richardson and Monro (2012, 127) as the five possible responses enacted by local councils in relation to LGBT citizenship claims: 'proactive' ("something we positively support"); 'compliance' ("we do it because we have to"); 'omission' ("we would if we could"); 'erasure' ("is there a need?"); 'active resistance' ("we oppose LGBT equality").

Governance and Networking in Italy: the Turin LGBT Office

In February 2001, the Turin City Council, after a proposal by the "GLBT Turin Pride Coordination" (the Coordination hereafter),[9] founded the 'Office for the overcoming of discriminations based on the grounds of sexual orientation and gender identity' (later officially renamed 'LGBT Office'). The LGBT Office's explicit, albeit narrow aim (as clearly stated in its very name) of fighting discrimination on the grounds of sexual orientation and gender identity can be explained by the fact that the most legitimizing discourse regarding LGBT issues in Italy centres around guaranteeing personal security to a discriminated minority that needs to be safeguarded. As the Director of the Turin Provincial Council declared, the strategy of supporting policies against homophobia was shared by all administrations, "irrespective of their political orientation" (interview excerpt, 2010). The approach of the LGBT Office challenged this paternalistic focus, considering it just as a small step towards the main objective of achieving positive visibility:

> We'll have to exit the logics of discrimination, I mean. . . if we want to overcome it, we shouldn't keep sticking to it.
>
> (interview excerpt, 2010)

Visibility was matched with a strong political commitment to promoting social rights by the City Councillor that provided legitimacy to the new-born LGBT Office through its 'proactive approach' (Richardson and Monro 2012) to LGBT equalities. Although policies were still presented in terms of overcoming homophobia, the Office reframed these into issues of citizenship rights through three different levels of action: via the academy, the Municipality and the Coordination. As a staff member of the LGBT Office declared:

> [LGBT] Organizations revealed who homosexual and transsexual people were in their everyday life. The research further stressed the most important aspects to be taken into account [in pursuing sexual citizenship]. The Municipal deliberation carried out such information and aimed at handing it over in order to change Public Administration.
>
> (interview excerpt, 2010)

In this quote, the LGBT Office presents its legitimation strategies: an on-going dialogue with the Coordination who participated in the designing of both the research and the deliberation. The research was conducted by the University of Turin (Bertone et al. 2003) and provided data to counteract the institutional approach of 'erasure' defined by Richardson and Monro (2012), which questions the existence of a specific need carried by LGBT citizens in a heteronormative society. The Municipal deliberation on the establishment of the Office provided a commitment to LGBT issues and to pursuing a thorough analysis of the social needs that the LGBT Office could address (as we will see in more detail in the next section). The LGBT Office, rather than focusing on civil rights only (the realm of liberty of each citizen, such as the right to freedom, property, personal security and marriage), kept the centrality of social rights (the need to recognize citizens as members of a community, and protected by the welfare state in order to limit social inequalities). As defined by the Italian Constitution, the latter includes protections and services provided by all levels of governance to ensure a social safety net, through rights to education, healthcare, pensions, social security, social services, employment, strike, trade union participation and family formation. In order to grant these social rights, the LGBT Office turned to networking, because fields of intervention and competence in these matters are assigned to different levels of governance.

Therefore, the LGBT Office started to build and has continued to rely on different nodes of networking, which are:

a) The Municipality Piloting Group, in which each department's representative brings to the fore the practical needs that emerge in their sector, trying to identify effective measures to address them. All the interviewed members of this Piloting Group seemed enthusiastic about this mainstreaming which allowed them to share duties and responsibilities within the administration at large, as stated by a member of the Piloting Group:

> It is a group that has grown over time, a group with little chitchat and lots of results [. . .]. This is a group that walks the talk. Things might take their time, [but] the involvement has always been tangible: the fact of working out how to link up between us to work on shared projects.
>
> (interview excerpt, 2010)

Fundamentally, this pragmatic mainstreaming aimed not only at welcoming citizens' demands in a more inclusive way, but it also helped out LGBT employees working within the administration.

b) The Coordination, strengthened by the LGBT Office, which emphasises agency rather than victimization (Bertone and Gusmano 2013). As declared by the Coordination, working with public institutions represented a challenge:

> When you work with institutions you know they have their *modus operandi*, their ignorance, their rigidities: they aren't the movement. They are another kind of animal. However, I am sure we never felt crushed [. . .]: we kept our constructive, autonomous and plural soul.
>
> (interview excerpt, 2010)

In order to grant an autonomous space to the associations which comprise the Coordination, the solution was to explicitly identify the dimensions of collaboration. As a result, associations could maintain their independence, their specific aims and activities that continued beyond the institutional dialogue.

c) The Turin Provincial Council, which decided not to create a structure specifically devoted to LGBT rights but, rather, to use the expertise already developed by the Municipality.

d) The Piedmont Regional Council, a partnership defined by the regional representative as "a small miracle" (interview excerpt, 2010), because in Italy there has always been stiff competition between Provinces, Regions and

Municipalities. Networking represented a tool to overcome obstacles linked to the 'active resistance' (Richardson and Monro 2012) in the approach to LGBT equalities. This was possible, for example, when the 'Regional Observatory on bullying' did not acknowledge the relevance of homophobic bullying in schools. After the suicide of a gay teenager in Turin in 2007, the Coordination asked the Observatory to focus on this issue, but the Observatory failed to do so, despite the intervention of the regional administration. It was only in 2010, after the intervention of the LGBT Office, that the Observatory acknowledged the specificity of homophobia as one of the variables for bullying.

e) RE.A.D.Y, a national network comprising local administrations fighting discrimination on the grounds of sexual orientation and gender identity, aimed at sharing LGBT good practices throughout the country in order to avoid the 'omission' approach (Richardson and Monro 2012). The strength of this initiative is that the proposal of sharing best practices was an autonomous decision taken by local administrations in order to cope with discrimination.

In conclusion, networking was identified as the necessary strategy to concretely develop positive actions for LGBT people inside a framework of both civil and social rights. Based on this case study, the next section will explore further differences in how civil and social rights have been pursued in Turin in the choices made by the LGBT Office in order to translate LGBT claims in the institutional language of public administration.

Pursuing Sexual Citizenship Through Civil and Social Rights

In 1999, the political struggle for the legalization of civil unions in Turin was defeated by the opposition of conservative parties, notwithstanding the long process of negotiations in which LGBT associations had engaged to achieve this goal. After this political defeat, the same associations refused to only accept funding for their activities, and decided to set up the GLT Coordination in order to present themselves as united in their common demands, insisting that the administration should take active responsibility in order to safeguard citizenship rights and equal treatment for all. As the Coordination affirmed, "LGBT rights [. . .] are not a question of safeguarding a minority, but a question of citizenship as a whole" (interview excerpt, 2010). Responding positively to this, from the start, the Municipality decided to frame LGBT demands as citizenship rights, seeing them as its public duty to guarantee them. The Equal Opportunity Councillor, who took up the task of addressing these demands by allowing the creation of the LGDT Office, recognized the political insightfulness of the Coordination in forcing the administration to comply with its duties, namely granting rights for all citizens, rather than providing an ideological resistance against the civil unions defeat. She stated: "It is unfair that rights are granted only to some citizens, while others have to rely on the voluntary work of associations" (interview excerpt, 2010).

An emphasis on rights was pursued by the Pride Coordination, the board created to host the 2006 Turin national Pride. Its aim was to revitalize the topic of rights, visibility and full citizenship, and this was considered a great success in terms of participation, as declared by one of its members. The emphasis on rights was kept in subsequent regional editions of Pride: in 2010 the event was organized in collaboration with feminist and migrant associations, giving voice to other identities who found themselves under attack, in this instance as a result of the success in the regional elections by the *Lega Nord*, a racist right-wing party. Thus, the 2010 Pride was described by the Coordination as "a counter-tendency in a moment of crisis" and "an extraordinary richness to counter the misery of politics" (interview excerpt, 2010). This focus and commitment to both civil and social rights had already been reached in the resolution leading to the foundation of the LGBT Office, which declared the following actions at the basis of its activities:

- the safeguard of rights in every aspect of social, cultural and working life;
- information about access to employment for transsexual people;
- widespread awareness-raising on LGBT issues;
- cultural events fostering dialogue between and beyond differences;
- healthcare information and prevention;
- training for staff operating in the education, schooling, social assistance and healthcare sectors;
- networking with associations to spread their work, promote training and develop joint activities.[10]

In this way, since in 2001 the LGBT Office started to 'practice' mainstreaming by a commitment to include LGBT issues in well-established national events (e.g. Memory Day, March 8th, Book Fair, etc.), emphasizing inclusion among citizenry and all City Council departments. The Equal Opportunities Provincial Councillor presented this move as follows:

> The issue of human rights is an issue of justice and equity [. . .]: our idea was to offer welcoming, sharing, and a work within the Municipality and the territories aimed at involving citizens in the struggle for LGBT people's rights.
> (interview excerpt, 2010)

The overarching aim was to organize public events in such a way that the entire public administration would be able to promote a culture free from prejudice within the city, "transcending what today we call the heterosexist look" (interview excerpt, 2010). As a result, in 2008 one of the Turin Municipality Districts contacted the Office to help broaden the scope of their family policies by including LGBT parents' needs and experiences, and with a view to improving LGBT families' access to public services. This is an important accomplishment, especially considering that in Italy institutions tend to ignore or silence any LGBT relational claim. In this instance, the inclusion of LGBT families' needs can be viewed as a commitment to social rights, because it facilitated a change of perspective by the public administration which made an unprecedented effort to meet the social needs of citizens who are more frequently excluded from these initiatives.

Regarding the impact of local authorities, another effective way of pursuing social rights is through the provision of public services. This entails not only the cultural role of the authority as a public institution that shows commitment to its citizens' wellbeing, but also the provision of material support thus facilitating a fairer distribution of resources in all fields of local intervention. A fairer provision of public services was reaffirmed in the City Council resolution with a view to complying with the needs emphasised by the research (Bertone *et al.* 2003), which showed a substantial lack of attention to LGBT needs in schools, workplaces, healthcare and public services. In the education sector, in 2003 the University of Turin was the first Italian academy to promote the possibility for trans students (still in transition) of having a second *libretto universitario* (university student's record booklet) with their preferred gender identity stated on it.[11] In the same year, the Turin Municipality carried out a four-year European project on the social and labour inclusion of trans people in Turin. As far as public services are concerned, greater emphasis was placed on mainstreaming within the entire city administration through the creation of the Piloting Group addressing LGBT actions in all city departments.

Moreover, in order to challenge the administration's heteronormative assumptions, the LGBT Office identified training as another key response to the needs of the LGBT community—for example, by ensuring that staff working in the registry office were competently addressing the needs of transgender people. Training has thus become an effective action, at the local level, for promoting the social and civil rights of LGBT subjects through a cultural and political commitment to positively presenting LGBT experiences. It is a tool to reduce heteronormative policies and practices within the administration, and is also used as an instrument to tackle homophobic bullying in schools. However, training, a practice that started 15 years ago alongside the emergence of the LGBT subject as a 'victim', could be seen as limiting the opportunities for collective action by stressing the individual responsibility of the administrative staff to overcome inequality, as opposed to tackling the actual structural conditions of inequality.

Uncomfortable Bargains: Some Concluding Thoughts on Coming to Terms With Neoliberalism

As we have seen with training, backlashes are 'always around the corner' and, notwithstanding the commitment towards civil and social rights demonstrated by the LGBT Office, a few uncomfortable bargains were struck with local institutions, which can be understood in the context of neoliberal politics.

One example regards the image on the very first LGBT Office's presentation leaflet, which was designed in consultation with the GLT Coordination that defined it as "a little watered down compromise [that] was not very queer" (interview excerpt, 2010). The cover depicted stylized humans, defined by the GLT Coordination as "anorexic sticks aimed at not bothering anyone", disembodying the "explosive power" of lesbian women, gay men, bisexual and transsexual people. The GLT Coordination would have preferred a more embodied representation of LGBT differences, but had to bargain with the institution that opted for a less disruptive portrayal of bodies, which were replaced by dull sticks.

Another uncomfortable bargain relates to the Office having to face the institutional 'active resistance' (Richardson and Monro 2012) of the Municipality's director of the education sector regarding a training course on LGBT policies. The director insisted that the course should be cancelled unless the Office accepted to change its title into the generic "sexual discrimination", rather than positively naming sexual orientation and gender identity. The LGBT Office accepted the 'generic' new title, but also addressed its inadequacy during the course itself. This is an example of the powerful incidence of the security discourse, whereby naming sexual orientation and gender identity is feasible only inside the framework of the well-established victimization discourse.

As far as the shift in LGBT demands is concerned, it would be useful to compare the differences perceived by the GLT Coordination (active at the end of the 1990s), and the subsequent Pride Coordination (still active). In the interviews it was possible to grasp these differences, starting from the GLT Coordination eliciting doubts about coming to terms with institutions:

> I wondered how, at a certain point, GL associations stopped being oppositional and tried to find strategies to collaborate, and what this collaboration implies in terms of validating the institutional counterpart and giving it credit which remained to be proven.
>
> (interview excerpt, 2010)

On the other hand, the more recent Pride Coordination embraced involvement both within political parties, and the Council. What the GLT Coordination deemed "a risk of diminishing the political meaning of collective action" (interview excerpt, 2010), was now defined by the Pride Coordination as a way of getting through the dense complexity of institutional apparatus by establishing personal relationships of trust within. Another difference here is the fact that business enterprises, for example a gay sauna, have now become part of the Pride Coordination, while they were not present in the previous GLT Coordination since, according to a member of the latter, "business trading has a logic that is incompatible with a shared political dimension because it has other priorities" (interview excerpt, 2010).

Notwithstanding these compromises, the focus on civil and social rights in Turin has remained a constant objective of the demands taken forward by both the GLT and Pride Coordination, mirroring changes within the national hegemonic discourse: from the radicalism of collective movements in the 1970s to the active participation in political parties in the 1980s; from the focus on sexual citizenship of the 1990s to the focus on a victimization approach in the 2000s; and finally, since 2008 in particular, the subject of the mainstream LGBT discourse is the responsible citizen achieving civil rights despite austerity.

During this time, the LGBT Office has constantly emphasized visibility when planning initiatives in the city, by developing tools for mainstreaming, networking and training. When the dominant discourse was that of victimization, the LGBT Office chose to positively name sexual orientation and gender identity as a priority, acknowledging that the discourse of discrimination hides the 'positive self' that was at the centre of politics in the 1970s. Finally, the long-sustained focus on social rights during the current economic crisis could be viewed as a way to foster queerness, while institutions at all levels of governance call for austerity through the privatization of both identities (sexual identity is considered a private matter) and responsibilities (citizens are in charge of their social needs). By showing how local authorities can reorient their policies to comply with LGBT social needs through networking with grassroots associations, the LGBT Office offers a proactive alternative to the victimization discourse by continuing to pursue with associations sexual citizenship rights that counteract the neoliberal model based on privatization of social rights, victimization and reproduction of institutional heteronormativity.

Notes

1 This work has been partly developed within the project "*INTIMATE—Citizenship, Care and Choice. The Micropolitics of Intimacy in Southern Europe*", funded by the European Research Council— Starting Grant n. 338452 (2014–2019), hosted by the Centre for Social Studies, University of Coimbra, and coordinated by Ana Cristina Santos.
2 With an urban population of almost 1 million people, Turin is an economic and cultural centre in the northern-west part of Italy, in the Piedmont Region. Since the X century, Turin was home to Savoia, a royal family that led the Italian unification in 1861: therefore, Turin became Italy's first capital city. It has always been a major European centre for what it concerns arts, culture, university, cinema, public television, radio, press, publishing, industry and trade. It was the symbol of economic upturn after WWII, accommodating migrants from the South arrived to work in the automotive industry, since Turin was the third economic productive pole in Italy. It is also the city where an Italian LGT collective gathered for the first time.
3 The project, funded by the European Commission, involved local authorities, universities and LGBT associations in Spain, Italy, Germany, England and Hungary. For the research, refer to Coll-Planas (2011); for the Italian case study, refer to Gusmano and Bertone (2011) and Bertone and Gusmano (2013).
4 This contested term can be understood in many different ways. In this chapter I draw on Lister's definition: "*Neo-liberalism rejects [social] rights. It argues that citizens have their own responsibility to ensure themselves against social risk [. . .]. It has attempted to break down the relation between social and political citizenship. Furthermore, it focuses strongly on the obligation citizens have towards themselves and towards other citizens*" (Lister et al. 2007, p. 52).
5 Historical facts regarding the gay and lesbian movement in Italy are based on Gianni Rossi Barilli (1999) and Elena Biagini (2011).
6 Namely, MHAR (*Mouvement Homosexuel d'Action Révolutionnaire*) in Belgium, FHAR (*Front Homosexuel d'Action Révolutionnaire*) in France, and GLF (*Gay Liberation Front*) in the United Kingdom.

7 The liberal party that was in the first line in the fights for civil rights such as divorce and abortion. It was the first party to foster homosexual rights, as well.

8 In Italy, only heterosexual marriage is possible, while civil unions are not recognized, neither for homosexual nor heterosexual people. Moreover, there is no recognition of same-sex parenting.

9 Since 1999 to 2003, the board of LGBT associations in Turin was called "Turin GLT Coordination"; in 2003 they passed through a moment of standstill; with the national Pride in Turin in 2006, the board of associations changed its name in "GLBT Turin Pride Coordination". Unless specified differently, hereafter both will be addressed as "Coordination".

10 City Council resolution no. 905/42 of February, 13th 2001.

11 Even though things are changing, according to law 164/1982 of April, 14th 1982, changes in official documents are possible only by providing a final judicial decision which assigns that person a different sex after the surgical intervention that implies sterilization.

References

Bertone, C., and B. Gusmano. 2013. "Queerying the Public Administration in Italy: Local Challenges to a National Standstill." In *Queer Presences and Absences*, edited by Y. Tylor and M. Addison, 260–278. London: Palgrave Macmillan.

Bertone, C., Casiccia, A., Saraceno, C. and P. Torrioni. 2003. *Diversi da chi? Gay, lesbiche, transessuali in un'area metropolitana*. Milano: Guerini e Associati.

Biagini, E., ed. 2011. *Una ribellione necessaria. Lesbiche, gay e trans: 40, 30, 20 anni di movimento*. Firenze: Stampato in proprio.

Brenner, N. and N. Theodore. 2002. "Building "Euro-regions": Locational Politics and the Political Geography of Neoliberalism in Post-Unification Germany." *European Urban and Regional Studies* 7 (4): 317–343.

Coll-Planas, G. 2011. *Combating Homophobia: Local Policies for Equality on the Grounds of Sexual Orientation and Gender Identity: A European White Paper*. Barcelona: Ajuntament de Barcelona, Direcció Drets Civils.

Cooper, D. 2006. "Active Citizenship and the Governmentality of Local Lesbian and Gay Politics." *Political Geography* 25 (8): 921–943.

Dall'Orto, G. 1988. "La 'tolleranza repressiva' dell'omosessualità.' In *Omosessuali e Stato*, edited by Arcigay, 37–57. Bologna: Cassero.

Duggan, L. 2003. *The Twilight of Equality? Neoliberalism, Cultural Politics, and the Attack on Democracy*. Boston: Beacon Press.

Gusmano, B. and C. Bertone. 2011. "Partnership and Legitimation in LGBT Local Policies." In *LGBT Local Policies: Italy and the Piedmont Case*, edited by CIRSDe & Turin City Council LGBT Office, 13–60. Turin: Città di Torino.

Harvey, D. 2005. *A Brief History of Neoliberalism*. Oxford: Oxford University Press.

Kapur, R. 2005. "The Tragedy of Victimisation Rhetoric: Resurrecting the "native" Subject in International/Postcolonial Feminist Legal Politics." In *Erotic Justice: Law and the New Politics of Postcolonialism*, 95–136. London: The Glass Press.

Lister, R., Williams, F., Antonnen, A., Bussemaker, J., Gerhard, U., Heinen, J. and A. Ganavas. 2007. *Gendering Citizenship in Western Europe: New Challenges for Citizenship Research in a Cross-National Context*. Bristol: Policy.

Richardson, D. 2000. *Rethinking Sexuality*. London: SAGE.

Richardson, D. 2005. "Desiring Sameness? The Rise of a Neoliberal Politics of Normalisation." *Antipode* 37 (3): 515–535.

Richardson, D. and S. Monro. 2012. *Sexuality, Equality and Diversity*. New York: Palgrave Macmillan.

Rossi Barilli, G. 1999. *Il movimento gay in Italia*. Milano: Feltrinelli.

Santos, A.C. 2013a. "Are We There Yet? Queer Sexual Encounters, Legal Recognition and Homonormativity." *Journal of Gender Studies* 22 (1): 54–64.

Santos, A.C. 2013b. *Social Movements and Sexual Citizenship in Southern Europe*. Basingstoke: Palgrave Macmillan.

13 Transgender Offenders Within the Prison Estate

A Comparative Analysis of Penal Policy

Joanna Jamel

This chapter undertakes a comparative analysis of penal policies relating to transgender offenders in Australia, Canada, England and Wales, and the United States of America addressing the following key areas. Firstly, it considers theoretical perspectives, transgenderism and imprisonment. Secondly, legislation and the application of penal polices to the placement transgender prisoners in the above territories are compared. Thirdly, notions of 'legitimate' victimhood and the transgender prisoner are discussed. Finally, the practical implications of facilitating gender equality and gender symmetry in prisons are outlined. Overall, this chapter illustrates how the accommodation of trans people in the prison estate raises questions regarding taken-for-granted aspects of penal policy based on the socially prescribed gender binary.

Introduction

This chapter undertakes a comparative analysis of penal policies pertaining to the accommodation of transgender offenders in Australia, Canada, England, Wales and the USA. The following are examined: (i) key definitions, (ii) the overrepresentation of these offenders in prison; (iii) legislation; (iv) policy administration; (v) access to medical resources and the impact on prisoners' well-being; and (vi) the implementation of gender equality and gender symmetry in prisons. This chapter illustrates how transgender prisoners challenge the normative aspects of penal policies based on a socially prescribed gender binary.

Few studies have examined the impact of penal policies on transgender offenders which is in stark contrast to the extensive research on female offenders (see Carlen and Worrall 2004; Chesney-Lind and Pasko 2013; Heidensohn 1985; Mallicoat and Estrada Ireland 2014) and young and ethnic minority offenders (e.g., Lieber, Mack, and Featherstone 2009; Piquero and Brame 2008). Most research focuses on transphobic victimisation of the transgender community outside of prison (e.g., Schilt and Westbrook 2009; Stotzer 2009). In 63 international jurisdictions in Australia, Canada, Denmark, England, Germany, Ireland, Sweden, Switzerland and the USA; 20% had some form of formal policy; a further 20% had informal ones and 44% would consider the initiation of hormone treatment for transgender inmates on a case-by-case basis (see Petersen et al. 1996). Despite being a small minority transgender offenders have complex and diverse medical and psycho-social needs which can exacerbate their prison experience, these are discussed next. After which this penal policy discourse will be contextualised within gender equality and gender symmetry debates discussed later.

'Gender identity' is pivotal within penal policies. The International Commission of Jurists and the International Service for Human Rights (2007) define it as an individual's internal and personal experience of gender, which may differ from their natal sex. Their corporeal sense is then achieved through bodily modifications via medical and surgical interventions altering their appearance and gender presentation and encompasses modes of dress, speech and related gendered nuances. *Gender identity disorder (GID)* has now been removed from the DSM V (due to the stigmatisation of being labelled 'disordered') and replaced with *'gender dysphoria'* (APA 2013). WPATHCGID [WPATH Standards of Care (SOC) for Gender Identity Disorders (formerly known as the Harry Benjamin International Gender Dysphoria Association)] (2009). "Gender dysphoria is manifested in various ways, including strong desires to be treated as the other gender or to be rid of one's sex characteristics, or a strong conviction that one has feelings and reactions typical of the 'other gender'" (American Psychiatric Association 2013, 3) for a minimum of six months. Transgender individuals must be diagnosed with gender dysphoria to access treatment, those rejecting medicalisation are denied access to the 'treatment' required to achieve their self-definition of gender (Maruri 2011).

The SOC guidelines version 7 published in 2012 are universally used by physicians and therapists to determine the treatment of gender identity/gender dysphoric patients and more recently, includes prisoners. Based on western centric research (World Professional Association for Transgender Health [WPATH] 2015), gender and cultural diversity remain neglected (see Cole, Denny, Eyler and Samons 2000). The key stages are (i) GID diagnosis; (ii) psychotherapeutic interventions; (iii) RLE (Real Life Experience); (iv) hormone therapy; and (v) GRS [Gender Reassignment Surgery] (surgical interventions to masculinise/feminise the body). RLE relates to living and may include working in one's desired gendered role, although, finding employment may be difficult due to discrimination (Schilt and Westbrook 2009, Brown 2009) and societal intolerance (Dickey 1990). There are conflicting findings regarding the socio-economic status of transgender individuals as Whittle, Turner and Al-Alami (2007) stated it was higher than the national average. In contrast, Munson and Cook-Daniels (2010) found high levels of unemployment may be experienced. Consequently, Merton's (1957) Strain Theory may be adapted to explain pressures on transgender or gender non-conforming people to achieve socially prescribed gender goals and norms through GRS. This creates a financial 'strain' and subsequent use of illegitimate means (see Tarzwell 2006), e.g. solicitation offences etc. to access GRS that can result in incarceration. It is a medical necessity to continue treatment in prison as rapid withdrawal from hormone treatment may result in self-harming behaviour, the reversal of acquired physical attributes, e.g., the reduction of breast tissue, chemical imbalances, and risk of depression and autocastration (Brown and McDuffie 2009; Tarzwell 2006) increasing the punitive experience for transgender offenders.

Relevant Legislation and International Penal Policies on the Housing and Treatment of Transgender Offenders

Legal provisions do not specify special protection for transgender prisoners, none-theless, they do protect all prisoners from discrimination. Australia, Canada, England and Wales, and the United States are all signatories to the following covenants, rules and commissions: the Universal Declaration of Human Rights, International Covenant on Civil and Political Rights, United Nations Convention against Torture and other Cruel, Inhuman or Degrading Treatment of Punishment, United Nations Standard Minimum Rules for the Treatment of Prisoners and the Body of Principles for the Protection of All Persons under Any Form of Detention or Imprisonment apply (UNODC 2009), The International Commission of Jurists and the International Service for Human Rights (2007) Principle 9.; nevertheless, the extent of their adherence to these is discretionary. The next section will focus on the two strategies used respectively which underpin all formal and informal penal policies.

Transgender prisoners present a unique challenge to the gender binary prison estate exacerbating negative gendered experience for them (Tarzwell 2006). Penal placement policies are based on either (i) genitalia-based placement or (ii) identity-based placement. Genitalia-based placement involves placement according to one's anatomical sex even if one self-identifies as the opposite gender. This places the Male To Female (MtF) inmate at a significant risk of being beaten, raped or killed. Whereas identity-based placement is assigned according to one's self-identified gender irrespective of their having undergone GRS. Brown and McDuffie (2009) suggest these inmates are more likely to be targeted by predatory offenders, experience restricted access to appropriate health care, and more affected by rules about how prisoners wear their hair and make-up. Penal authorities suggest the feminisation of MtF inmates through the transitioning process increases their risk of physical and sexual assault, and use this to deny the initiation of hormone treatment. Therefore the maintenance of hormone therapy is the preferred option of prison authorities. The most popular prison policy is the 'freezing' of hormone treatment on incarceration (which has significant negative side-effects see above), despite 85% of respondents from correctional services departments across 65 jurisdictions in federal, state and provincial authorities in Canada, Australia, Ireland, Sweden, Denmark, Finland, Germany, Switzerland and the USA stating that the risk management of physical and sexual violence against transgender inmates was not a significant issue (see Petersen et al. 1996). A comparative analysis of Australian, American, Canadian, English and Welsh penal policies highlighting best practice and suggesting recommendations is provided in the next section.

Transgender Offenders in Prison in Australia, Canada, England, Wales and the USA

Penal Policies in Australia

The number of transgender inmates housed within the Australian prison system is quite small (Graycar as cited in Blight 2000) and statistics are rare as gender identity may not be disclosed on admission, their transgender status or ethnicity may not be recorded. Placement of transgender offenders is based on three criteria, (i) relevant safety concerns and laws; (ii) reduction of the risk of self-harm or sexual assault to all inmates; and (iii) a determination on what basis hormonal or surgical intervention will be provided to inmates. There are two classification approaches (i) *social-based*, focusing on the social aspects of identity and presentation and self-identification; and (ii) *surgery-based approach* based on whether the inmate has had GRS or not. Hormone therapy is universally provided in prisons if inmates were undergoing therapy pre-incarceration. The provision of GRS is variable due to a lack of standardisation and being at the prison medical staff's discretion. Gender dysphoria/gender identity disorder are recognised as medical disorders in Australia, so, 'adequate health care' must be provided otherwise it contravenes transgender inmates' civil rights. Transgender inmates are placed in protective custody for their own safety, reserved for vulnerable prisoners, for examples, sex offenders at risk of violence from the general prison population. This approach may safeguard transgender inmates; however, it can result in discrimination against them; due to limited recreation periods and access to educational classes (UNODC 2009), further increasing the retributive experience for these offenders. Australian regions differ in their placement policies, nonetheless, examples of best practice were identified in New South Wales below.

New South Wales (NSW) has a progressive penal policy based on Gender Identification Placement. MtF prisoners are placed in female prisons and FtM (Female to Male) inmates are usually placed in female institutions (regardless of self-identification due to the potential risk of sexual assault in a male institution) unless they have legally changed their birth certificate. MtF inmates are evaluated and screened on a case-by-case basis; if they self-identify as female they are placed in a female prison unless a risk is posed to their individual safety or female inmates. The NSW progressive approach allows transgender inmates to have their own toilet and shower facilities and permits the wearing of gender appropriate clothing. Prison management and administrators also help maintain transgender inmates' self-esteem and self-identity by using their chosen name and gender identity. This staff policy extends beyond prison and probation officers. In addition, transgender inmates may start hormone therapy or have elective SRS in prison if self-financed this contrasts with American penal policies discussed later.

Penal Policies in Canada

In the Canadian prison population in 2000, ten out of 12,500 were pre-operative transgender inmates representing a minority of the general prison population (Mann 2006). In 2015 in Ontarian facilities 25 inmates identified as transgender. Although a minority, transgender inmates have diverse health and welfare requirements which are the most challenging to address in prison. There is also a lack of information regarding the ethnicity of transgender offenders compared to their counterparts in American Prisons. Also in 2015 a more progressive policy was instituted accommodating inmates in facilities according to their self-identified gender identity and preferences. They will be referred to by their name and pronouns (such as he, her or the gender-neutral ze), and permitted to retain prosthesis used for gender expression and choose the gender of staff performing searches (Strapagiel 2015). Transgender inmates are evaluated and screened on a case-by-case basis (Mann 2006) and previously hormone treatment in prison was not provided unless initiated prior to incarceration. The Commissioner's Directive 800, sections 33–42 now emphasise a continuity of care, inmates with diagnosed GID can initiate or continue hormone therapy prescribed by a psychiatrist with recognised expertise in this area or other relevant specialists. For all placement and program decisions, individual assessments are conducted to ensure offenders diagnosed with GID are accommodated recognising their vulnerabilities and needs including safety and privacy. GRS may be permitted if medically warranted under the SOC and if deemed essential then the Correctional Services of Canada will fund it. Transgender inmates are regularly assessed to ensure their needs are met and are permitted to wear gender appropriate clothing according to their acquired gender (Correctional Service Canada 2013). *Kavanagh vs Attorney General of Canada*, was an important case regarding the revision of penal placement policy and improved conditions for transgender prisoners in Canadian prisons. Synthia Kavanagh[1] complained to the Canadian Human Rights Commission that her human rights were violated. Her legal challenge to Sections 30 and 31 resulted in: (i) pre-operative transsexuals now being placed in an institution according to their anatomy and correctional facilities ensuring the needs of pre-operative transgender inmates are met; (ii) section 31 considered discriminatory and no longer applied; and (iii) a new policy developed providing inmates' access to GRS. Thus, significant improvements were made, the next section examines the English and Welsh penal policies.

Penal Policies in England and Wales

There is no official monitoring of gender identity in UK prisons which is problematic when addressing the needs of transgender prisoners and the level of resourcing required. However, anecdotal accounts from prison officers suggest that the numbers are small (Whittle and Stephens 2001) but significant considering the complexity of the needs of transgender inmates. Transgender individuals are overrepresented in the prison population in England and Wales (Poole, Whittle and Stephens 2002; Whittle and Stephens 2001). However, estimates vary as such data is not consistently recorded. In 2001, a pilot study was commissioned by the Home Office Research Directorate on the Probation Service response to Transgender Offenders (see Whittle and Stephens 2001). Their recommendations included (i) there should be better training for prison and probation staff, (ii) transgender prisoners should be able to contribute to medical decision-making about their case, (iii) have complete medical files kept, (iv) standard confidentiality provided and (v) disclosure of their transgender status should not be given without their prior permission (Poole, Whittle and Stephens 2002).

A key case was *R (on the application of AB) v Secretary of State for Justice* [2009] EWHC 2220 (Admin) (*New Law Journal* 2009), her human rights were contravened as she had a GRC and was still housed in a male prison. She challenged the Secretary of State's decision to refuse her transfer to a female prison a consequence of which was the denial of her GRS (as this was dependent on her RLE, living as a woman in a female prison). The judge agreed Article 8 of the ECHR was breached due to the denial of her autonomy resulting in her being held in a male prison which was disproportionate to the denial of liberty inherent in imprisonment.

In comparison to other regions considered here, England and Wales in many respects have been the most progressive regarding the rights of transgender individuals being recognised under the Gender Recognition Act (GRA) 2004. This Act established the Gender Recognition Certificate (GRC) enabling holders to change their British birth certificate to their acquired gender (HM Courts and Tribunal Service 2007). To obtain a GRC a person must be diagnosed with gender dysphoria, live as their authentic gender for two years, agree to live as their authentic gender until death and complete the SOC. To have undergone GRS is not a prerequisite to obtain a GRC (Jones and Brookes 2013). The GRA 2004 is criticised by Hines (2007) as although the rights of transgender individuals are legally recognised, it reinforces the gender binary and gender essentialism. Furthermore, it empowers medical professionals as the sole determinants of the construction and legitimate recognition of transgender identities (Davy 2011). This has significant consequences within the prison estate when managing transgender offenders. The aforementioned Whittle et al.'s (2001) recommendations were eventually addressed in 2011 by the Prison Service Instruction on the Care and Management of Transsexual Prisoners (despite the commitment being undertaken in 1997) (Jones and Brookes 2013) developed to comply with the Equality Act (2010) where 'gender reassignment' is specified as a protected characteristic under s.7. "A person has the protected characteristic of gender reassignment if the person is proposing to undergo, is undergoing or has undergone a process (or part of a process) for the purpose of reassigning the person's sex by changing physiological or other attributes of sex". The prison estate must therefore provide medical treatment to transgender offenders of the same standard received through the NHS if they were receiving this treatment outside of the prison environment to comply with this legislation. Placement within the prison estate in complex cases, require a case conference to be held with a multi-disciplinary risk assessment to decide on the most appropriate placement. Transgender inmates should also be permitted to wear gender appropriate attire and be referred to by their adopted gender appropriate name. This policy being similar to that followed in Canada and NSW. However, Canadian transgender inmates are more disadvantaged than inmates in the other regions. In 2013, Bill C-279 revising Canadian Human Rights Act and Criminal Code (318 as an aggravating circumstance to be taken into consideration under section 718.2 at the time of sentencing) protecting transgender individuals from discrimination (House of Commons 2013) is still under revision in 2015. Next, the management of transgender prisoners within the American penal state is examined.

Penal Policies in the USA

The majority of research on transgender offenders has been conducted in the USA (Jones and Brookes 2013). A study in San Francisco (Minter and Daley 2003) found at least one in seven transgender individuals has been incarcerated at one time; and 14% is approximately twice the average incarceration rate in the USA (Human Rights Watch 2006). The combined estimates of federal and state prisons in 2010 state there were less than 1,000 transgender inmates (see Brown 2010), thus, they are a significant minority considering their disproportionate and complex medical and mental health needs compared to those of the general prison population (Brown 2014). Sexton, Jenness and Sumner (2010) found the demographics of transgender offenders contrast with those of the general prison population as they are more likely to be aged between 36 and 45 years of age and are White or Black rather than being more ethnically diverse such as Hispanic, Asian/ Pacific Islander and Other. This demographic information for the other regions above was unavailable for comparison. Transgender offenders are incarcerated mainly for sex offences or property crimes, were less likely to identify as gang members, had a high rate of HIV prevalence and increased rates of physical victimisation (see Reback et al. 2001; Stotzer 2009; Witten 2003). Similar to the general prison population, 70% of transgender offenders experienced mental health issues during the course of their lives and drug and alcohol misuse.

Transgender prisoners' access to health care is variable across institutions according to Brown and McDuffie's (2009) study of housing and health care policies of 44 state prisons, the District of Columbia and Federal Bureau of Prisons found that most institutions allowed diagnostic evaluation; however, cross-sex hormone therapy, the initiation of treatment and whether surgical interventions for the treatment of gender identity disorder were denied, varied. The majority of prisons studied had no formal or informal policies addressing hormone therapy. Hormone therapy is not initiated but permitted if initiated pre-incarceration (Petersen et al. 1996). The denial of medical treatment was justified due to the prison's artificial environment making it difficult to assess the extent of gender dysphoria and for Real Life Experience to be gained. However, if the transgender inmate is incarcerated for a lengthy sentence then this is their RLE is it not and should be treated as such.

Lambda Legal (2012) conducted a national study, '*Protected and Served?*', exploring government misconduct by agents of the criminal justice system against sexual minorities and transgender (LGBT) inmates within jails or prisons, and those living with HIV in the United States. Of 2,376 people surveyed, 33% incarcerated in the last five years identified as transgender, genderqueer, gender-nonconforming, two-spirit or "other" gender identity (TGNC). The majority (60%) of incarcerated TGNC respondents reported being placed in a single-gender section of that institution incongruent with their gender identity. Furthermore, TGNC female identified prisoners stated they were incorrectly placed more frequently than TGNC respondents who identified as male. For example, 70% of TGNC female respondents and 47% of TGNC male respondents reported being incorrectly located (i.e. placed in jail or prison incongruent with their gender). In the USA, under the Eighth Amendment transgender and cisgender individuals alike should have access to 'adequate health care' irrespective of their imprisonment. Nevertheless, the interpretation of 'adequate' is contentious, and the courts not clinicians (Brown 2009) determine the extent of treatment provided which allows for discretion and potentially discrimination. The gender binary is present in penal policies in Canada, the USA and the majority of Australian territories.

Penal placement policies vary across American states, in California for example, San Francisco's progressive approach is discussed next. In San Francisco, segregation pods are provided for vulnerable prisoners. Prisoners are individually evaluated and screened by prison administrators to assess likelihood of heightened vulnerability if housed within the general prison population. Searches are conducted by prison officers whose gender is chosen by the inmate, or if it is not specified, the same gender (e.g., male for an FtM prisoner) is assigned (Human Rights Watch 2006). The small number of transgender inmates within respective prisons does not justify the expense of the provision of separate wards. San Francisco's penal policy is referred to as the most progressive in the USA. Nevertheless, there are limitations, it is expensive, requires extensive space and transgender inmates are still denied opportunities to attend school or access drug recovery programs routinely offered to other prisoners (Human Rights Watch 2006). In addition there is the lack feasibility of having a dedicated facility or ward just for transgender offenders (Mann 2006). Next, case studies are used to illustrate the incapability of prison systems to manage the complexity of the needs of transgender offenders and their appropriate placement in the penal estate.

In May 2012, Chrisshaun (CeCe) McDonald was arrested for murder of Dean Schmidt (for details see O'Hara 2014). This case captured the media's attention due to its intersectionality of gender and ethnicity. This case highlights bias or prejudice against transgender individuals and institutional racism within the criminal justice system. CeCe[2] spent four months locked in her single cell between 22–24 hours a day for 'her protection' in a male prison (which is excessive for administrative segregation), although she was allowed to shower alone. This penal policy is not unusual as in 2012 Minnesota Department of Corrections housed ten transgender inmates (all transgender women) in men's facilities. The above case evidences the increased punitiveness of the transgender inmate's experience which could be suggested as constituting 'cruel and unusual punishment' which contravenes the Eighth Amendment.

This inability to cope with the specific needs of transgender inmates is further exacerbated in military prison. The case of transgender woman Chelsea Manning (previously known as Bradley Manning) who received a 35-year sentence for treason in 2013.[3] This sentence was deemed cruel and unusual punishment by the media as military prisons are unequipped to manage transgender prisoners' complex and diverse health and welfare needs. Under military regulations she is denied hormone therapy or any transition-related treatment. If a gender dysphoria diagnosis is made she would be discharged from the army due to 'mental illness', however, this is not permitted while serving a sentence. Instead the options are (i) transfer Chelsea to a civilian prison to access treatment, (ii) deny her treatment and face legal challenges for contravening the Eighth Amendment or (iii) treat her in a military prison setting a new precedent. According to a leaked Pentagon document, a transfer request has been signed off to enable Chelsea Manning to receive treatment at a civilian prison; nonetheless, her attorney is sceptical of its legitimacy.

It will be interesting to see how military policy adapts to managing this case and the setting of precedents. The similarities and differences across the jurisdictions are examined using an adapted version of Mann's summary of penal policies with additional data included on England and Wales is presented in Table 13.1 below.

Transgender inmates with medically evidenced gender dysphoria should have access to the required medical and mental healthcare (UNODC 2009).

Table 13.1 A Summary of Penal Policies for Transgender Offenders (adapted from Mann 2006).

Penal Policies for Transgender Offenders

Australia	Canada	England & Wales	USA
Placement according to Gender Identity	Placement according to Anatomical Sex*	Placement according to Gender Identity under UK Law.	Placement according to Anatomical Sex
Facilitation of Hormone Therapy	Hormone Level Frozen on Incarceration*	Hormone Therapy provided on a case-by-case basis.	Hormone Level Frozen on Incarceration
GRS available at own expense	GRS available at own expense	GRS available via the NHS if requisite conditions are met as determined by the gender specialist/gender identity clinic and two medical supporting opinions and is then approved on a case-by-case basis.	No GRS
Protective Custody/ Segregation from the general prison population	Protective Custody/ Segregation from the general prison population	Protective Custody/ Segregation if deemed at risk from the general population.	Protective Custody/ Segregation from the general prison population

*This has now changed please see earlier discussion on penal policies in England and Wales and comparison to Canada

Nevertheless, access to GRS in prison is still disputed e.g., Kosilek Vs Spencer (see Brown 2014). The prohibitive factor is cost considering the already constrained budgets in the penal estate; the most practical approach would therefore be diversion out of the prison system for less serious offenders. Key to the management of transgender offenders is the 'risk of harm' but other pivotal factors which should also inform penal policy are gender equality and gender symmetry discussed next.

Risk and the Impact of Gender Symmetry and Gender Equality on Penal Policy

In the transgender community in San Francisco, 14% have suffered discrimination in jail or prison (see Minter and Daley 2003). A MtF inmate may be safer in a female prison, however, these are less well-resourced than male prisons. Concern is raised for female prisoners' safety due to the risk of rape by a pre-operative transgender woman. Peek rejects this risk and states the continuation of hormonal treatment results in the cessation of the sexual functionality of the penis. In contrast, the safety and well-being of the MtF prisoner housed in a male prison does not cause the same concern which raises the issue of gender equality and gender symmetry. Gender symmetry is the balance and proportionality between genders. Mann's (2006) summary of recommendations for the incorporation of gender equality and gender symmetry within penal policies is provided in Table 13.2 (below). Gender equality is the main objective, yet within the context of penal placement it can result in gender discrimination. For example, post-operative

Table 13.2 Universal Recommendations for Penal Policies Regarding the Placement of Transgender Offenders (Adapted from Mann 2006, p. 43).

Universal Recommendation

	Type of Transgender	Facility	Potential Harm	Hormone Therapy	GRS	Psychotherapy
Gender equality through gender asymmetry	Pre-operative male-to-female	Female	No	Yes	Yes	Yes
	Pre-operative female-to-male					
Gender inequality through gender symmetry	Post-operative male-to-female	Female	No	Yes (if necessary)	N/A	Yes
	Post-operative female-to-male	Male	Yes			

placement of MtF in a female facility results in no increased risk of harm in contrast with the FtM inmate placed in a male prison. The promotion of gender symmetry consequently results in gender inequality. Thus, treating people equally does not necessarily mean treating them the same. The solution would therefore be to place both FtM and MtF in a female facility which promotes gender equality but not gender symmetry is discussed next.

This juxtaposition of gender equality and gender symmetry is therefore difficult to accommodate within penal policy particularly when balancing an inmate's safety, access to amenities and cost. Gender equality is problematic because if GRS is provided for MtF inmates it must also be provided for FtM inmates, which is more expensive. Furthermore, employing gender symmetry whereby a FtM inmate is placed in a male prison results in an increased risk of physical and sexual assault due to the hypermasculine environment and macho hierarchy inherent in male prisons. The male hierarchy in prison is based on the 'ability to fight' and characteristics of 'manliness' which they do not conform to and hence deviate from male inmate norms of behaviour and demeanour. Thus, the safest option is administrative segregation (Alexander and Meshelemiah 2010) resulting in discrimination due to limited access to resources which are easily available to the wider prison population and increasing the punitiveness of their prison experience.

Conclusions and Recommendations

This comparative analysis of the penal policies of England, USA, Canada and Australia demonstrates that extensive changes are required to improve the accommodation and treatment of transgender offenders in prison in relation to the following key areas: firstly, gender identity-based placement and safety; secondly, medical and psycho-social welfare (e.g., access to hormone therapy and GRS); and, thirdly, access to education and other facilities should not be limited or denied when in administrative segregation.

Suitable legal counsel provided and complaints taken seriously, appropriately trained staff on the issues affecting LGBT offenders, promotion and recruitment of LGBT staff members, and their retention by disciplining staff who harass them or transgender inmates. Transgender inmates should also choose the gender of the person who strip searches them, and this procedure carried out sensitively to maintain the dignity of the person. Records should also be kept to enable accountability and justification provided for the search (UNODC 2009). The issues of gender equality and gender symmetry and their appropriateness within the penal policy context are complex; however, this should not preclude their consideration. An evaluation of the policies and practices in the management of transgender offenders should be conducted to assess their effectiveness and revise policies where necessary to improve conditions for this marginalised population. Segregation is frequently the solution to housing transgender individuals in prison which denies them (i) access to educational and recreational programmes; (ii) the opportunity to socialise; and (iii) protection from harassment from prison guards and administrators. Access to separate basic amenities (showers and toilets) should also be provided.

Best practice regarding the management of transgender offenders was highlighted in San Francisco (though cognisant of the inherent resource constraints and limitations), New South Wales and in England and Wales. However, improved advocacy in prison is required and access to comparable medical and mental health services for transgender individuals equitable with community provisions. Although, such treatment services in the penal estate in the USA may be more accessible to inmates without medical insurance who could not afford these in the community. Enhanced training provided on the importance of the SOC, its limitations regarding intersectionality and increased vulnerability of transgender prisoners if medical treatment is restricted or denied. RLE should be more widely acknowledged as being possible within institutional settings particularly long sentences as the custodial context is their 'lived experience'. Hormone treatment should be maintained or started de novo for inmates where necessitated by specialist medical staff. Gender dysphoric natal males should be permitted cosmetics, female underwear; allowed longer nails and hair, and gender neutral prison uniforms similar to female inmates.

The experience of the transgender prisoner is therefore more punitive than that of prisoners within the general population and is exacerbated by their lack of access to appropriate health care and psychological treatment (Edney 2004). Thus, where feasible it is suggested that transgender offenders be diverted from serving custodial sentences in line with the good practice highlighted by the Transgender, Gender Variant and Intersex Project in California (www.tgijp.org/) which promotes alternative sentencing of offenders from these marginalised communities to maintain access to the required medical, social and economic services which is often more challenging to provide within a carceral context.

Notes

1 Synthia Kavanaugh was a MtF pre-operative transgender prisoner diagnosed with gender identity disorder and was approved for SRS prior to incarceration. She was convicted of second degree murder in 1989. Her frequent requests to transfer to a female institution were denied as was her hormone therapy (finally reinstated in 1993). She also challenged sections 30 and 31 Commissioner's Directive which she stated was a violation of Section 5 of the Canadian Human Rights Act (which states it is "discriminatory practice" to deny access to services readily available to the general public).
2 CeCe was interrogated without a solicitor present and pressured to plead guilty to second-degree manslaughter instead of self-defence to obtain a reduced sentence of 41 months. She was released early after 19 months due to good behaviour, time served and potentially media pressure.
3 Chelsea's offence was leaking classified government material regarding nefarious US military activity in Baghdad, Iraq, Afghanistan and Guantano Bay and Cuba to the website Wikileaks in 2010 (see Manning 2014). The military suggested she may not receive her mail as her records will still state her name as Bradley Manning despite identifying as Chelsea Manning.

Bibliography

Alexander, R. and C.A. Jaquelyn Meshelemiah. 2010. "Gender Identity Disorders in Prisons: What Are the Legal Implications for Prison Mental Health Professionals and Administrators." *The Prison Journal* 90 (3): 269–287.

American Psychiatric Association. 2013. *Diagnostic and Statistical Manual of Mental Disorders: Gender Dysphoria Fact Sheet*. 5th ed. Washington, DC: American Psychiatric Publishing: 2.

Blight, J. 2000. "Transgender Inmates." *Trends and Issues in Crime and Criminal Justice*, No.168: 1–6.

Brown, G.R. 2009. "Recommended Revisions to the World Professional Association for Transgender Health's Standards of Care Section on Medical Care for Incarcerated Persons With Gender Identity Disorder". *Internet Journal of Criminology* 11 (2): 133–139.

Brown, G.R. 2010. "Autocastration and Autopenectomy as Surgical Self-Treatment in Incarcerated Persons With Gender Identity Disorder." *International Journal of Transgenderism* 12 (1): 31–39.

Brown, G.R. 2014. "Qualitative Analysis of Transgender Inmates' Correspondence: Implications for Departments of Correction." *Journal of Correctional Health Care* 20: 1–9.

Brown, G.R. and E. Mcduffie. 2009. "Health Care Policies Addressing Transgender Inmates in Prison Systems in the United States." *Journal of Correctional Health Care*, 15: 280–291.

Carlen, P. and A. Worrall. 2004. *Analysing Women's Imprisonment*. Abingdon: Taylor & Francis.

Chesney-Lind, M. and L. Pasko. 2013. *The Female Offender: Girls, Women, and Crime*. London: Sage Publications.

Cole, S.S., Denny, D., Eyler, A.E. and S.L. Samons. 2000. "Issues of Transgender." In L. T. Szuchman & F. Muscarella (eds.), *Psychological Perspectives on Human Sexuality*. 149–195.

Cook-Daniels, Loree and Munson, Michael. 2010. "Sexual Violence, Elder Abuse, and Sexuality of Transgender Adults, Age 50+: Results of Three Surveys." *Journal of GLBT Family Studies*, 6 (2): 142–177.

Correctional Service Canada. 2013. *Commissioners Directorate, Gender Identity Disorder, s.33 42*. Accessed April 24, 2014 www.csc-scc.gc.ca/text/plcy/cdshtm/800-cde-eng.shtml.

Davy, Z. 2011. *Recognizing Transsexuals: Personal, Political and Medicolegal Embodiment*. Farnham: Ashgate.

Dickey, R. 1990. "Gender Dysphoria and Anti-Social Behavior." In *Clinical Management of Gender Identity Disorders in Children and Adults*, edited by R. Blanchard and B.W. Steiner, 192–199. Washington: American Psychiatric Press.

Edney, R. 2004. "To Keep Me Safe From Harm." *Deakin Law Review*, 9: 327–338.

Equality Act. (2010). http://www.legislation.gov.uk/ukpga/2010/15/contents

Gender Recognition Act (GRA). 2004. http://www.legislation.gov.uk/ukpga/2004/7/pdfs/ukpga_20040007_en.pdf

Heidensohn, F.M. 1985. *Women and Crime: The Life of the Female Offender*. New York: New York University Press.

Hines, S. 2007. "(Trans)forming Gender: Social Change and Transgender Citizenship." *Sociological Research Online* 12: 1–12.

HM Courts and Tribunal Service. 2007. *Explanatory Leaflet: A Guide for Users: Gender Recognition Act 2004* (Updated April 2007). London: Author.

House of Commons. 2013. *Bill C-279*. Accessed April 19, 2015. www.parl.gc.ca/House-Publications/Publication.aspx?Language=E&Mode=1&DocId=6256603&File=27&Col=1.

Human Rights Watch. (2006). https://www.hrw.org/

Jones, L. and M. Brook. 2013. "Transgender Offenders: A Literature Review." *Prison Service Journal*, No. 206: 11–18.

Lambda Legal. (2012). http://www.lambdalegal.org/sites/default/files/publications/downloads/ps_executive-summary.pdf

Mallicoat, S.L. and C.E. Ireland. 2014. *Women and Crime: The Essentials*. London. Sage.

Mann, R. 2006. "Treatment of Transgender Prisoners, Not Just an American Problem-A Comparative Analysis of American, Australian, and Canadian Prison Policies Concerning the Treatment of Transgender Prisoners and a Universal Recommendation to Improve Treatment, The." *Law and Sexuality: Rev. Lesbian, Gay, Bisexual and Transgender Legal Issues* 15: 91–133.

Manning, C. 2014. 'Chelsea Manning: Why Speaking Out Is Worth the Risk". Accessed January 26, 2015. www.amnesty.org.uk/blogs/global-voices/chelsea-manning-%E2%80%98why-speaking-out-worth-risk%E2%80%99.

Maruri, S. 2011. "Hormone Therapy for Inmates: A Metonym for Transgender Rights." *Cornell Journal of Law and Public Policy* 96: 807–832.

Merton, R. 1957. *Social Theory and Social Structure*. New York: The Free Press.

Minter, S. and C. Daley. 2003. "Trans Realities: A Legal Needs Assessment of San Francisco's Transgender Communities." *Transgender Law Center* 4: 1–50.

New Law Journal. 2009. "Human Rights—Transgender Person—Gender Status for Prison Allocation". Retrieved from: www.newlawjournal.co.uk/nlj/content/law-reports-106. 12 May 2015.

O'Hara, M.E. 2014. *My Struggle Started When I Entered This World: Vice News Interviews CeCe McDonald*. Accessed January 26, 2015.https://news.vice.com/article/my-struggle-started-when-i-entered-this-world-vice-news-interviews-cece-mcdonald.

Parker, M.M. 2014. "Chelsea Manning's Attorney Accuses Pentagon of 'Strategic Leak'. *The Advocate*. Accessed January 26, 2015.www.advocate.com/politics/transgender/2014/05/14/chelsea-mannings-attorney-accuses-pentagon-strategic-leak.

Petersen, M., Stephens, J., Dickey, R. and W. Lewis. 1996. "Transexuals Within the Prison System: An International Survey of Correctional Policies." *Behavioural Sciences and the Law* 14 (2): 219–229.

Piquero, A.R. and R.W. Brame. 2008. "Assessing the Race—Crime and Ethnicity—Crime Relationship in a Sample of Serious Adolescent Delinquents." *Crime and Delinquency* 54: 390–422.

Poole, L., Whittle, S. and P. Stephens. 2002. "Working With Transgendered and Transsexual People as Offenders in the Probation Service." *Probation Journal* 49 (3): 227–232.

Reback, C.J., Simon, P.A., Bemis, C.C. and B. Gatson. 2001. *The Los Angeles Transgender Health Study: Community Report*. Los Angeles: Van Ness Recovery House, Prevention Division: 1–35.

Schilt, K. and L. Westbrook. 2009. "Doing Gender, 'Doing Heteronormativity': Doing 'Gender Normals', Transgender People, and the Social Maintenance of Heterosexuality." *Gender and Society* 23 (4): 440–464.

Sexton, L., Jennes, V. and J.M. Sumner. 2010. "Where the Margins Meet: A Demographic Assessment of Transgender Inmates in Men's Prisons." *Justice Quarterly* 27: 835–866.

Stotzer, R.L. 2009. "Violence Against Transgender People: A Review of United States Data." *Aggression and Violent Behavior* 14 (3): 170–179.

Strapagiel, L. 2015. "Ontario Will Now Assess Transgender Inmates Based on Identity Not Anatomy." *National Post*, 26 January. Accessed April 24, 2015. http://news.nationalpost.com/news/canada/ontario-will-now-assess-transgender--inmates-based-on-identity-not-anatomy.

Tarzwell, S. 2006. "The Gender Lines Are Marked With Razor Wire: Addressing State Prison Policies and Practices for Management of Transgender Prisoners." *Columbia Human Rights Law Review* 38: 167–219.

The International Commission of Jurists and the International Service for Human Rights. 2007. "The Yogyakarta Principles: Principles on the Application of International Human Rights Law in Relation to Sexual Orientation and Gender Identity", 1 35.

The White House—Office of the Press Secretary. 2014. *Fact Sheet: Taking Action to Support LGBT Workplace Equality Is Good for Business*. Accessed September 17, 2014. http://Www.Whitehouse.Gov/The-Press-Office/2014/07/21/Fact-Sheet-Taking-Action-Support-Lgbt-Workplace-Equality-Good-Business-0.

United Nations Office on Drugs and Crime. 2009. *Handbook On Prisoners With Special Needs*. Criminal Justice Handbook Series. Vienna: United Nations Office on Drugs and Crime: 1–190.

Whittle, S. and L. Turner. 2007. "Sex Changes? Paradigm Shifts in 'Sex' and 'Gender' Following the Gender Recognition Act?" *Sociological Research Online* 12 (1): 1–12.

Whittle, S., and P. Stephens. 2001. *A Pilot Study of Provision for Transsexual and Transgender People in the Criminal Justice System, and the Information Needs of Their Probation Officers*. Manchester: The Manchester Metropolitan University: 1–36.

Witten, Taryn M. 2003. "Life-Course Analysis—The Courage to Search for Something More: Middle Adulthood Issues in the Transgender and Intersex Community." *Journal of Human Behavior in the Social Environment* 8 (2–3): 189–224.

World Professional Association for Transgender Health [WPATH]. 2015. *Standards of Care for Transsexual, Transgender and Gender Non-Conforming People*. Minneapolis: Author. WPATHCGID [WPATH Standards of Care for Gender Identity Disorders] (2009).

Worrall, A. 2001. *Offending Women: Female Lawbreakers and the Criminal Justice System*. London: Routledge.

14 Conducting Sex Work Research in a Politically Contentious Climate

Lessons from Ireland

Paul Ryan and Susann Huschke

This chapter explores the challenges faced by four leading researchers of commercial sex, working in both Northern Ireland and the Republic of Ireland. At a time when both the Irish Parliament in Dublin and the devolved Northern Ireland assembly in Belfast are due to debate the merits of criminalizing the purchase of sex, the chapter explores how these researchers have navigated a political climate that has increasingly placed the spotlight on their personal and professional allegiances as much as the merits of the research conducted. The chapter focuses specifically on conflicts which have emerged within previous feminist allies, the political scrutiny of researchers hired by Universities to conduct sex work research and the personal consequences when data produced is subjected to criticism and debate.

Introduction

Prostitution policy has emerged as one of the most divisive issues within contemporary debates on sexual politics on the island of Ireland. The production of expert knowledge on the sex industry has been transformed by the growth of abolitionist advocacy research, the rise of auto-biographical 'survivor' stories of lives within prostitution and media reporting that often portrays women within an exclusively coercive narrative (e.g. Dudley 2006; ICI 2009; Moran 2013; Reynolds 2003). Sex work research is now undertaken within what has been recognized as a "new moral framework" where governments have increasingly directed resources to both 'rescue' women from commercial sexual exploitation, while fostering individual responsibility through funded exiting programmes. This development has taken place as part of a wider neo-liberal regulation of intimate life (Hubbard et al. 2008; Scouler and O'Neill 2007).

The extension of a so-called Nordic system of criminalization of the purchase of sexual services, first introduced in Sweden in 1999, in Northern Ireland in 2015 and due to be enacted in the Republic of Ireland by the end of 2015, had been a key demand from anti-sex work feminist, anti-trafficking, religious and political organizations for many years. While similar demands for this legislation have been strongly resisted by a combination of sex workers' rights organizations, academics and sex positive feminist groups in countries such as Denmark and France and in other parts of the United Kingdom, namely England and Scotland, the situation across the island of Ireland has remained markedly different. In the absence of substantial sex worker organizing, political parties expressing opposition and the silence (or non-existence) of harm reductive health services, the critique of the so-called Swedish model has come largely from individual sex workers and academics conducting sex work research. This critique and the research undertaken by academics has, through the debate, come into conflict with advocacy research commissioned by non-governmental organizations campaigning for the criminalizing of the purchase of sexual services. Such a conflict has led to accusations of bias and a lack of methodological rigor amongst a relatively small group of academics, activists and campaigners.

This chapter explores the experiences of four academic researchers working in both the Republic of Ireland (Paul Ryan and Eilís Ward) and Northern Ireland (Susann Huschke and Graham Ellison) on aspects of the sex industry.[1] It explores the personal and professional costs of speaking publically from a position that runs counter to the dominant abolitionist view, and how these researchers have navigated relationships with individuals and groups that were often former allies, but now stand in stark opposition to research that advocates a more nuanced anti-abolitionist position. The chapter utilizes the concept of emotional labor (O'Connell Davidson and Layder 1994; Saunders 2006; Sharpe 2000) to describe the experiences of the researchers, focusing not as traditionally understood on the toil and distress of hearing stories from the sex industry, but on the consequences for academics when they deviate from a dominant narrative on prostitution in the public sphere.

The Legal Regimes Governing Prostitution in the Republic of Ireland and Northern Ireland

The Republic of Ireland and Northern Ireland share a similar legal framework regarding prostitution. In the past, prostitution was viewed mainly as an issue of public nuisance and policy measures mainly targeted at street-based sex work. Kerb crawling and soliciting as well as organizing and living off the proceeds of prostitution are criminalized. Across the island, the discourse changed dramatically with the advent of the Turn off the Right Light (TORL) campaign, spearheaded by the Immigrant Council of Ireland (ICI), which successfully reframed the debate as being both inseparable from sex trafficking while being intrinsically linked to violence against women.[2] It has proved hugely successful in lobbying trade unions, women's groups and political parties and bringing them together in a coalition to support the criminalization of the purchase of sex. The ICI (2009) published a research report they had commissioned which they claimed provided evidence supporting a legislative change. The current government initiated a public consultation and the subsequent report by the Joint Committee on Justice, Defence and Equality (2013) did recommend the adoption of the Nordic style sex purchase ban. In October 2014, the new Minister of Justice, Frances Fitzgerald, announced that she would bring such legislative proposal to government.

In Northern Ireland, Maurice Morrow, Member of the Legislative Assembly (MLA) for the Democratic Unionist Party (DUP), introduced the *Human Trafficking and Exploitation Bill* as a private member's bill in 2012, including a clause

that aims to criminalize those who pay for sexual services provided by sex workers. In April 2014, the Department of Justice commissioned a comprehensive,
mixed-methods study on sex work to fill the gap perceived by the Justice Minister.
The study (Huschke et al. 2014) clearly highlighted the complexity of sex work
and addressed the multiple vulnerabilities many sex workers across the island of
Ireland face. However, the findings of the study were largely ignored or dismissed
as 'biased' by policy makers, and the bill, including the sex purchase ban, passed
the Assembly in October 2014 and was subsequently enacted in January 2015.

Four Researchers of Sex Work

The four contributors to this chapter have all played a significant role in debates
about prostitution policy on the island of Ireland, both through their published
academic work and through public engagement. This has included work on policing and prostitution (Ellison 2012), drug use and sex work, and sex work activism
(Ryan et al. 2011), trafficking, sex work and state policy (Ward and Wylie 2007,
Ward 2010, Ward and Wylie 2010) and a study on the sex industry in Northern
Ireland (Huschke et al. 2014).[3] All four have opposed the introduction of a sex
purchase ban in both jurisdictions and have entered into a public debate on the
merits of such a policy with its supporters drawn from organizations advocating
for immigrant rights, women's rights including ex-sex worker perspectives.[4] This
section of the chapter charts their engagement, exploring how these researchers
have navigated both their academic environments and relationships with colleagues, and also their public engagement discussing sex work in the media, in
Parliamentary hearings and in community forums.

Saunders (2006, 450–1) argues that researchers have been slow to reflect on
those challenges although some reflective accounts of field research on the sex
industry exist (Hammond and Kingston 2014; Hart 1998; Hubbard 1999; Maher
2000; Melrose 2002; O'Connell Davidson 1998; O'Neill 1996; Sharpe 2000;
Shaver 2005). While the literature may emphasize the marginality of sexuality
research (Irvine 2014), much depends upon the route of entry into the field. This
can create either wider networks of allies, give an illusion at least of a greater
impartiality or be eased by a tradition of ethnography of marginalized or partially
hidden groups. Graham Ellison describes how his introduction to this research
area was mediated by his subject matter—policing—and also an initial interest in
male sex work. Male sex work traditionally has been located within a criminologi-
cal perspective (Ginsberg 1967; Reiss 1961), but in contemporary debates it has
been both its visibility within the gay community and its invisibility from public
debates that have been noteworthy. This invisibility has lent support to a radical
feminist view of prostitution as exclusively women's commodification by men
(Agustin 2006; Smith 2012). Ellison explains that:

> I think the [criminal justice] route is possibly easier and less controversial
> because I think the selling of sex is a really interesting prism to refract a
> whole range of issues on policing, the policing of public space and policing

sexuality. . . and I suppose in that way because you are not talking about sex or sexuality upfront so it is less controversial.

Ward had been involved with feminist activism on issues of reproductive rights and sexual violence against women and, in her academic career, with teaching and writing on issue of women and politics. While initially supportive of a radical feminist perspective on prostitution as an inherent patriarchal exploitation of women, Ward's position changed as she became interested in the topic of lap dancing and sought out research that privileged the voices of the women in sex work themselves. Not finding them, she embarked on research in the area (Ward and Wylie 2010). Ward explains.

> What struck me as a feminist researcher was that I never read anywhere or heard the voices of the women that were lap dancing and I thought: that's something a feminist researcher, who believes in validating women's voices, women's experiences, ought to do. Seeking out of voices of those involved: that's the first principle and start point of doing fieldwork.

While Ward's views on sex work increasingly recognized the agency of those women involved, it was not a position that was shared by many of the women she had campaigned with, something which would ultimately create tension between them. While her university remains supportive, some colleagues do greet the subject matter of her work with "puzzlement", a view supported by other sexuality researchers who feel often personally valued although their work is viewed as marginal (Irvine 2014, 650). Female researchers of sex work can also face greater concern from institutions and colleagues about the potential danger faced in the field, with Institutional Review Boards automatically labeling the work 'sensitive', where the safety of the researcher is often a disguise for protecting the reputation of the institution (Hammond and Kingston 2014; Saunders 2006).

Paul Ryan, by comparison, became involved in sex work research after previously researching LGBT history and activism during the 1970s and 80s and entered the field influenced by a tradition of pro-sex feminism and a commitment to the extension of labor rights to those working in the sex industry (Brunckert and Parent 2006; Saunders 2005). He describes how:

> Marginality was never an issue I guess, my work was already marginal but as stigma started to reduce around gay and lesbian issues I became convinced that if you were committed to a progressive sexual politics, it was those in the sex industry that were the really marginalized ones—stigmatized, experiencing violence and there was a huge silence around it even in 2009 when I became involved

Susann Huschke took yet another entry into the field of sex work research. In her previous work (Huschke 2013), she focused on undocumented migration and access to health care in Germany, combining ethnographic research with political activism (Huschke 2014). The close link between migration and sex work led her to investigate the selling of sex, initially with a focus on health and health care. In regard to choosing yet another politically sensitive field, she explains:

> When I first moved to Northern Ireland, the public debate about the sex purchase ban had just started. I was struck by the lack of research on this topic and the one-sidedness of the arguments, which appeared to be based mainly on stereotypical views of those who sell and buy sex. I found these to be good reasons to undertake research on this topic. Looking back though, I think: I had no idea what I was getting myself into in terms of politics. I was in no way prepared for the hostility that we faced by politicians and anti-sex work activists in Northern Ireland.

All four researchers started doing sex work research based on their commitment to social justice, gender equality and civil rights. Regardless of this—or perhaps because their notions of justice and rights contradicted those of conservative politicians and abolitionist feminists—they faced significant opposition by activists and politicians once they entered the public arena as sex work researchers.

Sex Work Researchers and Public Engagement

In a neo-liberal age universities are increasingly evaluated on the societal impact of the research they produce (Mullerleile 2014). The desire for greater public engagement has encouraged academics to become both public providers of knowledge through the traditional dissemination of their work but also through writing op-eds for newspapers, writing blogs or advising community groups (ibid. p. 507). As the narrative of prostitution increasingly became redefined solely into a discourse of exploitation of women and a number of organizations (e.g. ICI, Women's Aid Northern Ireland, Ruhama) reoriented their energies to advocate for a sex purchase ban, academic interventions were often fraught with reputational danger, and, rather than simply moving from the ivory tower to the public arena, they had the feel of "moving into a battlefield" (Loftus 2003, 84). For Ryan, speaking as a male academic about the sex purchase ban which was popularly defined as a measure to reduce violence against women was often especially difficult. He explains:

> I'd say around 2009, news organizations were delighted to have anyone on that would argue another side but I found that I was on radio up against people from organizations that had spent so much money on media training and were so on message—one message—that here I was trying to communicate something much more complex and it was always a struggle that left you feeling why am I bothering with this. . .

Not having *one* answer or solution to the complex issue of prostitution leaves academics exposed when engaged in research or speaking publically. Even worse is producing what might be perceived to be the 'wrong answer'. Ward and Wylie (2014, 6) document how their research into prostitution and trafficking brought out greater nuance in the experience of migrant women that left the researchers unable to categorize a singular experience rather different "shades of grey". The consequences for researchers of providing the 'wrong answer' can be significant. A well-funded anti-prostitution advocacy group excluded Ward and Wylie (2014) from tendering for a piece of research they were commissioning because the researchers' views were deemed incompatible with their organization. The subsequent research project (ICI 2009) marginalized Ward and Wylie's original contribution to the field. This tendency of research on the sex industry to undervalue diversity of experience in favor of dichotomies remains strong (Shaver 2005).

Ryan claims that a shift occurred in the debates on prostitution over the years, with news organizations increasingly relying less on academics and more on the autobiographical accounts of former sex workers who support criminalization (Annandale 2005; Moran 2013). Given the lack of sex worker activism across the island of Ireland[5] and the highly stigmatized nature of the work, this was not always an easy task. Nor were the media always upfront with the format of shows that researchers were invited on. Ryan recalls being asked to appear on Vincent Browne's current affairs TV3 show to speak about merits of the Nordic sex purchase ban:

> Before the show the host Vincent Browne came out to meet us and was chatting and then just said—'come on Paul, guys that buy sex, there must be something pathological going on there' and this was the host. . . I just knew it was going to be bad and then I was on the show and we both spoke and then they showed a 20 minute video insert of an ex-sex worker who told of her life in a brothel being raped 20 times a day. . . and this was never discussed with me and the camera came back to me and I was asked 'so what do you think about that?' so it all felt like an ambush.

The twitter feed of the show also revealed the public dissatisfaction that a man was appearing on the show and speaking 'for women' even though between 9% and 22% of sex workers in Ireland are male or transsexual (Huschke et al. 2014; Maginn and Ellison 2014). Twitter comments also made reference to his personal appearance and how his unshaven look made him look "shady"; comments that go to the heart of this "speaker's burden" when one speaks of sexuality (Irvine 2014, 635). While female researchers risk becoming sexualized by their involvement, male researchers risk being seen as apologists for a violent sex trade, or worse, pimps. Both suffer from critical or hostile responses that bear similarity to the treatment of sex workers themselves (Hammond and Kingston 2014).

Ward was always more circumspect about engaging with the media believing it to be a strategy of those proponents of a sex purchase ban to discredit and marginalize those who spoke out against. She believed this strategy created an assumption that if you did not support this campaign you were 'either directly benefiting from the sex trade or you were somehow validating rape and violence against women'. Despite her reservations, Ward did feel a responsibility to contribute to the debate and set about writing an opinion piece for the *Irish Times* newspaper.

> I felt obliged, and I really mean obliged, as a scholar in this area to give my opinions and I was absolutely terrified of doing that because I didn't want to bring down on myself this wrath. . . . I had wanted to write an opinion piece for the Irish Times and I had contacted them and they were interested and I subsequently had several anxious weeks encouraging myself to do it. I spoke to my Head of School about the tensions and he said if you feel that this is something you have to do then I fully support you.

For Huschke, the emotional labor of doing sex work research entailed predominantly feelings of frustration and anger. Her first direct interaction with proponents of the Bill took place during an oral evidence session of the Justice Committee, in which she spoke up against the sex purchase ban (together with Ellison) based on an on-going study on sex work in Northern Ireland (prior to the comprehensive study conducted in 2014). Committee members in support of the Bill dismissed her research findings and conclusions by labeling methods that are commonly used in social research on marginalized and hidden populations, such as online surveys and opportunistic sampling, as flawed and inadequate.

Huschke was confronted with allegations such as that 'a leading pimp [had] encourage[d] his workers to complete the survey', that she was somehow part of the 'pimp lobby' due to her alleged 'direct links with the largest prostitution website in Ireland' (because she had posted information about the study and links to the online surveys on Escort. Ireland and other websites), and that she had not interviewed or surveyed anyone who experienced negative sides of the sex industry—allegations that were simply nonsensical or wrong (cf. Huschke et al. 2014: chapter 6). Huschke explains how these attacks by policy-makers affected her:

> The most frustrating part was trying to discuss this topic with people who very clearly do not know much about research and methodology—and why would they, it is not their area of expertise—but come up with the most unfounded accusations that aim to destroy the research by making it look unprofessional. . . there was no way of explaining our methods and the research process to people like Paul Givan and Jim Wells (DUP representatives in the Justice Committee). They had made their minds up a long time ago about what sex work is and what is to be done about it, and were not going to be swayed by anything that we found in our study, or by anything sex workers themselves had to say about it.

Ellison's experience of public engagement in Northern Ireland also raises important concerns about the role of academics in public engagement, and specifically how a contentious issue like sex work seemed to have re-constituted the parameters of the debate leaving academic researchers more exposed and vulnerable.

Researchers, who conduct and publish research that contradicts dominant narratives, hegemonic worldviews or challenges powerful interests, may be portrayed as 'malicious, incompetent, unscientific, agenda-driven, and unethical' (Landman and Glantz 2009; Nutt 2009; Sleek 2013). Like Ward, Ellison knew that public opposition to Lord Morrow of the ruling Democratic Unionist Party's (DUP) attempt to introduce a sex purchase ban in Northern Ireland would identify him as someone "who could be attacked or ridiculed". This started when Ellison received a number of Freedom of Information (FOI) requests submitted by journalists known to be supportive of the Morrow Bill requesting him to release correspondence between himself and his respondents on a current sex work project. Ellison describes the impact on his work and Queen's University Belfast's response:

> The university quite rightly redacted [the communication] on the grounds that university. . . well I had signed an ethics approval form and the university had given my respondents a guarantee of anonymity and confidentiality. To release their correspondence to me would have released their names to the public. . . It was challenging not to say time consuming, there were over 1,000 emails that I had to produce and someone in the university had to go through them and decide what needed to redacted. I think it was basically an attempt to stymie the research.

In this case, it appears that the researcher's accountability as an employee of a public institution was used to hinder his work—albeit disguised as a commitment to openness about data production (cf. Martin 1999).

Another difficult situation arose when Ellison made a submission to the Justice Committee examining the provisions of the Morrow Bill and was called to give oral evidence. While reluctant, Ellison felt that as an academic he had a responsibility to contribute. Unknown to Ellison, the DUP had secured an email he had privately sent to Swedish feminist Gunilla Ekberg in which he had questioned her support for the DUP sponsored bill given the party's hostility to reproductive and gay rights. DUP members of the Justice Committee read the email out loud, labeled Ellison's communication with the Swedish researcher as 'abuse of a witness', threatened a formal complaint against Ellison with his university, and questioned his 'integrity' and 'motivation', suggesting that he had mainly opposed the sex purchase ban because of his 'prejudice against the DUP' not because of his research findings. Looking back, Ellison states:

> I thought it was part of my civic duty to give evidence to that committee. I'm sure in hindsight, given what happened whether I would have turned up (laughs), they basically had the email for a long time before I was called so I don't know if. . . I feel I was set up but the point was I was one of two people doing research in this area, I had some interesting data that basically was contradicting everything that Lord Morrow said about the issue and contradicted everything Women's Aid had said about the issue and simply there

was no evidence for what they were saying and I thought it was useful to put that in the public domain.

Revealing the email sent by Ellison at the Justice Committee on broadcast live on webcam, and the subsequent accusations that he was biased against the DUP and not a credible researcher had serious implications for the role of academics and their conduct in the public arena. According to Ellison, Queens University 'were thinking about whether they would advise their staff whether they should contribute in those types of civic engagements and structures'. Universities do have a duty of care to academics in such cases by offering, for example, communication specialists to advise staff before they enter the public arena (Mullerleile 2014). Furthermore, an open debate is needed, both within academia and beyond, about how powerful players—in this case, supporters of the sex purchase ban—may actively seek to suppress research by ignoring or discrediting results that run counter to the dominant discourse and by launching 'attacks on researchers who produce unwelcome results' (Martin 1999, 355).

Managing Personal Relationships in a Small Research Community

The experiences of public engagement in sex work debates can create tension at a personal level in how academics *manage* their research interest in the sex industry within a broader alliance of colleagues, activists and friends. Ward explains that when asked what her research area was she would often say 'gender and migration' rather than dealing with potentially negative reactions or heated debate. Israel (2002, 259) was involved in a similar process that deliberately obscured the focus of her research describing it as "diversity issues" or "gender issues". Hammond and Kingston (2014) also preferred to describe their work as 'gender' when discussing it with people they did not know, which became necessary after they were subjected to jokes about their research which was seen as an area unworthy of study. Both Saunders (2006) and Grenz (2014) describe how they were located as a potential sex worker by research participants or, in Grenz's case, also as asexual by the men in her study in contrast to male colleagues conducting research who were often viewed as peers (e.g. Walby 2012). It would appear that female researchers suffer an interrogation of both their academic and personal motivations for embarking on such research in a different way to men (Braun 1999). Ultimately Ward considered whether she should continue in a research field that created such divisions, particularly amongst former feminist allies (Ward and Wylie 2014, 9). She explains that—

I had a lot of sleepless nights wondering many times if I'll just walk away from this topic it's just too contentious. . . . I didn't want to always open that door and be always defending myself and I wanted to separate my work life from personal life; life is difficult enough, why don't I just study electoral systems. . . . Researchers are tough but behind it they are also human beings and they can feel things.

The idea that researchers can 'manage' their work lives in a manner that does not impinge on their private self is often difficult to achieve. Melrose (2002, 345) describes how she tried to separate both parts of her life only to realize that her working life was 'intimately connected to my total sense of self' and would involve her dissociating from part of herself.

For Ellison, Ryan and Huschke there is less conflict with their research and a wider peer network. For the latter, despite being a female researcher, this is mainly due to the fact that within her home discipline of (critical) medical anthropology, research on contested topics and marginalized populations is relatively common and not generally frowned upon. For the former two, as men, they are less likely to be judged for 'betraying' women by highlighting the agency involved in the choices women make in sex work. However, the researcher's gender identity can at the same time contribute to difficulties in this field. Ellison describes how organizations like Women's Aid would say 'you don't know what we know', suggesting there was a knowledge and understanding of prostitution which could only be accessed by women and remained external to male researchers. Hubbard (1999) argues that given sex workers are also an 'other' to all middle-class female academics being male should not necessarily exclude one from embarking on research in this field. He did recognize however that his interviews with women were often "difficult and stilted" due to his presence in the feminized space where he became fearful that women would view his presence as some academic pimp, exploiting their stories for career advancement (Hubbard 1999, 232).

The experiences of the researchers in this chapter reveal significant emotional labor in the conduct of their work. We argue that this exists beyond the collection of data that often proves distressing to listen to, transcribe and analyze (Melrose 2002; O'Connell Davidson and Layder 1994). While emotional labor may be benignly defined as 'the labor involved in dealing with other people's feelings' (James 1989, 21) or "efforts to understand others" (England and Farkas 1986, 91) it can, in politically contentious research, demand a degree of emotional robustness not experienced in other research fields. This robustness is demanded of researchers when there is trepidation of speaking in public about research findings lest accusations of bias are leveled at you, potentially damaging your academic reputation. It can manifest itself in politically motivated interference in the research process through the submission of FOI requests. This emotional labor requires the learning of new coping skills and a willingness to seek advice from others in coping with these difficult situations (James 1989).

Conclusion

This chapter raises new challenges for those undertaking sex work research. In the case of Ireland, (both North and South), the production of expert knowledge on prostitution has created competing versions of the *truth* where non-governmental advocacy research findings challenge traditional academic studies which have been conducted without a specific policy goal. The chapter argues that in the context of Ireland's conservative moral climate; when both sets of research enter the public domain, academic researchers remain at a significant disadvantage in communicating complex social realities of those in the sex industry. The politicized nature of the debate around the future of prostitution policy has exposed the researchers who contributed to this chapter to bullying and a suggestion that they are colluding with the sex industry in the sexual exploitation of women.

The chapter reveals that significant amounts of emotional labor are deployed in the management of public engagement activities. This "stigma by association" may discourage academics from embarking upon or defending their research in the public arena (Hammond and Kingston 2014, 330; Martin 1999). This would undermine the concept of the public intellectual reinforcing stereotypes of an 'ivory tower' whose funding leads to little social impact. However, the emotional labor described in this chapter also constitutes an opportunity to enhance research: becoming part of the moral economy of sex work politics may help researchers gain an empirically and experientially grounded understanding of the stigma attached to sex work and the moralities and power dynamics at play, and holds the potential for greater empathy and solidarity with sex workers.

In order to support researchers, especially at the early stages of their careers, to conduct research on this politically and emotionally sensitive topic (particularly in a social setting shaped by religious conservatism and sex negative attitudes such as the island of Ireland), universities must offer greater institutional support to their staff that bring their research into the public domain. Publically engaged sex work research is an important opportunity to support the struggle of a marginalized group, and the consequences of a withdrawal of expert knowledge from this field would leave both academia and society diminished. In order to reduce the negative effects of conducting research on sex work and engaging in the public discourse on this topic, media training as well as supervision and peer support should be provided to researchers in this field (and other similarly emotionally demanding research areas). Furthermore, preparation to engage in public debates and present research findings to the lay population could be (better) integrated into student education.

Last but not least, it is important to point out that it is one of the many roles of academic research to provide alternative views in the face of dominant paradigms and to push beyond the moral, political and social boundaries that (re)produce inequality in our societies. Thus, we may take it as a compliment that our research has stirred up the debate in our attempt to challenge stereotypes and homogenizing and marginalizing policies and discourses that negatively affect the lives of sex workers across the island of Ireland and beyond.

Notes

1 The data on which this chapter is based is the result of both informal conversations about the challenges facing sex work researchers and formal in-depth interviews. Ryan interviewed both Ward and Ellison about their experiences and then together with Huschke combined their more informal conversational interview data about working in Ireland.
2 www.turnofftheredlight.ie/
3 Graham Ellison is a reader in the School of Law in Queen's University Belfast, Paul Ryan lectures in the Department of Sociology in Maynooth University; Eilís Ward lectures in the School of Social and Political Science at the National University of Ireland

Galway and Susann Huschke was a postdoctoral research fellow at the Institute for the Study of Conflict Transformation and Social Justice at Queen's University Belfast for the duration of her study and is now a postdoctoral research fellow at the School of Public Health and the African Centre for Migration and Society, University of the Witwatersrand, Johannesburg, South Africa.

4 One of the authors of the ICI (2009) report Monica O'Connor was also invited to contribute to the chapter but declined.

5 This has changed since after the sex purchase ban was introduced in Northern Ireland. The advocacy group Sex Workers' Alliance Ireland has grown since and increasingly engages in the public debate on prostitution across the island.

References

Agustin, L. 2006. "The Disappearing of the Migrant Category: Migrants Who Sell Sex." *Journal of Ethnic and Migration Studies* 32 (1): 29–47.

Annandale, D. 2005. *Call Me Elizabeth*. London: Times Warner Books.

Braun, V. 1999. "Breaking a Taboo? Talking (and Laughing) About the Vagina". *Feminism and Psychology* 9 (3): 367–372.

Brunckert, C. and C. Parent. 2006. "The In-Call Sex Industry: Classed and Gendered Labour on the Margins." In *Criminalizing Women: Gender and (in) Justice in Neo-Liberal Times*, edited by G. Balfour and E. Cormack, 95–112. Halifax: Fernwood.

Dudley, R. 2006. *Crossing Borders: Preliminary Research on Human Trafficking in Northern Ireland*. Belfast: Women's Aid Federation Northern Ireland.

Ellison, G. 2012. "The Sex Trade in Northern Ireland: The Creation of a Moral Panic". *Social Science Research Network, Working Paper*. https://papers.ssrn.com/sol3/papers.cfm?abstract_id=2184040.

England, P. and G. Farkas. 1986. *Households, Employment and Gender*. Aldine: New York.

Ginsberg, K.N. 1967. "The Meat Rack: A Study of the Male Homosexual Prostitute American." *American Journal of Psychotherapy* 21: 170–185.

Grenz, S. 2014. "The Desire to Talk and Sex/Gender-Related Silences in Interviews With Male Heterosexual Clients of Prostitutes". In *Secrecy and Silence in the Research Process: Feminist Perspectives*, edited by R. Ryan-Flood and R. Gill, 54–66. London: Routledge.

Hammond, N. and S. Kingston. 2014. "Experiencing Stigma as Sex Work Researchers in Professional and Personal Lives." *Sexualities* 17 (3): 329–347.

Hart, A. 1998. *Buying and Selling Power: Anthropological Reflections on Prostitution in Spain* Oxford: Westview Press.

Hubbard, P. 1999. "Researching Female Sex Work: Reflections on Geographical Exclusion, Critical Methodologies and 'useful' Knowledge." *Area* 31 (3): 229–237.

Hubbard, P., Matthews, R. and J. Scoular. 2008. "Regulating Sex Work in the EU: Prostitute Women and the New Spaces of Exclusion." *Gender, Place and Culture* 15 (2): 137–52.

Huschke, S. 2013. *Kranksein in der Illegalität*. Bielefeld: Transcript.

Huschke, S. 2014. "Giving Back: Activist Research With Undocumented Migrants in Berlin". *Medical Anthropology* 34 (1): 54–69.

Huschke, S., Shirlow, P., Schubotz, D., Ward, E., Probst, U. and C. Ní Dhónaill. 2014. *Research into Prostitution in Northern Ireland*. Accessed December 14, 2014. www.dojni.gov.uk/index/publications/publication-categories/pubs-criminal-justice/independent-research-into-prostitution-in-northern-ireland.htm.

Immigrant Council of Ireland. 2009. *Globalisation, Sex Trafficking and Prostitution: The Experiences of Migrant Women in Ireland*. Dublin: Immigrant Council of Ireland.

Irvine, J. 2014. "Is Sexuality Research 'dirty work'? Institutionalized Stigma in the Production of Sexual Knowledge." *Sexualities* 17 (5/6): 632–656.

Israel, T. 2002. "Studying Sexuality: Strategies for Surviving Stigma". *Feminism and Psychology* 12 (2): 256–260.

James, N. 1989. "Emotional Labour: Skill and Work in the Social Regulation of Feelings." *The Sociological Review* 37: 15–37.

Joint Committee on Justice, Defence and Equality (2013), Report. http://www.oireachtas. ie/parliament/oireachtasbusiness/committees_list/about/committee-reports/

Landman, A. and S.A. Glantz. 2009. "Tobacco Industry Efforts to Undermine Policy-Relevant Research." *American Journal of Public Health* 99 (1): 45–58.

Loftus, E.F. 2003. "On Science Under Legal Assault." *Daedalus (Journal of the American Academy of Arts and Sciences)* 132 (4): 84–86.

Maginn, P.J. and G. Ellison. 2014. "Male Sex Workers/Escorts in Ireland: Geography and Regulation". In *Male Sex Work and Society*, edited by V. Minichiello and J. Scott. 426–461. New York: Harrington Park Press.

Maher, L. 2000. *Sexed Work: Gender, Race and Resistance in Brooklyn Drug Market*. Oxford: Oxford University Press.

Martin, B. 1999. "Suppressing Research Data: Methods, Context, Accountability, and Responses". *Accountability in Research* 6: 333–372.

Melrose, M. 2002. "Labour Pains: Some Considerations on the Difficulties of Researching Juvenile Prostitution". *International Journal of Social Research Methodology* 5 (4): 333–351.

Moran, R. 2013. *Paid For: My Journey Through Prostitution*. Dublin: Gill and Macmillan.

Mullerleile, A. 2014. "European Studies and Public Engagement: A Conceptual Toolbox." *Journal of Contemporary European Research* 10 (4): 505–517.

Nutt, D. 2009. "Governments Should Get Real on Drugs". *New Scientist*. Accessed February 26, 2015. www.newscientist.com/article/dn18099-david-nutt-governments-should-get-real-on-drugs.html#.VO9MCvnF-So.

O'Connell Davidson, J. 1998. *Prostitution, Power and Freedom*. London: Routledge.

O'Connell Davidson, J. and D. Layder. 1994. *Methods, Sex and Madness*. London: Routledge.

O'Neill, M. 1996. "Researching Prostitution and Violence: Towards a Feminist Praxis". In *Women, Violence and Male Power*, edited by M. Hester, L. Kelly and J. Radford, 130–147. London: Open University Press.

Reiss, J.R.A. 1961. "The Social Integration of Peers and Queers". *Social Problems* 9 (2): 102–120.

Reynolds, P. 2003. *Sex in the City: The Prostitution Racket in Ireland*. London: Pan Books.

Ryan, P., Whitaker, T. and G. Cox. 2011. "Stigmatization Among Drug-Using Sex Workers Accessing Support Services". *Qualitative Health Research* 21: 1086.

Saunders, T. 2005. "It's Just Acting: Sex Workers Strategies for Capitalizing on Sexuality." *Gender, Work and Organisation* 12 (4). 319–42.

Saunders, T. 2006. "Sexing Up the Subject: Methodological Nuances in Researching the Female Sex Industry." *Sexualities* 9 (4): 449–468.

Scouler, J. and M. O'Neill. 2007. "Regulating Prostitution: Social Inclusion, Responsibilization and the Politics of Prostitution Reform." *The British Journal of Criminology* 47 (5): 764–778.

Sharpe, K. 2000. "Sad, Bad and (Sometimes) Dangerous to Know: Street Corner Research With Prostitutes, Punters and the Police." In *Doing Research on Crime and Justice*, edited by R. King and E. Wincup. 363–372. Oxford: Oxford University Press.

Shaver, F. 2005. "Sex Work Research: Methodological and Ethical Challenges." *Journal of Interpersonal Violence* 20 (3): 296–319.

Sleek, S. 2013. "Inconvenient Truth-Tellers: What Happens When Research Yields Unpopular Findings." *Observer* 26 (9): 24–29.

Smith, N.J. 2012. "Body Issues: The Political Economy of Male Sex Work". *Sexualities* 15 (5/6): 586–603.

Walby, K. 2012. *Touching Encounters: Sex, Work and Male-for Male Internet Escorting*. Chicago; University of Chicago Press.

Ward, E. 2010. "Prostitution and the Irish State: From Prohibitionist to a Global Sex Trade". *Irish Political Studies* 25 (1): 47–65.

Ward, E. and G. Wylie. 2007. *The Nature and Extent of Trafficking of Women Into Ireland for the Purposes of Sexual Exploitation 2000–2006*. Galway: Galway Social Science Research Centre, October, 2007, 1, 48.

Ward, E. and G. Wylie. 2010. "Lap-Dancing Clubs and Right Milieu: A Context for Sex Trafficking of Women to Ireland." In *Human Trafficking in Europe: Character, Causes, Consequences*, edited by G. Wylie and P. Redmond, 108–122. Basingstoke: Palgrave Macmillan.

Ward, E. and G. Wylie. 2014. "Reflexivities of Discomfort: Researching the Sex Trade and Sex Trafficking in Ireland". *European Journal of Women's Studies* 21 (3): 251–263.

15 Medicalized Virilism Under Scrutiny

Expert Knowledge on Male Sexual Health in Italy

Raffaella Ferrero Camoletto and Chiara Bertone

Treatments for male sexual dysfunctions work at transmitting cultural scripts which reinforce normatively gendered expressions of sex focused on a phallocentric coital imperative and on a naturalized notion of male sexual desire, assumed as always present and unproblematic. Drawing on the analysis of documentary material and in-depth interviews with medical experts involved in awareness campaigns on male sexual health this chapter shows how medical discourses, setting male sexual health as a new public issue, construct both the masculinity to be fixed and the new forms of medical expertise legitimized to treat it. By focussing on the plurality of accounts experts give for their clinical experience, the chapter discusses to what extent there is some room for negotiating or challenging over-medicalized frames from within the medical field.

Introduction

The "Viagra phenomenon" is the most visible, and studied, expression of a broader global process of medicalization of male sexuality. Associating male health with self-control and the expression of sexual potency, this process is giving shape to a new public discourse on masculinity, taking the form of a medicalized virilism: legitimized by scientific bases, it restores the foundations of a naturalized notion of man and his sexuality.

Medical discourses have a crucial part in this process, setting male sexual health as a new public issue, and thereby constructing both the masculinity to be fixed and the new forms of medical expertise legitimized to treat it. By analyzing documentary material and interviews with medical experts in Italy, this chapter shows, however, that medical discourses are far from being just a cog in the medicalization machine. Medical discourses work at transmitting cultural scripts which reinforce normatively gendered expressions of sex focused on a phallocentric coital imperative and on a naturalized notion of male sexual desire, assumed as always present and unproblematic. Nevertheless, they also include elements of ambivalence, tension and problematization: an indication that the medicalization process, and the interpretive frames that it implies, are an object of possible redefinition not only by end-users—patients—but also by those actors, experts in the male sexual-health field, who are supposed to be the means of propagating and legitimizing it. By focussing on the plurality of accounts experts give for their clinical experience, we discuss which forms negotiations or challenges of medicalized frames take *from within* the medical field.

Medicalization Through Viagra: a Multidimensional Process

The advent of Viagra in 1998 and, subsequently, of other erectile enhancement medications (EEM)[1] like Cialis, Levitra and—more recently—Spedra, has provided a unique entry point for expanding the understanding of the intersections of health and well being with sexuality, gender and ageing, already explored in different streams of critical studies, dealing with men's health, sexuality and ageing (Gott 2004).

A wide-ranging body of scientific literature has developed, acknowledging the "Viagra phenomenon" as a crucial case of a construction of masculinity through medicalized practices. The so-called Viagra studies have mainly investigated cultural discourses in marketing, media and medical documentary materials (e.g. Baglia 2005; Ferrero Camoletto and Bertone 2012; Johnson and Asberg 2012; Katz and Marshall 2003; Mamo and Fishman 2001;Wienke 2006).

Discourses and consumption practices involving EEM have mostly been interpreted as reinforcing naturalized understandings and experiences of male sexuality, thereby disempowering emerging possibilities of a questioning of such visions of men as "sex machines" (Potts and Tiefer 2006, 270). The social construction of the disease and of the pharmaceutical treatment supports in fact a definition of an adequate masculinity based on the association between men's health and sexual potency (Potts 2000). This understanding redefines male sexual standards, promoting the expectation of a bodily functioning more effective than nature itself and erasing the uncertainty and instability of sexual performance (Marshall and Katz 2002), thereby underpinning expectations of health consumerism. As a tool for "male enhancement", "Viagra, commonly seen as a quality-of-life drug, can also be seen as an identity drug, promising men the opportunity to 'do' masculinity and better perform sexually with the help of the pill" (Loe 2004, 173). Viagra echoes the feature of men as cyborgs, blurring the boundaries between the organic and the synthetic (Potts 2005): via the sexuo-pharmaceuticals embodiment, men are able to enact drug-assisted erections, thereby envisaging a limitless male body reprogrammed to behave better, that is to enact a properly functional sexuality.[2]

Cyborg configurations can disrupt certain boundaries—like nature/culture while protecting and entrenching others—like the gender binary (Balsamo 1996). Therefore, while redefining and reinforcing masculinity, EEM also sustain heteronormative assumptions, influencing the definition of which lifestyles and relational contexts are considered convenient for sexual activity (Mamo and Fishman 2001): a healthy sexuality is seen as functional for the heterosexual couple and thereby for society at large (Marshall and Katz 2002). The impact of EEM in the redefinition of ageing as a pathological process and in promoting the expectations of an active physicality in the life course (Gott 2006) has triggered other directions of enquiry on what Marshall (2008) has described as a post-Viagra 'men's health' industry, expanding the medicalization of masculinity and male sexuality in later life, especially via the construction of the 'male menopause' as an andro-gen deficiency in the aging male.

Besides focussing on reproduction of hegemonic discourses on male sexual-ity and masculinity, these studies have also explored possible resistant and/or alternative ones, in particular among male consumers and their female partners. Research on consumers in fact has often been identified as the crucial step for broadening and problematizing our understanding of the clinical, cultural and social implications of the Viagra revolution (Tiefer 2006), and to open the door to more meaning-making oriented investigation (Tiefer 2008). However, such research has remained limited to a few local instances, covering countries where the possibility of direct-to-consumer advertising of prescription drugs has implied a greater visibility of the marketization of EEM, namely the USA (Loe 2004), New Zealand (Potts et al. 2003, 2006) and Mexico (Wentzell 2013).

These studies have detected how people using Viagra and other EEM exceed and resist the hegemonic discourses accompanying the diffusion of these drugs, displaying a broader range of meanings of sexuality and revealing more flexible and open-to-change masculinities. Interviews with the partners of EEM consum-ers in heterosexual relationships have shown the "downside" (and the dark side) of the Viagra revolution, but they have also challenged the implicit assumption, within Viagra studies themselves, of these drugs as "inherently oppressive" tech-nologies because of their efficacy (restoring erection) being conflated with pen-etrative heterosexual sex.

While providing a multifaceted picture of patients, these critical studies often assign instead to medical experts the role of transmission chains of a top-down process of medicalization. In what is depicted as medical experts' compliance with the engine of pharmaceuticalization, little room seems to be left for their resistance,[3] except for their attempt to contrast the marginalization of their profes-sional role (what was defined as "medical dominance") in the therapeutic process, reducing them to suppliers of the magic bullet.

A closer look into medical experts' experiences and practices reveals instead their active role both in reproducing and questioning the notions of male sexual health and masculinity conveyed by the marketing of EEM. The following discus-sion on medical discourses on EEM in Italy is based upon an analysis of visual and written material produced by the main national awareness campaigns on male sexual health that professional medical associations have promoted or supported in Italy since the advent of Viagra, and upon interviews and a roundtable with medical experts in the field of male sexual health, identified as andrology, who have been involved in these campaigns. In Italy andrology is still a contentious field, disputed by different professional positions (urologists, endocrinologists, sexologists, sex counsellors) (Salis 2013). For the purposes of this chapter, in which homosociality and constructions of masculinity are central issues, we have limited the analysis to male medical experts (five urologists, four endocrinologists, one urologist/sexologist, one specialist in general medicine, one sex counsellor).[4]

Medical Experts Restoring the Male Sex Machine

Viagra and the following EEM have had widespread success in Italy: in 2013 Federfarma described an Italian EEM market of 170 millions of euro. Their diffusion has not been accompanied by advertising aimed at consumers, which in Italy (as in the rest of the European Union) is forbidden for prescription medicines, but by insistent national awareness campaigns on male sexual health, promoted by professional associations of physicians and supported by pharmaceutical companies as well as, often, by public institutions.

In our previous analyses of these campaigns (Ferrero Camoletto and Bertone 2012) we have argued that, while they can be fully inscribed in the current, global construction of a medicalized virilism, they also provide a juxtaposition of a plurality of themes and male sexual scripts (Bertone and Ferrero Camoletto 2009) that carries a potential for tensions and contradictions. The analysis of doctors' interviews offers another fruitful perspective to interpret medical knowledge as an arena of plural and contested discourses claiming for hegemony in the diagnostic and therapeutic field of male sexual health problems. By questioning a simplifying representation of medical experts as the actors endorsing a process of medicalization, and pharmaceuticalization, of male sexual health, we therefore look at pharmaceutical devices as cultural tools used by experts themselves in accounting for their medical practice.

In this section we discuss how, in making sense of their clinical experience with ED, the specialists mostly rely upon the dominant discourses on male sexual health and masculinity embedded in EEM as gendered technologies, thereby contributing to their reproduction.

Medical Experts Handling EEM: Between Diagnostic Expansion and Therapeutic Revolution

All the interviewees, without exception, admit a general increase in ED diagnoses since EEM came onto the market. Rather than to a growth in the epidemiology of the problem, however, they ascribe it to an increased turnout by more self-confident and motivated patients.

EEM are seen as "*useful available tools*" (endocrinologist) and "*an important aid*" (urologist) providing doctors with a powerful magnet to attract Italian men, who are stereotypically depicted as historically and culturally reluctant to seek medical help for sexual matters. EEM are welcomed as "the" previously lacking solution, providing an effective, simple and immediate therapy. Many doctors declare their use of EEM as preliminary tests (the "Viagra test") or as start-therapy, justifying this approach as a considerable saving of time and energy for both doctors and patients: why indeed should one "*go to the trouble of doing a battery of—possibly invasive—tests when one can simply swallow a pill?*" (endocrinologist). "*We do the Viagra test [. . .] and we couldn't care less about doing a pile of diagnostic tests*", another urologist explicitly admits. This diagnostic and therapeutic shortcut is justified in the name of patients' well being and happiness: "*I believe this is right, because we must address first the happiness of a person, so that he can solve the problem without stressing him too much, without upsetting him, indeed we must remove his distress*" (sex counsellor). Goal-oriented diagnostic procedure, however, tends to reify and decontextualize the "pharmaceutical" option as "the" solution, and to reproduce a specific definition of the problem to be solved.

Moreover, EEM reinforce an understanding of having a good erection as a symptom of a more general health condition, likewise any other dysfunctional condition reducing one's well being. Similarly to the normalization, and democratization, of aesthetic surgery, fixing erectile dysfunction becomes a mundane pharmaceutical treatment allowing men just to restore their more broadly defined "optimal conditions".

> Erectile dysfunction can be total, but also partial; it may be that a middle-aged person can have his erection anyway, but that he is not able to maintain it long enough, or that the penis may not be so firm as it should be, so there is a mild dysfunction. So, practically, Viagra can be useful to keep his erection as long as it is needed. It's like when your eyelid drops, you can undertake a rhinoplasty and you restore your optimal conditions. You may ask: 'Why are you doing that? For aesthetic reasons?'. But often, as it has occurred to one guy in the local café, he told me [. . .] he undertook this operation because he could no longer see well, I had never noticed it, I never look at men [smiling].
>
> (sex counsellor)

This account not only seems to endorse a diagnostic expansion, subsuming milder forms of underperformance under the ED definition, but also to make erectile quality an integral part of the contemporary societal requirement to always stay in shape and look after oneself in order to keep up with today's ever-rising standards of functionality (Conrad 2007; Tiefer 1994).

The Old and the Young: Accounting for the Real Patient

Diagnostic expansion is outspokenly supported by medical experts when they portray the two extreme poles of the age range: the oldest patients, often facing a loss of sexual potency, and the youngest ones, who often go through difficulties in managing their sexual and relational inexperience.

As an urologist states, EEM pluralization has allowed to segment the male population into market niches·

> The young man, who doesn't suffer from coronary diseases, can have access to a pharmaceutical lasting till 30 hours; for the old man, who may have coronary problems, it is better if the drug lasts only 4 hours: so sildenafil for the latter and tadalafil for the former. Or if one needs an erection on demand, it's ok the vardenafil, short duration but ready to go.

Ageing men have represented the main expected target for EEM. Many doctors welcome EEM advent as an expansion of therapeutic options meeting ageing men's expectations of a never ending sexual vitality centred upon the capability to perform penetrative sex. Medical experts, significantly with no relevant differences in relation to their specializations, often seem to share, or at least to acknowledge as "normal", elderly men's aspirations to "stay in the game", handling their request with a winking male complicity:

> Taking a step back in the past, the man of a certain age who lived in the family with the idea of getting older, he was content with the old wife as a companion and so on, he smoothly dragged himself towards old age, and. . . boom! There was the shake because he could use this drug giving him the possibility to get back to the game again [laughing].
>
> (urologist)

> The average age is about 40. I also see the old guy who at 80 still wants his part, his sexual performance [smiling]. And that's very. . . they are the nicest.
>
> (endocrinologist)

The youngest patients' demand for a chemical aid, on the contrary, is accounted for as an anxiety-trap problem, due to sexual inexperience and to peer group and broader societal pressures to gain adult masculinity by having penetrative sex. In this case, doctors admit the prevailing psychological dimension of the problem: some of them tend to prescribe EEM as a pharmacological start-therapy at low dosages, a halfway between a supplement and a placebo.

> Performance anxiety is undoubtedly a source of insecurity in one's relations with oneself and with others, which can be, even if only in a banal sense, situational, I mean, if I don't know where to have sex with someone it causes me anxiety because doing it in a car creates anxiety, if I do it at home with my parents who are opposed to the idea, if they catch me at it, it's not an ideal situation, nor is it an ideal situation if I do it in my friend's house because I am not in my own home, I don't have my own world around me giving me serenity. . . in those situations you can use fast-acting anxiolytics plus Viagra or its brothers. . . and at once the situation is under control [. . .] I help him with that, he is aware of desiring a sexual relationship, so he triggers off the mechanism and the erectile system starts up, and so I manage to get a good erection.
>
> (endocrinologist)

In their medical practice, the majority of the specialists interviewed convey a notion of a full masculinity to be acquired by the youngest as well as to be maintained by the oldest through a sexual performance centred upon penetrative skills. In this way, they are underpinning the coital imperative as a testing ground for a masculinity always under scrutiny, whose centrepiece is a firm and lasting erection.

Potency to be Fixed: Reproducing the Coital Imperative

In medical experts' accounts, male patients' notion of sexual functioning is focussed on (or rather reduced to) the symbolic significance of the erect penis, reproducing a highly performative vision of male identity, essentially based upon sustained sexual performance. "*If I have a good erection, it means that I am a strong man*", refers a urologist, adding "*If I can have an erection, why not having a better one, even if mine is already optimal?*". Medical experts remark at the same time that men's phallocentric synecdochical identification (Potts 2000) seems to be so deeply rooted that full control of solid erectile functionality takes form as an essential prerogative, independently of the successful execution of the sexual act:

> We see it in prostatectomies [. . .] Even over-60s. . . male identity as such is associated with erection, so that if these patients lack sexual activity, if they do not have a female partner, the fact that they can no longer have an erection drives them up the walls.
>
> (urologist)

The conflation of erectile potency and masculinity can lead some patients to use EEM as a check-up for evaluating their erectile quality, irrespective of sexual satisfaction itself:

> Men have two options during the erection: to have sex with a totalizing involvement, so that pleasure will be 100%; or, and that's human as well, not to aim at satisfaction but to aim at checking on their erectile functioning, so they take the pill, have sex and watch if it works, if they reach that rigidity, that duration, that kind of ejaculation. That kind of performance where there is no satisfaction or total involvement body and soul with the partner, but there is a check, and this is human, it's normal. [. . .] The aim of the andrologist is to reproduce what the patient requires, a good erection, then the patient will use it as he prefers.
>
> (urologist)

This extreme case is emblematic of how, for men, penetrative potency and sexual performance work at vouching not only for sexual satisfaction, but also for a wider pleasure of doing masculinity (Ferrero Camoletto and Bertone 2010).

In the whole picture provided by medical experts, however, what male desire is remains unquestioned. Medical experts' accounts return a portrait of ED as a matter of an organic-vascular machine in trouble to be repaired: a picture in which desire, interpreted as a biologically determined sexual drive, is taken for granted.

Deconstructing Masculinity: Signs of Counter-Discourses

As we have seen, male sexual health appears as a jurisdictional arena contested by multiple professional skills (urological, endocrinological, sexological) and colonized by dominant pharma-oriented narratives. These tensions open up a space for negotiating and questioning the process of reproduction of dominant discourses we have described above, and for the emergence of alternative or counter-arguments.

Normative Timings: Resisting the "Forever Functional"

Most interviewees state that a large part of their over-65 patients are literally experiencing a "pharma-mediated second youth" through the use of EEM to fight against typical ageing sexual decline. Nowadays, also in the Italian context, "positive ageing" has assumed the features of artificial maintenance of typically youthful physical skills (Maturo 2012), like a kind of sexual vitality "*not any more adequate to biological age*" (urologist). Older men, in fact, seem to be aware of having, thanks to Viagra, "*more possibilities to have, in some way, an acceptable sexual life with their partner*" (urologist), and of being able to employ them to re-open a chapter of their life that was already closed, following what is perceived as an innate male desire "*to never end the game*" (urologist).

The new opportunity for older men to live the myth of a second youth may easily lead to what the doctors have called a "Peter Pan syndrome". EEM work therefore as a support not only for older patients, but also for those adult men who do not in any way accept getting old and losing their capability to live up to the coital imperative standard. As a urologist critically points out:

We are here to try to make people and couples, first of all, feel better [. . .] we are absolutely not available—and I talk on behalf of the majority of my colleagues that work professionally and not just for money—to eroticism, that is, if the patient, as it happens, comes to tell me 'When I was 20–30 my sexual activity was xxx, now that I am 60 it is only double x', I reply 'That's it, thank you', I am not here to make a 60 year old person come back to 20. [. . .] You should always interpret the evolution of Mother Earth, right, and sexuality should be comparable to what should be the right one for each age of life.

Doctors have therefore to face expectations of "*a patient of a certain age who has an adolescent-like relationship [. . .] who in his 60s buys a motorcycle and goes for a passionate weekend with his partner*".

(urologist and sexologist)

The threshold of what is considered dysfunctional is lowered and the sense of inadequacy engendered by those standards is handled through medicalized solutions, from aesthetic surgery to pharmaceutical treatment, in a vicious circle where the use of biomedical devices becomes, more and more, the only possible way to ensure an always-first-class performance:

The point is that these drugs, and the campaigns and media too, make it impossible for the patient to get old any more. [. . .] Therefore it becomes a disease; in the past, without the drug, people came to terms with it [. . .] the age of the patients using these drugs has decreased because sexuality is seen as a performance, like going to the fitness centre [. . .] so men cannot give up therefore they need doping, they need Viagra to maintain these good performances. [. . .] it's the media's fault that today having a long-term relationship with someone you marry and you love is considered out of fashion, look at all those movies asking "What? Are you still together with your wife? Are you still having sex with her?", well, because of this kind of message men must do, must have an affair. Then, if at 50 I base my extramarital relationship only on sex, I will need Viagra, it's inevitable, but this doesn't mean I suffer from ED [. . .] I often have patients who are adolescent till their 50s.

(urologist and sexologist)

The technologically assisted normative standard of an ageless sexual functioning is questioned firstly by claiming for the need to re-orient patients' demand to a more "natural timing": the reference to a "biological age" or to "mother Earth" conveys a process of renaturalization of sexuality in relation to ageing. The "forever functional" standard is also problematized by referring to a "moral timing", by which a never-ending sexual activism is paradoxically depicted as a form of demasculinization: the shade of a "decadent machismo" (as a urologist stated) is evoked by the cultural imagery of the elderly man chasing after young chicks, losing the individual control and social respectability warranted by his marital status.

However, the envisaged alternative of a return to "sexual retirement" fails to question a heteronormative framing of male sexuality as centred upon the capacity to penetrate a female body.

Medical Professions Between Cure and Enhancement

Medical experts are concerned about the expectation of a forever functional sexuality conveying an ideal of a hypermasculinity—always ready, always in control—as a new yardstick men of all ages have to measure against. The expansion of patients' demand for medical help in sexual matter is problematized as a drift to health consumerism which endangers the doctors' power to define the pathology and its treatment.

Pharmaceuticals as effective as EEM risk becoming a two-edged sword which, precisely because of their therapeutic strength, may weaken the diagnostic process, thereby disempowering medical experts. As a urologist states, "*we are not suppliers of pharmaceuticals at all costs*": medical experts react by reaffirming their power to define the "real patient", and thereby the criteria for defining the "legitimacy of the cure".

In their accounts, while setting boundaries based on age (not only "not too old", but also "not too young"), they acknowledge the difficulty to draw the line between legitimate and illegitimate motivations. In fact, the effectiveness of these drugs "independently of the cause" makes it possible to use them in a way which is not strictly therapeutic, aimed only at enhancing and standardizing sexual performance according to an ideal—if not idealized—functionality. A urologist admits the limitations of his diagnostic power in not being able to "*check whether he [the patient], who previously performed 100 times, now does it 50 times, or whether he who now performs 100 times has become possessed and wants to do 120*", recognizing the difficulty of distinguishing between effective deficit and optimization. Moreover, many doctors complain about the spread of a consumer-approach among patients, stimulated by the market availability of a quick-fix technological solution.

> The problem is that today we are facing demands which go beyond the aim of such drugs. . . Sometimes we find requests for treatment and verification which we would define as non-medical because they concern performance, performance increase, playful objectives—these are the request we receive from users—and this poses ethical problems because—perhaps more in this field than in others—we have the problem of objectivising the dysfunction.
> (endocrinologist)

The complexity of defining and managing the boundary between the "real patient" and the playful-recreational use of pharmaceutical treatments, and therefore of establishing the legitimate forms of andrological therapy, potentially opens up to the last level of problematization, which has however a marginal place in medical experts' accounts: the distancing from biological reductionism in the understanding of male sexuality.

Pluralizing Sexual Functioning, Contextualizing Desire

The problematization of the notion of the male sex machine, whose functioning is unaffected by contextual conditions, is more outspoken and articulated by those experts with a sexological training who believe it is necessary to pay attention not only to symptomatic organic evidence, but rather and mainly to the context within which the sexual health problem is located. Focussing on the context promotes a wider and deeper understanding of ED within a diagnostic and therapeutic process that is more complex and comprehensive than simply taking a pill. It takes into account the type of relationship the patient is involved in, the stage in his life course, his reference models and other social factors.

This interdisciplinary management of the medical problem is associated with a more comprehensive notion of erectile function itself, which is not reduced to a mere on/off mechanism, but is acknowledged as "*an ongoing situation, not something that you can say—here today, gone tomorrow—there can be ups and downs, there can be [. . .] degrees*" (endocrinologist).

This leads to questioning an understanding of pleasure as a taken-for-granted by-product of penetrative sex, creating space for a wider definition of what can trigger men's sexual arousal and pleasure. Discussing the last question (measuring the level sexual satisfaction) of the self-assessing questionnaire (IIEF-5) used in the diagnosis of ED problems, a urologist and sexologist admits: "It's an ambiguous question because I can feel pleasure also by touching a woman's breast, without penetrating her".

Some interviewees also point to a more comprehensive understanding of the variety of sexual functions, questioning the notion itself of a decontextualized sexual standard.

> Sexuality is very variable [. . .] there are some normative standards on the average duration of intercourse, then the problem is to make these standards converge with one's own need. But actually there is a large variety: the problem then is not who lasts 3 hours and who lasts 3 minutes, these are only two differences both within normality, that is they are not pathological, but it is a difference that can be stigmatized into a pathology.
>
> (endocrinologist)

Desire itself is acknowledged in its variability against a representation of EEM efficacy assuming an omnipresent and unproblematic drive.

> I always ask, when I meet a couple, does she always get an orgasm. And the answer is usually 'No'. Assuming it as a normal thing. Applying this to the male, when the male loses excitement, the penis flops down. . . but the problem is that if I have an excitement disorder because I have a sexual aversion towards the woman at my side, [the standard ED diagnostic tool] transforms it into an erection-problem [. . .]
>
> (urologist and sexologist)

Not only patients, but doctors themselves are criticized for reifying the organic symptom of ED and conflating it with the cause of the problem, overlooking other dimensions which are made invisible: it is the risk "*to send a boy who is not hungry to the dentist. The dentist cannot fix the problem*" (urologist and sexologist).

Nevertheless, discourses on the lack of desire remain framed in therapeutic terms as an abnormal condition: whatever the cause (organic, psychological, relational), desire must be restored. This understanding have double-edged implications for the medicalization of male sexuality: while some interviewees point to a variability of desire depending on contextual and relational conditions which can be actively changed, others envisage new frontiers of medicalization targeting male desire itself as a matter of hormonal level.

Conclusion

The therapeutic and cultural revolution engendered by EEM has promoted the emergence of a socially available public discourse on male sexual inadequacies, providing a physical-organic definition (ED), a reassuring medical solution (Viagra and the like) and a legitimate medical expertise (in Italy, the andrological field).

At a closer look, this seemingly linear representation of an exemplary top-down process of medicalization, via pharmaceuticalization, constructing a new form of medicalized virilism, reveals tensions and contradictions, opening up space for alternative understandings of sexual health and masculinity. Forms of resistance and counter-discourses have been detected in research on patients/consumers and their partners, as opposed to the other actors of the process, assuming a complicity between pharmaceutical companies and medical experts. In this chapter, we have interpreted doctors' clinical experience with ED as forms of cultural use of EEM, where we see coexisting elements of reproduction and questioning of the dominant meanings attached to EEM.

Medical experts' accounts mainly draw upon, and thereby sustain, idealized sexual standards of readiness, rigidness and endurance as a testing ground for an ageless masculinity. These standards, however, prove to be controversial, triggering forms of reflexivity that pluralize the understandings of the problem to be addressed, the treatment to be prescribed and the role of medical experts.

Through the lens of a discussion on the age-relatedness of male sexual functioning, we see a problematization of the ideal of a forever sexually functional man as the enactment of an always-ready and always-in-control hyper-masculinity.

Some doctors in fact take distance from a notion of EEM as more natural than nature itself, envisaging risks of misuse and abuse: they wonder which are the boundaries between a real patient, asking for a cure of his male dysfunction, and a consumerist patient demanding a support for enhancing the quality of his performances. In this quest for an optimization of sexual functioning, they see an illegitimate attempt to overcome its "natural" limits embodied in a respectable masculinity. Through the notion of those limits, the idea of control as a core dimension of masculinity takes a different meaning: rather than control over an always-successful sexual performance, it refers to men's capacity of self-containment in accepting the social and natural limits of their sexuality.

By addressing consumerist attitudes towards sexual health, critical accounts reclaim medical professional dominance in defining what healthy sexual standards are and how they can be achieved. Rather than pluralizing the notion of sexuality, these counter-discourses reinforce normative assumptions on the legitimate times and spaces for appropriate male sexuality. the meaningfulness of sex is grounded not so much on performance, but on its relational and affective dimensions, that is on the primacy of coupledom.

A few medical experts acknowledge the contextual variability of sexual functioning, and of sexual desire itself. However, these situational accounts of lacking arousal do not question an understanding of desire as a constitutive pillar of masculinity: the desiring man, epitomized and embodied by the erect penis, remains the core dimension of male subjectivity. What seems written out is instead the very possibility of redefining the legitimate expressions of male sexuality towards a radical remapping of the male erotic body.

Notes

1 This definition is proposed by Pantalone et al. 2008.
2 Potts discusses the Viagra case under the guise of a wider literature of cyborg, pointing at the cyborg male body as a site for connecting restorative, normalizing and enhancing technological uses and purposes.

3 The "Challenging the Medicalization of Sex" campaign (www.newviewcampaign.org/) in the USA is one of the few attempt of mobilizing a resistance involving medical experts.
4 The interviews have partly been carried out by Francesca Salis. For an analysis of the construction of the andrological field through the awareness campaigns on male sexual health, see Salis 2013.

References

Baglia, J. 2005. *The Viagra AdVenture: Masculinity, Media and the Performance of Sexual Health*. New York: Peter Lang.

Balsamo, A. 1996. "Technological Embodiment: Reading the Body in Contemporary Culture". In *Cyberspace/Cyberbodies/Cyberpunk: Cultures of Technological Embodiment*, edited by Featherstone, Mike, and Burrows, Roger, 43: 215–238. London: Sage.

Bertone, C. and Raffaella Ferrero Camoletto. 2009. "Beyond the Sex Machine? Sexual Practices and Masculinity in Adult Men's Heterosexual Accounts." *Journal of Gender Studies* 18 (4): 369–386.

Conrad, P. 2007. *The Medicalization of Society: On the Transformation of Human Conditions Into Treatable Disorders*. Baltimore: The Johns Hopkins University Press.

Ferrero Camoletto, R. and C. Bertone. 2010. "Coming as a Man: Pleasure in the Construction of Italian Men's Sexuality." *Italian Studies* 2: 235–250.

Ferrero Camoletto, R. and C. Bertone. 2012. "Italians (Should) Do It Better? Medicalisation and the Disempowering of Intimacy." *Modern Italy* 17 (4): 433–448.

Gott, M. 2004. *Sexuality, Sexual Health and Ageing*. Buckingham: Open University Press.

Gott, M. 2006. "Sexual Health and the New Ageing." *Age and Ageing* 35 (2): 106–7.

Johnson, E. and C. Åsberg. 2012. "Enrolling Men, Their Doctors, and Partners: Individual and Collective Responses to Erectile Dysfunction." *Science and Technology Studies* 25 (2): 46–60.

Katz, S. and B. Marshall. 2003. "New Sex for Old: Lifestyle, Consumerism and the Ethics of Aging Well." *Journal of Aging Studies* 17: 3–16.

Loe, M. 2004. *The Rise of Viagra: How the Little Blue Pill Changed Sex in America*. New York: New York University Press.

Mamo, L. and J. Fishman. 2001. "Potency in All the Right Places: Viagra as a Technology of the Gendered Body." *Body and Society* 7 (4): 13–35.

Marshall, B. 2008. "Older Men and Sexual Health: Post-Viagra Views of Changes in Function." *Generations* 32 (1): 21–27.

Marshall, B. and S. Katz. 2002. "Forever Functional: Sexual Fitness and the Ageing Male Body." *Body and Society* 8 (4): 43–70.

Maturo, A. 2012. *La società bionica*. Milano: Franco Angeli.

Pantalone, D.W., Bimbi, D.S. and J.T. Parsons. 2008. "Motivations for the Recreational Use of Erectile Enhancing Medications in Urban Gay and Bisexual Men". *Sexually Transmitted Infections* 84 (6): 458–62.

Potts, A. 2000. "The Essence of the Hard On: Hegemonic Masculinity and the Cultural Construction of 'Erectile Dysfunction'". *Men and Masculinities* 3 (1): 63–103.

Potts, A. 2005. "Cyborg Masculinity in the Viagra Era". *Sexualities, Evolution and Gender* 7 (1): 3–16.

Potts, A., Gavey, N., Grace, V. and T. Vares. 2003. "The Downside of Viagra: Women's Experiences and Concerns." *Sociology of Health and Illness* 25 (7): 697–719.

Potts, A., Grace, V., Vares, T. and N. Gavey. 2006. " 'Sex for Life'? Men's Counter-Stories on 'erectile dysfunction', Male Sexuality and Ageing". *Sociology of Health and Illness* 28 (3): 306–329.

Potts, A. and L. Tiefer. 2006. "Introduction." *Sexualities* 9 (3): 267–272.

Salis, F. 2013. *Medicalizzare la società: il ruolo dei saperi esperti nella costruzione sociale dell'impotenza.* Torino, Italy: Tesi di Laurea Magistrale in Sociologia, Università degli Studi di Torino.

Tiefer, L. 1994. "The Medicalization of Impotence: Normalizing Phallocentrism." *Gender and Society* 8 (3): 363–377.

Tiefer, L. 2006. "The Viagra Phenomenon." *Sexualities* 9 (3): 273–94.

Tiefer, L. 2008. "Prognosis: More Pharmasex." *Sexualities* 11 (1–2): 53.

Wentzell, E. 2013. *Maturing Masculinities: Ageing, Chronic Illness and Viagra in Mexico.* Durham and London: Duke University Press.

Wienke, C. 2006. "Sex the Natural Way: The Marketing of Cialis and Levitra." In *Medicalized Masculinities*, edited by D. Rosenfeld and C.A. Fairlcloth, 45–64. Philadelphia: Temple University Press.

16 Challenging the Use of Heteronormative Categories in Childlessness Studies

Gerardo Zamora

Most research on childless individuals has focused on the factors that "cause" childlessness, its apparent consequences on health and wellbeing, and its risk of social isolation in old age. This generalised perspective exudes a strong heteronormative assumption linking sexuality and reproduction and confirms that childless individuals confront, too, the stigma of leading a life that does not comply with the standard script of expected parenthood and grand-parenthood. The chapter discusses whether childlessness can be an identity and if so, how it is linked to sexuality. It considers how one "becomes" childless and the extent that LGB and childless individuals face common discriminations and challenges.

Introduction

Becoming a parent is considered to be one of the key markers of adulthood (Benson and Furstenberg Jr. 2006), indeed the paramount confirmation of adulthood itself (Aronson 2008) and also a social confirmation of good (procreative) citizenship (Roseneil et al. 2013). Parenthood is a key organiser of social relations and the life course (Dykstra and Hagestad 2007a) and those '*failing*' to become parents, or even discarding parenthood, usually undergo various types of stigmatisation, unless they have a socially accepted waiver (e.g., celibacy in certain religions). Providing explanations for why one decides not to become a parent or why one does not have children are commonly experienced by those adults and older adults who are not parents (Dykstra and Hagestad 2007b; Rijken and Merz 2014). The 'childless' are often represented as 'The Other' and are subject to all sort of representations and stereotyping (Dever and Saugeres 2004; Giles, Shaw, and Morgan 2009; Graham and Rich 2014; Peterson 2014). Despite growing social acceptance of non-parenting adulthood and old age (Koropeckyj-Cox and Pendell 2007; Tanturri and Mencarini 2008), at different points in their lives, those who are not parents are frequently the target of searching questions about their sexualities (Lampman and Dowling-Guyer 1995; Park 2005; McDavitt et al. 2008; Warren 2010).

In sociology, demography and other social sciences, those adults of so-called reproductive age who are not parents are called 'child*less*', whilst those who are parents are called 'child*ed*', although the latter term is less frequently used. These categories are also employed for the study of aging and old age (Silverstein and Giarrusso 2010). The study of childlessness has received much attention within sociology and demography, especially in recent decades, as important population transformations occur, such as demographic aging in low fertility societies (Dannefer and Phillipson 2010; Uhlenberg 2009) alongside other changes in social behaviors affecting population dynamics such as fertility, marriage, cohabitation or reproduction. Furthermore, childlessness, as a concept, has been critiqued for its narrow focus on women (dichotomously referred to as 'mothers' and 'non-mothers' or childless women), which has led to the construction of new concepts such as 'childfree by choice', 'childfree lives' or 'childfreedom' in order to challenge the implicit message of failure to comply with normative behavior that is imbued in the concepts childless and childlessness (Agrillo and Nelini 2008; Basten 2009; Moore 2014).

Parenthood has been socially—and sometimes legally—considered as reserved for heterosexual individuals and couples. Yet, many lesbian, gay, bisexual, transgender or queer (LGBTQ)[1] people become parents. Some LGBTQ individuals have children within previous heterosexual relationships at certain points in their lives and others have had children within their non-heterosexual relationships, through for example, surrogacy, in vitro fertilization (IVF), adoption or partnering with someone who is already a parent. Social stigmatisation and legal restrictions have not prevented LGBTQ individuals from becoming parents and building their own families (Dewaele et al. 2011; Galán-Pichardo 2009); nonetheless, others have been faced with significant barriers to becoming parents (Hicks 2011; Silin 2014). Although LGBTQ people have resisted, subverted and countered the social expectation of not becoming parents, the social and legal recognition of parenthood outside the heterosexual couple is still very recent.

Childless individuals have been the object of sociological inquiry mainly in terms of comparison with childed individuals (Blackstone 2014), rather than being themselves worthy objects for research (Kendig et al. 2007). The study of childlessness amongst LGBTQ people and their families have been indirectly researched within the sociology of families because of research on LGBTQ kinship and 'families of choice', in addition to the study of LGBTQ aging and care relationships in later life (Cronin and King 2014; Dewaele et al. 2011; Fredriksen-Goldsen and Muraco 2010; Fredriksen-Goldsen et al. 2014; Gabb 2005). Some studies have also directly addressed the issue of childlessness and parenting amongst non-heterosexual individuals (Berkowitz 2007; Patterson and Riskind 2010; Riskind and Patterson 2010). Research on men and childlessness is still limited and even scarcer in non-heterosexual men. Research on childlessness in heterosexual individuals has been carried out mainly by demography and the sociology of population to understand its apparent 'causes and consequences' on health, well-being and social support (Huijts, Kraaykamp and Subramanian 2013; Jeffries and Konnert 2002; Keizer, Dykstra and Poortman 2010) and also to examine its impact on demographic dynamics (Mencarini and Tanturri 2007; Mills et al. 2011; te Velde et al. 2012). Yet, research is still scant with respect to the relationship between childlessness and sexualities, or to assess if childlessness studies are also heteronormative.[2]

This chapter will contribute to filling this gap. The following section outlines three, basic, key categories in childlessness studies (i.e., voluntary, involuntary, temporary) and how they are based on women's (normative) fertility. The next section then proposes a critique of these categories and suggests that they are not completely suitable to understand LGBTQ childlessness. New and complementary categories to approach LGBTQ childlessness are then put forward for discussion. Finally, the concluding section briefly examines the alternative concept of 'childfree by choice' and the questionable freedom of choice LGBTQ people experience with respect to decisions about parenthood; it also posits that the examination of the social worlds of childless non-heterosexual men can enhance the breath and scope of sexualities research. To build these arguments, I use research data from Spain coming from different sources (e.g., my own research,[3] population data and legislation).

Setting the Scene: Childlessness and Sexualities

Research on childlessness has been growing since the 1950s, despite the apocalyptic prediction by some demographers that voluntary childlessness would become extinct or was almost extinct at that time after surveying a sample of "*wives in the reproductive ages*" in the United States (Whelpton, Campbell and Patterson 1966). In fact, empirical studies suggest that childlessness is increasing (Silverstein and Giarrusso 2010; Tanturri and Mencarini 2008) and that a greater share of adults born after 1950 are childless older persons. This can be seen in Table 16.1, which shows data only for women because research on childlessness has overwhelmingly focused on women. As Table 16.1 shows the proportion of childless women varies greatly across Europe. Estimates suggest that 27% of women born in 1960 in West Germany did not have any children when they were 52 years old (in 2002), almost four times the proportion of women born in the same year in Portugal. Data on *childless* men collected at national level across all European

Table 16.1 Proportion of *Childless* Women Born in 1960 Surveyed in 2002 (selected European countries and the United States)

West Germany	27.8	Belgium	13.7
United Kingdom	21.5	Denmark	12.0
Finland	18.0	Spain	11.0
Netherlands	17.7	Norway	10.8
United States*	15.6	France	10.7
Ireland	15.1	East Germany	7.9
Italy	14.7	Iceland	7.3
Sweden	13.8	Portugal	7.2

*as of 2005

Adapted from Tanturri and Mencarini (2008) except data from the United States (Kirmeyer and Hamilton 2011).

countries is far less common, frequent or accessible. Sociologists and other scientists have been interested in this issue (Dykstra and Keizer 2009; Magarick and Brown 1981), but the absence of national representative data hinders studies on male childlessness with the same depth, scope and historical extension as those focusing on women's childlessness (e.g., through the use of fertility statistics).

Although challenged by theorists and activists, the assumption that raising children is the foremost marker and aim of adulthood prevails in Western societies, where, ironically, the percentage of adults who are not parents as a permanent state is growing; as is the personal preference to be a childless adult (the desire not to have any children). The proportion of women and men aged 18–40 who do not *intend* to have children, i.e., to be childless adults, also varies greatly across Europe (see Table 16.2 below) and is expected to keep growing. Table 16.2 shows the difference between women and men who do not intend to be parents. In a few countries more women than men aged 18–40 years of age do not intend to have children (e.g. Cyprus, Greece and Belgium). In others, almost as many women as men do not intend to be parents (e.g. Germany, Hungary, Switzerland or Denmark). And quite interestingly, in quite a few countries the proportion of men aged 18–40 years of age who intend to be childless is certainly greater that the proportion of women (e.g. Finland, Romania, Luxembourg, Italy, Sweden, Spain or the Netherlands).

Traditionally, studies on the topic classify three types of childlessness: voluntary, involuntary and temporary. These categories are based on women's fertility

Table 16.2 Proportion of Women and Men Aged 18–40 Who *Intend to be Childless* Adults in the Eurobarometer 2011 (selected European countries) (n = 4373)

Country	Women (mean = 5.2)*	Men (mean = 7.0)*	Difference (Women-Men)
Cyprus	6.0	2.9	3.1
Greece	8.5	5.7	2.8
Belgium	11.7	9.8	1.9
UK	10.0	9.8	0.2
Germany-W	8.6	8.5	0.1
Hungary	5.6	5.9	−0.3
Switzerland	14.6	15.0	−0.4
Denmark	5.5	6.1	−0.6
Germany (total)	9.2	10.0	−0.8
Finland	5.3	7.0	−1.7
Romania	4.8	7.3	−2.5
Luxembourg	12.9	16.3	−3.4
Germany-E	11.2	15.1	−3.9
Austria	9.2	13.4	−4.2
Italy	4.2	9.3	−5.1
Sweden	5.2	11.2	6.0
Spain	4.0	10.7	−6.7
Netherlands	10.2	19.1	8.9

*The mean for 27 European Union countries (except Croatia), and it does not include Switzerland either. Adapted from Miettinen and Szalma (2014)

behavior and are premised on two basic assumptions: first, at some point during their lives women decide whether to become a mother or not; and second, once this decision is made, those women who decide to become mothers actually enter motherhood and others do not. Hence, *voluntary childlessness* refers to the decision not to become a parent (mother), be it biologically or through adoption, and then '*remain childless*', as it has been customarily phrased (González and Jurado-Guerrero 2006; Heaton, Jacobson, and Holland 1999; Silka and Kiesler 1977). *Involuntary childlessness* indicates the condition in which biological factors, i.e. infertility or fertility problems, impede reproduction, or the condition of fertile women who postpone motherhood for so long that they end up having no children, albeit involuntarily. *Temporary childlessness* refers to the state in which the aspiration to become a parent (mother) is present, but there is still time to postpone parenthood (motherhood); or when such postponement is due to temporary fertility problems or other social barriers preventing parenthood (e.g., delay of marriage, early divorce, employment, studies, housing).

Some researchers have critiqued these categories and their underlying rationale for several reasons: because the difference between *voluntary* and *involuntary* childlessness is sometimes vague or imprecise (Rowland 1988); because the increasing availability of infertility treatments blurs these differences (Miettinen and Szalma 2014); or because the explanations derived from using these categories are inadequate for the study of (heterosexual) childless men (Waren and Pals 2013). Furthermore, I contend that these categories are not completely suitable for the study of childlessness amongst LGBTQ people because their life circumstances, characteristics and opportunities are very much unique when compared to their heterosexual and/or cisgendered counterparts. In fact, many LGBTQ persons have moved from a status of individual pathology to individual and group identities (Herdt and de Vries 2004); they have faced social, political and legal barriers to enjoy full citizenship rights; they have been criminalised, medicalised and ostracised because heterosexuality and cisgender[4] have been as a prerequisite to citizenship (Brandzel 2005) and despite their resilience and social support, if available, they have often suffered from cumulative homophobia, biphobia and/or transphobia and discrimination across their lives. The risk of denied citizenship extends not only to LGBTQ persons but also to "those who do not marry and have children, [and] lesbians and gay men who did not marry heterosexually and bear children [have been] the most obvious and vulnerable" (Herdt and de Vries 2004, xvii). For an LGBTQ person becoming a parent has been and still is a form of social contestation and resistance to heteronormativity. Therefore using the traditional approach of childlessness studies (why the status of childlessness occurs—focusing on women—and whether it is a choice) to research childlessness amongst LGBTQ people may not be appropriate. First, it overlooks the fact that childlessness amongst LGBTQ persons is a form of compliance with the heteronormative policy of heterosexual and/or cisgendered family formation. Second, it assumes that LGBTQ persons enjoy the same rights to family recognition as do heterosexual and/or cisgendered individuals. Third, in line with their restricted citizenship, it neglects the differences and specific difficulties in implementing the decision to become a parent amongst non-heterosexual and/or transgender couples or individuals.

Each of the three traditional categories used in childlessness studies are heteronormative and require a critique that further expands their scope before they can be used to research LGBTQ childlessness and the unique and differentiated experiences of childlessness amongst LGBTQ people. As a first approach to build and support the critique for each of the three categories, I use qualitative data from a small sample of gay men in Spain and data coming from other sources (e.g., legal documents, statistics, and surveys). Although the critique draws only from the analysis of the gay men in my sample, I argue that it is, however, a pertinent first step for putting together a general critique of childless categories in LGBTQ-related research that looks into the wide spectrum of significant differences of childlessness in non-heterosexual and transgender individuals.

Critiquing the Categories Used in Childlessness Studies

Voluntary Childlessness: When Choosing Is Not a Choice

Ironically, apparently very private and personal decisions, such as choosing to become a parent or not, are indeed not entirely private and personal. Voluntary childlessness is widely understood as something that is reflected upon deeply, because it is a decision that will denaturalise what has been socially naturalised: heteronormative reproduction. If this is a question of choice, how do a lesbian woman, a gay man, gay and lesbian couples 'choose' not to become parents? Are they at all in a position to choose parenthood or not in the same form as their heterosexual counterparts? Are they at all able to choose? This is even more complex if we examine inequities in access to parenthood via assisted reproduction amongst LGBTQ individuals or couples and analyse how choice operates in these circumstances.

In the case of gay men, I argue that they do not reject parenthood and become voluntary childless individuals or couples. In fact this decision has been already made, it has been 'socially' decided in compliance with heteronormative expectations about who is allowed to and who is denied parenthood. Gay men do not 'remain childless' as has been traditionally phrased in the childlessness literature; they are already 'socially' childless. If voluntary childlessness is usually seen through the lens of choice, then there is no possible choice within heteronormative reproduction. Conversely, it is the decision to become a parent that really challenges heteronormative expectations of childlessness in non-heterosexual men. Being gay and being childless is still assumed to be conjoined conditions in many social discourses. As one of my informants said:

> I think that in the future there will be more people like us—people without children.
>
> (50, partnered)

The traditional category 'voluntary childlessness' is problematic for gay men. The focus of this category is on the intentional and deliberate choice to not comply with the normative expectation of becoming a parent. Yet, for the case of gay men this is inadequate because it is already socially proscribed. If any decision is to be examined it is the intentional and deliberate choice to become a parent, not otherwise. Therefore, 'voluntarily child*ed"* could be a more appropriate category to capture the confrontation and resistance to heteronormative childlessness in non-heterosexual men. Not all gay men who wish to be "voluntarily child*ed*" become parents, though. The category 'voluntarily childed' can enrich childlessness studies in that it expands the scope of this field of inquiry by including the standpoint of those who were childless without a choice and highlights connections between sexuality and childlessness, an overlooked topic in most childlessness studies. Yet, the other traditional category 'involuntary childlessness' is not fully suitable either as will be discussed in greater detail in the following section.

Involuntary Childlessness: Personal Aspirations Versus Social Expectations

As stated previously, most gay men are not voluntarily childless because social expectations already construct them as childless. The pervasiveness of heteronormative reproduction indicates that non-heterosexual men should be excluded from parenthood and this is clearly understood also by gay men themselves. The following excerpt from another one of my informants illustrates this understanding:

> We [him and his partner] have discussed what it would be like if we had children. We don't want that now. When I was young I felt the need [to be a parent], but now I am happy the way I am. My family stopped asking questions [about becoming a parent] when I was 35 and I introduced [my partner] to them, they stopped and didn't ask any more questions. . . [laughs].
>
> (55, partnered)

The rationale operating behind 'involuntary childlessness' is the assumption that there are either physiological reasons (infertility) or other barriers (e.g. lack of housing, employment, sufficient income, suitable partner, student status) contributing to a delay in the decision to become a parent. This category is problematic for many gay men. They could be physiologically able to reproduce (fertile), willing to become parents, whether they are a single person or in a couple, and not facing any of the barriers usually found in involuntary childlessness; however, they would still face the force of heteronormative childlessness; i.e., the socially expected and accepted condition of childlessness in non-heterosexual men. For example, de Vries and Blando (2004, 5) write:

> Herein lies an interesting difference between the prospective and new parental experience of heterosexual adults and lesbians/gay men: in the case of the former, upon hearing of the pregnancy, congratulations are typically expressed by both family and friends; in the case of the latter, upon hearing of the pregnancy (or adoption), queries about the reasons for such actions are typically posed by both family and friends.

Non-heterosexual men are usually unable to enter parenthood if other mechanisms besides heterosexual intercourse are not put in place to effectively make parenthood feasible. Sometimes, however, these mechanisms are legally forbidden or provided only to women in heterosexual couples.[5] The traditional category 'involuntary childlessness' does not capture this complexity when it comes to non-heterosexual men. "Socially childless" is, therefore, suggested as a category to capture such difference.

Temporary Childlessness: Not Just a Question of Time

The reasoning behind 'temporary childlessness' is the assumption that adults (traditionally, women) postpone parenthood (motherhood) for different reasons: because they are too young, they are not married, they are focusing on their careers, they have temporary fertility problems or because they face other barriers (e.g., affordable housing, unemployment). The literature on childlessness is rich and robust on temporary childlessness and delayed parenthood. Yet, this reasoning implies that the social aspiration to become a parent is not questioned; it is only postponed. The normative expectation about becoming a parent (mother) is not contested or challenged. Although this may be so for many heterosexual individuals and couples, it might not work in the same way for gay men: one cannot postpone what in the first place was never expected, or wanted and yearned for (due to being socially childless). Assuming that gay men or gay couples are *postponing* childbearing does not acknowledge that they do not begin at the same starting point and baseline conditions to bear children as heterosexual persons or couples. Not only is any aspiration from gay men or gay couples to become parents problematic with respect to logistics, legal terms and finance, it also challenges the naturalisation of heteronormative reproduction. Likewise, lesbians who wish to be mothers usually go through a reflexive process of decision making (Goldberg 2006; Hayman et al. 2013), including contesting social norms, family expectations and other barriers to lesbian motherhood. This is because they are actually challenging the assumption that *they are not postponers: they are lesbians!* They are expected to be childless (Barker 2004) and consequently they should not postpone. Similarly, non-heterosexual men might be subject to comparable social expectations, especially if they want to be single parents (Brinamen and Mitchell 2008; Schacher, Auerbach, and Silverstein 2005). The pervasiveness of heteronormativity is discernable in the enduring perception of 'lesbian' and 'mother' or 'gay' and 'father' as oppositional categories in many legal systems and social worlds, let alone transgender or bisexual people who are not regarded as parents either. Meanwhile, the pervasiveness of heteronormativity is also visible in the presumably timeless perception of older adults as grand-parents, i.e., as individuals who did reproduce, had children and whose off-spring are, obviously, also child*ed*. Decoupling the social identities of older persons (age) and grand-parents (social role) is almost socially impracticable in certain settings, such as social and health policy, healthcare or the media. Therefore, using the category 'temporary childlessness' for non-heterosexual men neglects the fact that they face several barriers to actually becoming parents and that they are not postponing, but actually dealing with socially constructed hurdles.

Some of the gay men I interviewed reflected upon the normative social forces that expect them to be childless and then decided to remain childless adults. As one of my informants explained:

> They [his aunts] are two very normal persons. They got married and didn't have any children. They never had children and, nonetheless, they've had a very normal life. And then I think of them [. . .] and me.
>
> (61, single)

The category 'reflexive childlessness' may be more suitable to catch the intricate and complex process of reflection and decision-making that some non-heterosexual men go through in order to be and live as non-parents. Rather than accepting what is socially expected (to be childless), they may go through a process of awareness of how heteronormative childlessness operates. 'Reflexive childlessness' captures the process of awareness of heteronormative childlessness by non-heterosexual men and/or trans women. It does not point out how heteronormative childlessness is contested (i.e., socially childed) or operates (i.e., socially childed), but rather it seeks to highlight the reflexive process of those who are aware of the social expectations of non-parenthood bestowed upon them.

Conclusion

The critique of the three traditional categories used in childlessness studies draws on both existing literature and the emerging themes in the interviews I conducted

Table 16.3 Suggested Complementary Categories to Approach LGBTQ Childlessness

Socially childless	Voluntary childed	Reflexive childlessness
Unlike heterosexual persons and couples, non-heterosexual men are expected to be childless in order to comply with heteronormative reproduction; they are socially constructed as childless. It is not their choice or decision to '*remain*' childless, but it is rather the heteronormative social forces driving sexual and gender relations across society that mandates they should be childless (heteronormative childlessness).	Non-heterosexual men are expected to be childless in order to comply with heteronormative reproduction; therefore, their aspiration and choice to become parents challenges the heteronormative order. The connotations of 'voluntary' with respect to childlessness should denote therefore the will to subvert this heteronormative order. The study of voluntary child*ed* individuals can inform, too, the breadth of childlessness studies.	Non-heterosexual men are expected to be childless in order to comply with heteronormative reproduction. A reflexive and meditated decision to stay childless implies understanding the social forces of heteronormative childlessness. Childless gay men sometimes sabotage their expected state of "socially childless" and embrace it as a meditated trajectory.

with a sample of gay men. Further refinement and theoretical discussion is certainly needed to extend this proposal. Table 16.3 (below) summarises the key components of the suggested three categories.

Some authors have suggested other categories to approach childlessness such as *childfree by choice, childfree lives* or *childfreedom'* (Agrillo and Nelini 2008; Basten 2009; Moore 2014). Although useful to challenge the traditional categories used in childlessness studies and widely used to precisely denote the pervasiveness of heteronormative reproduction, these categories may fail to apprehend and capture the unique complexity of LGBTQ childlessness, especially because of the centrality of "choice" in their rationale. In the case of non-heterosexual men, choice is not always an option. Research is expanding on the 'childfree by choice' population, especially amongst women; yet, most of these women are heterosexual and cisgender, who choose not to become mothers, rather than non-heterosexual and trans women reflexively adopting childlessness (instead of just complying with heteronormative childlessness). Other researchers (Taylor 2003) argue that the category 'childfree by choice' and the rhetoric of 'choice' avoids more profound discussions about the place of parenthood, motherhood and fatherhood in society.

Research on childlessness needs to be further explored, including more research to build suitable categories to approach LGBTQ childlessness that can be used with traditional categories. Three categories have been suggested in this chapter to examine childlessness amongst gay men: socially childless, voluntary childed and reflexive childlessness, which may also contribute to research on and understanding of the experiences of childlessness amongst LGBTQ people. Ultimately, queering demography and childlessness studies can also contribute to strengthen and expand the breadth and depth of sexualities research more broadly.

Acknowledgements

I am deeply grateful to the editors of this book, especially Andrew King, for their detailed and constructive reviews of the various versions of this chapter.

Notes

1 The choice to use the identity-based categories lesbian, gay, bisexual, transgender or queer (LGBTQ) does not neglect that diversity in sexual identities expands beyond them. Asexual, intersex, questioning or unsure are other identity-based categories and all of them try to reflect the '*diversity of social identities of those who stand outside of the heteronormative sexual order*', although it is difficult to fully transmit the complexity of intersecting social identities (Cronin and King 2010: 876).
2 Heteronormativity is the production and reproduction of heterosexuality as the natural normal, taken-for-granted sexuality. It assumes that individuals, families, organizations and institutions celebrate heterosexuality and are organized to reproduce it.
3 A sample of nine self-identified gay men (aged 50–65; eight childless, one parent) was constructed as part of my final dissertation "*Care expectations in old age and health behaviours in non-normative ageing [Expectativas de cuidado en la vejez y comportamientos de salud en procesos de envejecimiento no normativos]*" for the Master of Science in Health Research, Universidad Pública de Navarra in 2011. Along with other type of

data (e.g. laws, national statistics and surveys), these nine interviews were also used in my thesis for Doctorate in Public Health, which is due for public defense in 2015.

4 Cisgender is a concept used to express the alignment between the sex assigned at birth and the identities, experiences and gender expectations corresponding that. It is a complement to the transgender concept.

5 Heteronormative childlessness in LGBTQ persons has been exemplified by the recent decision of the Government of Spain to modify the current law on publicly funded assisted reproduction in order to make this service only accessible to under 40-year-old, childless, heterosexually married or coupled women suffering from medically diagnosed infertility after 12 months of 'unsuccessful' vaginal sexual intercourse. Despite intense contestation from human rights, women's and LGBTQ groups, the Minister of Health explained that 'the lack of a man is not a medical problem' as a reason to limit this publicly funded service, which is now more inaccessible to lesbians and/or single women. The superseded law granted this service to all women, irrespective of their marital status and sexual orientation.

References

Agrillo, C. and C. Nelini. 2008. "Childfree by Choice: A Review." *Journal of Cultural Geography* 25 (3): 347–63.

Aronson, P. 2008. "The Markers and Meanings of Growing Up: Contemporary Young Women's Transition from Adolescence to Adulthood." *Gender and Society : Official Publication of Sociologists for Women in Society* 22: 56–82.

Barker, J.C. 2004. "Lesbian Aging: An Agenda for Social Research." In *Gay and Lesbian Aging: Research and Future Directions*, edited by Gilbert H. Herdt and Brian de Vries, 29–72. New York: Springer Publishing Company.

Basten, S. 2009. *Voluntary Childlessness and Being Childfree.* The Future of Huma N Reproduction: Working Paper 5. Oxford, UK: St. John's College, Oxford, and Vienna Institute of Demography.

Benson, J.E. and F.F. Furstenberg Jr. 2006. "Entry Into Adulthood: Are Adult Role Transitions Meaningful Markers of Adult Identity?" *Advances in Life Course Research, Constructing Adulthood Agency and Subjectivity in Adolescence and Adulthood* 11: 199–224.

Berkowitz, D. 2007. "A Sociohistorical Analysis of Gay Men's Procreative Consciousness," *Journal of GLBT Family Studies* 3 (2–3): 157–90.

Blackstone, A. 2014. "Doing Family Without Having Kids." *Sociology Compass* 8 (1): 52–62.

Brandzel, A.L. 2005. "Queering Citizenship? Same-Sex Marriage and the State." *GLQ: A Journal of Lesbian and Gay Studies* 11 (2): 171–204.

Brinamen, C.F. and V. Mitchell. 2008. "Gay Men Becoming Fathers: A Model of Identity Expansion." *Journal of GLBT Family Studies* 4 (4): 521–41.

Cronin, A. and A. King. 2010. "Power, Inequality and Identification: Exploring Diversity and Intersectionality Amongst Older LGB Adults." *Sociology* 44 (5): 876–92.

Cronin, A. and A. King. 2014. "Only Connect? Older Lesbian, Gay and Bisexual (LGB) Adults and Social Capital." *Ageing and Society* 34 (2): 258–79.

Dannefer, D. and C. Phillipson. eds. 2010. *The SAGE handbook of social gerontology.* Los Angeles, London, New Delhi, Singapore, Washington, DC: SAGE Publications.

Dever, M. and L. Saugeres. 2004. "I Forgot to Have Children! Untangling Links Between Feminism, Careers and Voluntary Childlessness." *Journal of the Motherhood Initiative for Research and Community Involvement* 6 (2)116–126.

De Vries, B. and J.A. Blando. 2004. "The Study of Gay and Lesbian Aging: Lessons for Social Gerontology." In *Gay and Lesbian Aging: Research and Future Directions*, edited by G.H. Herdt and B. de Vries, 3–28. New York: Springer Publishing Company.

Dewaele, A., Cox, N., Van den Berghe, W. and J. Vincke. 2011. "Families of Choice? Exploring the Supportive Networks of Lesbians, Gay Men, and Bisexuals." *Journal of Applied Social Psychology* 41 (2): 312–31.

Dykstra, P.A. and G.O. Hagestad. 2007a. "Roads Less Taken Developing a Nuanced View of Older Adults Without Children". *Journal of Family Issues* 28 (10): 1275–1310.

Dykstra, P.A and G.O. Hagestad. 2007b. "Childlessness and Parenthood in Two Centuries Different Roads—Different Maps?" *Journal of Family Issues* 28 (11): 1518–32.

Dykstra, P.A. and R. Keizer. 2009. "The Wellbeing of Childless Men and Fathers in Mid-Life." *Ageing and Society* 29 (8): 1227–42.

Fredriksen-Goldsen, K.I. and A. Muraco. 2010. "Aging and Sexual Orientation: A 25-Year Review of the Literature." *Research on Aging* 32 (3): 372–413.

Fredriksen-Goldsen, K.I., Hoy-Ellis, C.P., Golden, J., Emlet, C.A. and N.R. Hooyman. 2014. "Creating a Vision for the Future: Key Competencies and Strategies for Culturally Competent Practice With Lesbian, Gay, Bisexual, and Transgender (LGBT) Older Adults in the Health and Human Services." *Journal of Gerontological Social Work* 57: 80–107.

Gabb, J 2005. "Locating Lesbian Parent Families: Everyday Negotiations of Lesbian Motherhood in Britain." *Gender, Place and Culture* 12 (4): 419–32.

Galán-Pichardo, J.I. 2009. "(Homo)sexualidad y familia: cambios y continuidades al inicio del tercer milenio." *Política y Sociedad* 46 (1): 143–60.

Giles, D., Shaw, R.L., and W. Morgan. 2009. "Representations of Voluntary Childlessness in the UK Press, 1990–2008." *Journal of Health Psychology* 14 (8): 1218–28.

Goldberg, A.E. 2006. "The Transition to Parenthood for Lesbian Couples." *Journal of GLBT Family Studies* 2 (1): 13–42.

González, M-J. and T. Jurado-Guerrero. 2006. "Remaining Childless in Affluent Economies: A Comparison of France, West Germany, Italy and Spain, 1994–2001." *European Journal of Population/Revue Européenne de Démographie* 22(4): 317–52.

Graham, M. and S. Rich. 2014. "Representations of Childless Women in the Australian Print Media." *Feminist Media Studies* 14 (3): 500–518.

Hayman, B., Wilkes, L., D. Jackson and E. Halcomb. 2013. "De Novo Lesbian Families: Legitimizing the Other Mother." *Journal of GLBT Family Studies* 9(3): 273–87.

Heaton, T.B., C.K. Jacobson and K. Holland. 1999. "Persistence and Change in Decisions to Remain Childless." *Journal of Marriage and Family* 61(2): 531–39.

Herdt, G. and B. de Vries. 2004. "Introduction." In *Gay and Lesbian Aging: Research and Future Directions*, edited by G.H. Herdt and B. de Vries, xi–xxii. New York: Springer Publishing Company.

Hicks, S. 2011. *Lesbian, Gay and Queer Parenting*. Basingstoke: Palgrave Macmillan.

Huijts, T., Kraaykamp, G. and S.V. Subramanian. 2013. "Childlessness and Psychological Well-Being in Context: A Multilevel Study on 24 European Countries." *European Sociological Review* 29 (1): 32–47.

Jeffries, S. and C. Konnert. 2002. "Regret and Psychological Well-Being Among Voluntarily and Involuntarily Childless Women and Mothers." *International Journal of Aging and Human Development* 54 (2): 89–106.

Keizer, R., Dykstra, P.A. and A-R. Poortman. 2010. "Life Outcomes of Childless Men and Fathers." *European Sociological Review* 26 (1): 1–15.

Kendig, H., Dykstra, P.A., R.I. van Gaalen and T. Melkas. 2007. "Health of Aging Parents and Childless Individuals." *Journal of Family Issues* 28 (11): 1457–86.

Kirmeyer, S.E. and B.E. Hamilton. 2011. "Transitions Between Childlessness and First Birth: Three Generations of U.S. Women." *Vital and Health Statistics. Series 2, Data Evaluation and Methods Research* 153 (August): 1–18.

Koropeckyj-Cox, T. and G. Pendell. 2007. "Attitudes About Childlessness in the United States Correlates of Positive, Neutral, and Negative Responses." *Journal of Family Issues* 28 (8): 1054–82.

Lampman, C. and S. Dowling-Guyer. 1995. "Attitudes Toward Voluntary and Involuntary Childlessness." *Basic and Applied Social Psychology* 17 (1–2): 213–22.

Magarick, R.H. and R.A. Brown. 1981. "Social and Emotional Aspects of Voluntary Childlessness in Vasectomized Childless Men," *Journal of Biosocial Science* 13 (2): 157–67.

McDavitt, B., Iverson, E., Kubicek, K., Weiss, G., C.F. Wong and M.D. Kipke. 2008. "Strategies Used by Gay and Bisexual Young Men to Cope With Heterosexism," *Journal of Gay and Lesbian Social Services* 20 (4): 354–80.

Mencarini, L. and M.L. Tanturri. 2007. "High Fertility or Childlessness: Micro-Level Determinants of Reproductive Behaviour in Italy." *Population (English Edition)* 61 (4): 389–415.

Miettinen, A. and I. Szalma. 2014. "Childlessness Intentions and Ideals in Europe." *Finnish Yearbook of Population Research* (49): 31–55.

Mills, M., Rindfuss, R.R., McDonald, P. and E. te Velde. 2011. "Why Do People Postpone Parenthood? Reasons and Social Policy Incentives." *Human Reproduction Update* 17 (6): 848–60.

Moore, J. 2014. "Reconsidering Childfreedom: A Feminist Exploration of Discursive Identity Construction in Childfree LiveJournal Communities." *Women's Studies in Communication* 37 (2): 159–80.

Park, K. 2005. "Choosing Childlessness: Weber's Typology of Action and Motives of the Voluntarily Childless." *Sociological Inquiry* 75 (3): 372–402.

Patterson, C.J. and R.G. Riskind. 2010. "To Be a Parent: Issues in Family Formation Among Gay and Lesbian Adults." *Journal of GLBT Family Studies* 6 (3): 326–40.

Peterson, H. 2014. "Absent Non-Fathers: Gendered Representations of Voluntary Childlessness in Swedish Newspapers." *Feminist Media Studies* 14 (1): 22–37.

Rijken, A.J. and E-M. Merz. 2014. "Double Standards: Differences in Norms on Voluntary Childlessness for Men and Women." *European Sociological Review* 30: 470–482.

Riskind, R.G. and C.J. Patterson. 2010. "Parenting Intentions and Desires Among Childless Lesbian, Gay, and Heterosexual Individuals." *Journal of Family Psychology* 24 (1): 78–81.

Roseneil, S., Crowhurst, I., Santos, A-C and M. Stoilova. 2013. "Reproduction and Citizenship/Reproducing Citizens: Editorial Introduction." *Citizenship Studies* 17 (8): 901–11.

Rowland, D.T. 1988. *Cross-National Trends in Childlessness*. Working Papers in Demography 73. Canberra: Research School of Social Sciences, Australian National University.

Schacher, S.J., C.F. Auerbach and L.B Silverstein. 2005. "Gay Fathers Expanding the Possibilities for Us All." *Journal of GLBT Family Studies* 1 (3): 31–52.

Silin, J. 2014. "What Makes a Queer Family Queer? A Response to Cristyn Davies and Kerry H. Robinson." *Contemporary Issues in Early Childhood* 14 (1): 54.

Silka, L. and S. Kiesler. 1977. "Couples Who Choose to Remain Childless." *Family Planning Perspectives* 9 (1): 16–25.

Silverstein, M. and R. Giarrusso. 2010. "Aging and Family Life: A Decade Review." *Journal of Marriage and Family* 72 (5): 1039–58.

Tanturri, M.L. and L. Mencarini. 2008. "Childless or Childfree? Paths to Voluntary Childlessness in Italy." *Population and Development Review* 34 (1): 51–77.

Taylor, E.N. 2003. "Throwing the Baby Out With the Bathwater." *Women and Politics* 24 (4): 49–75.

Te Velde, E., Habbema, D., Leridon, H. and M. Eijkemans. 2012. "The Effect of Postponement of First Motherhood on Permanent Involuntary Childlessness and Total Fertility Rate in Six European Countries since the 1970s." *Human Reproduction Update* 27 (4): 1179–83.

Uhlenberg, P. 2009. *International Handbook of Population Aging.* Dordrecht, The Netherlands: Springer.

Waren, W. and H. Pals. 2013. "Comparing Characteristics of Voluntarily Childless Men and Women." *Journal of Population Research* 30 (2): 151–70.

Warren, C.A.B. 2010. "Pride, Shame and Stigma in Private Spaces." *Ethnography* 11 (3): 425–42.

Wholpton, P.K., Campbell, A.A. and J.E. Patterson. 1966. *Fertility and Family Planning in the United States.* Princeton, NJ: Princeton University Press.

Index